MW00776080

Unglued

Unglued

A Bipolar Love Story

JEFFREY ZUCKERMAN

Boyle
&
Dalton

AUTHOR'S NOTE

By providing candid details about my experience, I attempted to combat the stigma of mental illness and discrimination against those who have such an illness. By request, I changed several names and two locations.

Book Design and Production
Boyle & Dalton
www.BoyleandDalton.com

Cover photo provided by the author

Copyright 2020 by Jeffrey Zuckerman
All rights reserved

This work is the intellectual property of the author.
Your cooperation with and support for U.S. copyright law is appreciated.

LCCN: 2018956680
Paperback ISBN: 978-1-63337-376-1
E-book ISBN: 978-1-63337-378-5

Printed in the United States of America
1 3 5 7 9 10 8 6 4 2

For my family

Contents

Rinse, Repeat

Lamentations

Behold, the Winter Is Past

Preface

The January blues are hardly uncommon in the Upper Midwest, where my wife Leah and I have frozen like human Popsicles for nearly four decades. Over the years, the weight of wintertime was particularly punishing to Leah. Her doctors suggested she might be struggling with seasonal affective disorder, and to lighten her load they prescribed the antidepressant Prozac. For a long time that helped well enough, along with one of those million-watt therapy light boxes, like the kind used as lighthouse beacons or along the top of prison fences.

Frigid winters notwithstanding, we loved raising our two kids in Minnesota. Leah flourished in long careers in social work and public health, and each spring she emerged from hibernation with gusto. She cultivated a big backyard flower garden and set bouquets of lilacs and peonies atop the dining room table. Most years I worked two jobs to help make ends meet. Each summer I played softball and Leah entertained our friends with well-executed dinners on our deck. She and I eventually made enough money to take a few memorable trips, and off to college went our adult children.

In 2015, our marriage was sucked into a whirlpool.

In May, a turbulent weekend in New York City and Leah's tumultuous trip to the Middle East.

In June, full-on mania.

In July, her uncorked rage.

In August, a diagnosis of bipolar disorder.

In September, Leah's first hospitalization.

In late October, her first Great Depression, six months spent in the blackness of our bedroom under a blanket of melancholy and inertia.

In 2016, second verse, same as the first.

As Leah's life became unmoored by a late-onset mood disorder, I became unglued. I was terrified of her manic episodes and demoralized by her depression. I read unsettling advice about how to talk to someone who rejects his or her diagnosis, as well as a dispiriting set of essays by authors mired in depression. I listened to TED Talks and podcasts and watched videos on YouTube. I attended support groups and wrote in a journal and talked to clergy and read powerful memoirs written by men and women with mental illnesses, people not much different from Leah.

The spouses in those narratives were portrayed either as angels or as bit players in their husbands' and wives' dramas—which belied my experience. In my support groups, those of us who loved someone with a mental illness saw ourselves as neither heroic nor righteous. We bumbled along, day after day, month after month, often crushed by the weight of the stress and moral incertitude in our own roles as caregivers.

One night a husband in my group summed up his twenty-year marriage: "I have a love–hate relationship with my wife's bipolar disorder," he joked. "I love my wife, and I hate her bipolar disorder."

I laughed. It was funny, and it was honest.

And it was the book I most wanted to read. A story in which the spouse, like that guy in my support group, is top banana in a real-life tragicomedy. A morality play that captures the day-to-day and year-to-year struggle to maintain one's sense of humor, integrity, and emotional and physical health in the face of a friend or family member's harrowing chronic illness.

A story of resilience, and a story of hope.

This story: a memoir of enduring love.

Up

Chapter 1

Fly the Friendly Skies

Look, we weren't Jay Gatsby, with vast blue gardens and men and women coming and going like moths among the champagne and stars. Leah and I were two middle-class Midwesterners who in the winter shoveled snow and in the summer grilled salmon burgers over charcoal briquettes. We set plastic lawn chairs under the shade of a silver maple, and every ten years we invited a few dozen friends to our backyard for a Sunday afternoon bash to celebrate our health and good fortune.

The last such gathering was in September 2014, coming up on my sixtieth birthday and our thirtieth wedding anniversary. Our kids flew in—Sarah from New York and Joey from Portland. I mowed our patch of grass and hosed the dirt off the deck. There was white wine and cold beer and plates of finger foods and party dips assembled by Leah and Sarah. There was the sound of an electric piano on which Joey played jazz and the aromas and sights of late summer, citronella candles and hydrangeas, impatiens and purple Russian sage.

There was Leah, calm and content, with her chocolate eyes and broad smile and long brown hair with tints of red. There were

3

neighbors and laughs and a fading sun in an orange and lavender sky. And before our guests departed, I passed around an old bowling pin for our friends to sign, and I offered a farewell toast, with Leah's hand folded in mine.

"Thank you all so much for your friendship and love," I announced in the September twilight. "Leah and I want to invite you back here in ten years to celebrate our fortieth anniversary and my seventieth birthday. We hope these will be the best years yet in all our lives."

How charming.

And after what Leah and I endured during the next five years, how thoroughly naive.

MAY 2015, EIGHT MONTHS LATER, a springtime Sunday in Brooklyn, New York. Sarah and her fiancé Seth, their dog, and I were sprawled on their sectional, waiting for the other guests to arrive, yawning our way through a recorded episode of *Jeopardy!* Their apartment was small and dark and the toilet seat was broken, but they had a walk-out to the backyard where their dog did his business and where Seth would barbeque a big lunch later that afternoon.

"Famous Quotes for one thousand dollars," Alex Trebek read. "'Today I feel like the luckiest man on the face of the earth.'"

"Who was Lou Gehrig?" Seth shouted.

"Sarah, give Seth a thousand dollars."

"Daddy, who was Lou Gehrig?"

"The first guy with ALS!" Seth practically screamed. "Sarah, he was, like, one of the all-time great New York Yankees. You ever hear of Babe Ruth?"

In two months my Midwestern daughter would be marrying this unrestrained New Yorker, as exuberant and opinionated as the city he held dear. He wore size 14 shoes, had a heart the size of a moose, and could make a cadaver laugh. I adored the guy, and, best of all, he and Sarah had fallen in love.

Fast-forward through a commercial for Ex-Lax. A promo for yesterday's newscast.

A father visiting Brooklyn, embracing a moment of joy with his soon-to-be-married daughter and her beau.

"Pause the TV for a second, would ya? I drove all the way from Minnesota to tell you two something."

"What's that, Jeffrey?"

"Today . . . I feel . . . like the luckiest man on the face of the earth."

"That's so sweet, Daddy."

"But I'm Jewish," I said, "so I know my luck will run out."

It was supposed to have been a joke.

WHERE WAS LEAH?

I had driven in to Brooklyn from Minneapolis on the first leg of a sentimental journey through the Midwest, and she had flown in to join me. We were there to attend Sarah and Seth's engagement blessing[1] that weekend at a Long Island synagogue. On Monday I would head back home on a three-day excursion through my home state of Pennsylvania. Leah had a flight to catch from Newark to Israel, with a

---

[1] An *aufruf,* pronounced to rhyme with *woof-woof,* is an Ashkenazi Jewish tradition. The bride and groom are called before the Torah for a blessing and prayer for a sweet life. It's normally held a week before the wedding. But nothing that summer was normal. See https://reformjudaism.org/wedding-0.

layover in Belgium, to enjoy a few days of sightseeing. From Tel Aviv she would travel to Tunisia to volunteer for a couple of weeks with an international aid organization doing some kind of public health work I didn't quite understand.

She had been acting testy the past few days, sleeping poorly, and by Sunday morning she was glued to our bed at the Comfort Inn. She told me she had barely slept all night and wanted me to keep the curtains drawn and let her lie there in the dark.

"I need to get dressed," I said.

"So turn on the light and leave me alone. I want to get our money back for this fucking hotel room."

This fucking hotel room, that is, that I had found online. It wasn't the Taj Mahal, but come on. What do you expect for $95 a night in New York City?

"I'm getting a migraine. Just go to the barbeque without me."

Fine. If she's in a bad mood, too bad for her. It was a sunny spring Sunday in the Big Apple, too nice a day to mope around a hotel room. Sarah and Seth lived a couple miles away from the hotel in Carroll Gardens, a section of Brooklyn I liked, with its oddly small-town ambience. I took off on foot and left the car with Leah. For a little while I enjoyed the morning stroll—or at least I did until I came to the mucky Gowanus Canal, where I feared I'd see the decayed body of a gangster or a spent nuclear fuel rod floating atop the sludge.

"Where's Mom?" Sarah asked when she let me in the apartment.

"She said she has a migraine."

"Is she coming to the barbeque?"

"Beats me," I said, and I took their dog for a long walk around the neighborhood.

A while later Leah texted me that she was feeling better. She told me she just had to hop in the shower, and then she'd drive over.

Those were her words: "I just have to hop in the shower."

Over the next few hours I kept wondering how long it could possibly take a person to hop in the shower. It wasn't how much time Leah was spending once she was *in* the shower. The apparent lack of hopping was the issue. I couldn't understand why she had not already hopped or what was so important about this alleged hopping compared to enjoying the day with our future in-laws. I liked them. They were gregarious, these New Yorkers, generous and funny—but a bit raucous to my distressed Midwestern ears while I seethed over why Leah was taking so much time to hop.

"*Whaaayy-uh* is *Lee-er*?" they wanted to know. "*Aw* you *shoo-uh* she's all right?"

My mother was from the Bronx, and I can imitate a New York accent for a laugh. But I felt jittery and peevish.

She's been hopping in the shower the past two hours, I thought to myself.

I just shrugged.

When Leah finally pulled up in our car two and a half hours later, she looked stunning, wearing a tight white blouse and bright white pants, with those long brown curls dangling down her back. But she could read my face.

"I said I had a headache. And there was no hot water at the fucking Comfort Inn."

"Sorry—"

"And then Google Maps sent me the wrong *fucking* way."

It took her forty-five minutes to drive over, she said, growing more churlish. The one-way streets made no sense and she'd gotten lost, and if she was late that was her own business and no reflection on me and, anyway, no one comes to a party on time, and the crux of the problem was that as usual I was just too hung up on not being late.

She swigged a couple of glasses of wine. Spent maybe an hour at the barbeque.

I timed it: The drive back to the Comfort Inn took ten minutes. How had she gotten lost for three-quarters of an hour?

ONE OF OUR FRIENDS later told me Leah seemed a little off that entire month. Sharp-tempered and self-absorbed. Humorless and mouthy. Discombobulated.

No kidding.

The next day, a Monday, Leah couldn't get herself organized. She had barely slept and kept bloviating about the hotel. She said she was still pissed there was hardly any hot water and insisted she needed to yell at the hotel manager before we checked out. This is *bullshit,* she said, growing angrier by the hour. She wanted a full refund.

"Dear," I said, seeing her dawdle while she ranted, "are you watching the time? We have to drive through Manhattan to get to Newark."

"We have plenty of time! I'm going to get our money back for this dump. Why aren't you being more *supportive* of me?"

"Fine. If you miss your plane, you can deal with it. I'm driving to Pennsylvania this afternoon."

Which was when Leah told me she still needed to buy a new cell phone.

"Why? What's wrong with your phone?"

"It doesn't work right!"

Cripes, I thought, out of patience with her snarling. *Just take this mystery trip of yours to North Africa and leave me alone for a few weeks.*

I wasn't about to diddle around in the hotel room while Leah spent all day hopping in the shower. Instead, I walked a couple miles to the AT&T store with her old phone for a head start on the Leah-Suddenly-Needs-A-New-Phone Initiative. I figured I'd pay for the thing and walk back to the hotel while Leah's eight thousand pictures she'd been taking the past few months were transferred to the new phone. Meanwhile, she could load the car and I wouldn't have to be there when she berated the poor guy who managed the Comfort Inn.

Two hours later she finally finished packing. We loaded the suitcases and her backpack into the car and drove to the store for the new phone. I paced around outside, annoyed with Leah's indifference to my having spent the weekend walking all around Brooklyn while she complained about the hotel room and my inadequate regard for her travel stress and insomnia.

"I bought a new iPad," she said when she exited the store.

"How expensive was that?"

"Do you even *care* that I got a refund for the hotel room?"

Leah said the salesman added the iPad for only a hundred and fifty dollars. "When I get home from Tunisia," she gloated, "I'll sell it for three hundred dollars."

No, you won't, I thought.

IT WAS EARLY AFTERNOON when we made our way across the Brooklyn Bridge into a Manhattan traffic jam. In Tribeca a limo driver cut us off, and Leah jumped from the passenger seat and started blasting our car horn.

"I hate you rich fuckers!" she yelled through the driver's window.

I laughed, warily.

"It wasn't funny," Leah grumbled, freaking me out with her growing rage and incessant swearing.

Wait a second, I thought. *Who is this woman in my car? What happened to that Leah person I used to know in Minneapolis?*

After we emerged from a bottleneck at the Lincoln Tunnel, Leah suddenly demanded I pull over at the next turnpike exit. She hadn't eaten a thing *all day,* she said.

"Here. Get off here!"

She had a plane to catch, but by then it was no skin off my ass if she missed her flight. I exited the expressway into the North Jersey rubble and pulled into the parking lot of an abandoned factory. Leah leapt out of the car and yanked her suitcase and backpack from the trunk and dumped all her stuff onto the cracked blacktop and weeds and broken glass. Her clothes, toiletries, shoes, notebooks, pens, magazines. All of it. She said she hadn't had enough time to pack her suitcase right. Said she wasn't sure what should go in her suitcase and what should go in the backpack on the plane.

"Should I bring the old iPad with me or the new one? Or both?"

Okay, Leah had always been the calm one. The organized one. The one reminding me to hang my keys on a hook so I wouldn't spend half the morning looking for them. The one who folded her clothes so they wouldn't wrinkle. The one who brought a manila folder with flight information, hotels, phone numbers, and tourist spots.

Someone driving past that parking lot might have thought we were setting up a booth at a pop-up flea market.

"Just tell me what should go where!"

Holy cow. My wife was about to fly to Brussels and from there to Tel Aviv, and we had barely made it to frickin' New Jersey.

We never did find her a restaurant. When I finally pulled up to the United Airlines terminal, I got out of the car, lifted the suitcase from the trunk, and handed Leah her backpack.

Quick kisses.

Good-bye.

Good-bye.

And off I drove into the sunset on my journey back to Minnesota.

But I hadn't even exited the airport road for the freeway when it suddenly hit me: Even though Leah had been blowing her cork like a geyser the past few days, I sure was going to miss her.

Not only that: I was scared as hell. What was wrong with my wife?

FOR THE PAST TEN YEARS I had been healthier than at any time in my life. After a decade of my digestive misery, anemia, and weight loss, our family practitioner, Dr. Woody, had figured out I had been living with undiagnosed celiac disease. Not some bullshit gluten intolerance, I bragged. Full-on celiac sprue. I quit eating wheat, barley, and rye, figured out a way to reduce my stress, and in 2014 quit my job to work part-time as a freelance editor. As I had done for half my life, that summer I played on the Loons, a recreational softball team in St. Paul, fished for bass out of my kayak, and took long bike rides. In the winter, I snowshoed, skated, and cross-country skied.

If I were taller and better looking, I could have been one of those iStock models in an ad for AARP or Viagra.

Leah was physically healthy as well but had started seeing a psychologist a month before the New York trip in 2015. She mentioned it to me almost in passing, and I guess I should have been paying more attention. Years ago Leah had seen a therapist about her family of origin—specifically, about her relationships with her estranged brother and her deceased parents, whose ashes impiously inhabited a pair of cardboard boxes on a shelf in my clothes closet. I figured if she wanted to tell me why she was seeing a shrink, she would have done so. And if her problems involved me, Leah would have dragged me in with her for counseling.

Whether Leah's work with a therapist unsealed a portal to her becoming sick with a mood disorder, I don't know. Or was it because she'd been laid off from her university job two years earlier? Or because she missed a few doses of Prozac that week and quit her Trazadone cold turkey? Or because the Golden State Warriors won the NBA championship in 2015?

Or was it an act of God, in whom Leah did not believe and I had my doubts?

About 20 percent of Americans experience mental illness each year.[2] About 10 percent of cases of bipolar disorder have onset after the age of fifty.[3] Statistically, then, at least one person aboard a jumbo jet heading to Brussels was likely to be experiencing the effects of a diagnosed or undiagnosed mental illness.

That person was Leah.

One hundred percent of the ill person's family members are affected by their loved one's mental illness.

That person was me, Jeff, along with our children and everyone who knew us.

In time I stopped trying to figure out why Leah's mental health began to unravel. Instead, I focused on surviving a soul-crushing threat to my own well-being—and the near-collapse of our decades-long marriage.

---

[2]   https://www.nami.org/Learn-More/Mental-Health-By-the-Numbers.
[3]   https://www.ncbi.nlm.nih.gov/pmc/articles/PMC2848458/.

CHAPTER 2

Go Forth Yourself

In spring 1982, at the age of twenty-seven, I finished a master's degree in social work in Duluth, Minnesota. My father died in Arizona that summer, fretting that, despite a pair of college degrees, his son would spend his life stuffing women's feet into pumps at a J.C. Penney's, living in a tent, marrying, at best, a tabby from the Humane Society.

He wasn't far off . . . until I met Leah.

I stayed in Duluth through the summer, working at various odd jobs I strung together. In August a former professor invited me to a backyard party for the incoming graduate students, and I stopped by to snoop around and scrounge for food. Leah recognized my face from a picture in a departmental newsletter and walked up to me and said, "So you're Zuckerman. I heard you have a big mouth."

She was toting around an oversized satchel.

"Nice laundry bag," I said.

She had a long reddish-brown curly mane, dark brown eyes, smooth white arms, and a mischievous smile. We flirted over the professor's cocktail wieners and wine and heard each other's story. Leah was from Chicago and I was from Pittsburgh and we were the two young Jews in town. She offered me her phone number, and a couple weeks later I took her to a divey Chinese restaurant for stir-fry and nervous conversation.

"So, what are you majoring in?" Leah asked me.

That was her sense of humor right there, imitating a college freshman on her first date.

"If you're going to go out with me," I answered her, "you should know I have syphilis."

"Me, too."

After dinner, we shivered on Park Point while the Lake Superior spray smacked our faces like the *Edmund Fitzgerald*. Disenchanted with the arctic romance of the moment, and, I surmised, indifferent toward me, Leah said she wanted to go warm up somewhere.

"I think you'll like Tony's Cabaret. Have you been to Superior yet?"

We drove across the Blatnik Bridge to Wisconsin. Among the cheap bars and strip joints where the ore boat sailors unwound was Tony's, a smoky 1940s-era dance hall with a corny three-piece house band. The drummer played a small drum kit and had a blond beehive hairdo, and the trumpeter, one of few Blacks in that part of Wisconsin, would play a straight-up Dizzy Gillespie version of songs he liked to sing, like "The Flat Foot Floogie with a Floy Floy" and "Rompin' and Stompin' at the Savoy."

Near the end of the night the band handed the mic to one of the regulars, the guy with the pompadour.

"Check this guy out," I said.

He used to sit by himself in a booth next to the bandstand, dragging on cigarettes all night, patiently anticipating his big moment like it might be the next stop before his Las Vegas debut. It was always the same song: the Engelbert Humperdinck ballad "After the Lovin." You never heard a version so slow and slightly off-key or saw a guy so tormented in a place so thick with smoke and despair. I couldn't read Leah but feared maybe Tony's Cabaret was a bad idea for a first date.

"Hey, that was a lot of fun," she said when we left.

It was after midnight and we drove back to Duluth via a spooky back road across the St. Louis River estuary. Leah lived in a big apartment overlooking Lake Superior and invited me up. Her roommates were asleep, and we made out like teenagers in the living room.

"Has anyone ever mentioned your eyes are like doves?"

It was a pick-up line from the first chapter of the Song of Solomon in the Bible.

"Yes," she answered, which was funnier and more seductive than it was grating. She was a wisenheimer, and we got back to business, both intent on not screwing things up.

A month later Leah and I crashed on a friend's couch, because Duluth was like the McMurdo Station in Antarctica and even in October if it was late you stayed put, and we made love for the first time.

Back then Duluth's economy was a wreck, and so was my so-called career. I was living in a garret behind an eastside mansion and teaching Hebrew to a pack of hormonal wolverines enrolled in an after-school program. I was too cheap to turn on the oil furnace and sat at my desk wrapped in an electric blanket. Leah and her two roommates shared a four-bedroom apartment with a magnificent view of the south shore of Lake Superior on the rare days the fog lifted. There was no doorbell, so if you stopped by her building you had to stand on the front stoop and tug on a string we'd rigged up to a bell in the apartment.

One of the roommates liked me well enough, but the other one was ornery and hated my guts. After I slept over a couple of times, the nasty one said to Leah, "Tell Jeff not to say hello to me in the morning," which Leah and I thought was stupendously funny.

It had been a long time since either of us had dandled that much. Leah had trouble studying and I kept getting asthma attacks and needing my inhaler. Through the early winter we got to know each other better and snowshoed in the state parks and went to the movies, and romance blossomed like winter jasmine in frigid Duluth.

MANY YEARS LATER, now in her mid-fifties, Leah's career came to a halt. Nothing personal, she was told. Budget crunch. Strategic objectives. A golden opportunity for you, Leah, to pursue other interests.

More like a golden opportunity to find out no one wanted to hire a fifty-seven-year-old woman with a pair of twentieth-century social work and public health degrees. So Leah bought a MacBook and enrolled in a certificate program at a community college.

"What's the first course you'll be taking?" I asked her.

"Typography. It's a class in fonts."

Fonts! My wife would be getting certified in fonts!

Actually, the certificate was in graphic design, and I trusted Leah knew what she was doing because Leah always did. I had long admired her intuition and self-confidence. Over the years she had served on the board of directors of numerous nonprofit agencies, in part out of compassion and a sense of social justice, in part because she was the queen of networking.

And it paid off. One day she received an email from a contact in Chicago who mentioned an international volunteer trip with a nonprofit agency doing public health work in Tunisia.

"This aid group is solid," Leah told me. "The Chauncey Greene said I should look into it."

The Chauncey Greene. Ha. Longtime couples and their inside jokes. Leah used to put the article *the* before a person's name. *The*

Beyoncé has great hair. *The* Michelle Obama is coming to town next week.

The Chauncey Greene was a family practice doctor Leah first met during a college internship. We would see him every few years, and he finally remembered my name after the sixth or seventh introduction. Whatever. If the Chauncey Greene could get Leah a job "doing" global public health and fonts, swell. I knew she was fervent about doing it, whatever *it* was.

"One more thing," Leah said.

"What's that?"

"What would you think if I wanted to stop in Israel on my way to Tunisia? It would be expensive."

We were blowing the travel budget. There was the visit to New York, the trip to Jamaica two months later for our daughter's wedding, and a flight to Los Angeles a week later for a cousin's wedding. That was a lot of travel, and with Leah volunteering in Tunisia, we would be spending a boatload of money.

But I wanted to be supportive of Leah's visit to Israel. She had been rooting around on Ancestry.com, and with the help of a distant cousin, she found out her great-great-grandfather was buried in Jerusalem. I had lived in Israel in the mid-1970s, and Sarah and Joey had traveled there during college. Leah was the only one of us yet to visit the country.

I checked in with our financial gal. "You'll be okay," she said, "as long as you don't spend your savings like a couple of drunken sailors." I didn't ask her how drunken sailors spend their savings. I guess drinking.

"I think you should do it," I said to Leah.

Neither of us wanted to end up like her Depression-era parents, who spent their lives hoarding ketchup packets and napkins from McDonald's. Instead, we would be the geezers with the annoying "We're

Spending Our Children's Inheritance" bumper stickers slapped on the side of our suitcase.

And what the heck. Drunken sailors didn't visit Great-Great-Grandpa on the Mount of Olives.

THE MORNING after I dropped her off in Newark, Leah phoned me from the Brussels airport. I was driving west through the Allegheny Mountains of central Pennsylvania, green and lush, a landscape I had never fully appreciated as a student at Penn State University. Leah sounded exhausted after her all-night flight from Newark. She spoke falteringly, her words inert and blurry, floating across the ocean like puffs of smoke.

"I can't hear you, dear," I said. "Leah? Are you there?"

She mumbled something.

"Leah, what did you say happened?"

"Don't yell at me! I'm just so tired."

I wasn't yelling. I asked her again what was wrong.

"I think my new iPad was in my backpack," she said. "I might have left it on the plane."

An announcement on an airport loudspeaker drowned out her voice.

"Hang on, Leah." I pulled over to the shoulder of Interstate 80. Surrounded by the forests of Union County, I was pondering not the beauty of this unspoiled landscape but how much this phone call was costing.

"Do you remember if I put it in the backpack? Or did I leave it in the car?"

"Leah, can you hear me? What did you leave on the plane? Your backpack or the iPad or both?"

"What?"

"Dear, do you have your meds? Were they in your backpack, too?"

"I'm a little confused."

She hung up the phone.

I felt my stomach juices rumbling, a conditioned, neurotic puree of that morning's granola bar and fear.

I knew that, in addition to Prozac, Leah had been taking a sleep medicine and some other new drug I wasn't sure about except, according to the packaging, if she skipped any doses her legs would fall off or her kidneys would explode or whatever terrors Walgreens warned us about in those forty pages of gibberish.

Having heard nothing else from Leah, I took a lengthy pit stop in State College and wandered around campus, desperately seeking to remember attending school there. According to my road journal, "I ululated outside the apartment where Carole with an e broiled my heart and tossed it in a salad dressed with vinegar and bile."

Leah phoned me back that afternoon.

"Found my backpack," she said blandly. "It was in a restaurant."

Someone stole her iPad, she said. Or maybe it was in her suitcase, getting loaded on her connecting flight to Israel. She was trying to figure out how to call United Airlines so she could report it missing.

"Leah, dear. Dear, do you have your meds with you?"

She sounded woozy, hardly the spirited woman I'd known half my life and a day earlier had kissed goodbye at the airport.

"I'm so tired. I need to board the plane."

And away she flew.

AFTER MY STOP IN STATE COLLEGE I headed west to Pittsburgh, where I'd spent the first eighteen years of my life. I parked near my parents' old house and walked up and down the hills of the old neighborhood. I could still remember the names of the children who lived in those homes a half-century ago. The scary woman who lived two doors up the block from us. The houses with mean dogs. A bucktoothed blond-haired girl I was in love with in second grade. I had heard that the school district finally razed the asbestos-soused elementary school I'd attended. I saw a grass field in its place, and I vowed it was high time I threw away my report cards I had kept all those years. That night I slept on the couch at the home of a pal from high school, Beth, and her husband Larry. I cherished their friendship and left Pennsylvania treasuring the lucky life I'd lived as a child, reminded of my good fortune the past forty years in Minnesota.

Friday evening, a Motel 6 in Kokomo, Indiana.

Saturday evening, a campground in Rocky Arbor State Park in central Wisconsin. It was Memorial Day weekend and I grabbed the one remaining site for my tent, unaware until after I paid for it that the trucks on Interstate 94 were rumbling past only a quarter mile west of the park.

Leah phoned me from Israel as I was scrounging for kindling. After I hung up I jotted a note in my journal.

MAY 23, 2015

I hoped to relax and enjoy a campfire tonight, but the freeway noise is intense. I might as well have set up my tent in a bowling alley.

I'm worried about Leah. She just called me from Jerusalem. She was talking very weirdly on some Kuwaiti guy's phone.

One sentence, a benign peek into the unfolding havoc: "She was talking very weirdly."

She sounded frazzled. Hyper and loopy. Said she couldn't decide if she should take her dose of Prozac and the prescribed mystery medication in the morning or evening. Said she was heading to the Mount of Olives to find her great-great-grandfather's grave. Or maybe she'll go tomorrow, she said. Maybe today.

"Where did you say you are?" she asked.

"Wisconsin."

"What day is it in Wisconsin?"

She said her meds were in her hotel room and told me about the amazing poetry she had been writing. Told me some guy might be hitting on her. No, not this guy whose phone she was using. See, Leah explained, the guy with the phone was a Kuwaiti waiter she met, her new friend. This was a different guy. She told me that, yes, she was still planning to travel to Tunisia, that she just needed some sleep. Mentioned again she was unsure which pills she should be taking.

"Call the pharmacy," she instructed me. "Ask them if it's morning or night."

I was flabbergasted. Leah had long suffered from insomnia, but she had never been this disoriented. Only a few years earlier she had navigated Nairobi on a work trip. Other times she had wound her way fearlessly through the back alleys of Paris and London and Istanbul.

I wasn't worried about her "new friend." After so many years of marriage, you can smell a rat halfway around the world. And I trusted Leah more than anyone I knew.

But my gastrointestinal system was on high alert.

CHAPTER 3

The Life of Leah

A couple of months after our first date in Duluth, Leah invited me to spend Thanksgiving at her parents' house outside Chicago.

"Try to ignore them," she said. "They're a little crazy."

They lived in a ranch house in Skokie dominated by a nineteen-inch portable TV parked on a cart that blocked the narrow artery between the kitchen and the dining room. I couldn't hear anything in that house because Leah's mother kept screaming at her to turn up the volume. "Stop making so much noise! I can't hear the TV set!"

Leah's father, hiding in the basement, hollered, "Did you say something?" and the mother yelled back, "I can't hear you," and Leah withdrew to her bedroom to escape the bickering, just as she had done as a child.

On Black Friday Leah guided me on the Skokie Swift and the El to the Chicago Loop, her old stomping grounds during high school and college. Water Tower Place. The gift shop at the museum at the Art Institute. Kroch's & Brentano's bookstore near the lakefront. The wind was raw, practically blew us across a bridge over the Chicago River, and we rushed inside Marshall Field's to warm up. It was like a holiday movie, with harried customers hauling bags of gifts, cosmeticians attacking women with squirts of perfume. Leah led me to the kiosk where an attendant was giving out free boxes of Frango mints for filling out a credit-card application.

"Make up someone's name," Leah said. "They won't check. We can come back for more later."

By late afternoon the snow was swirling, and Leah suggested we duck out of the cold for a pastrami sandwich at Mort's Deli.

"You'll love the place," Leah said.

When we entered, Mort himself was guarding the restaurant. His white shirt was unbuttoned toward his navel, and a gold *chai* the size of a softball dangled from a choker around his neck, resting on his hairy chest like a nursing whelp.

Mort eyeballed the room for an open booth and took a drag of his cigarette. With a subtle nod of his gigantic head, he pointed us toward a clean table by the windows. When we sat down Leah brushed the snowflakes off the felt beret she used to wear in those days, and I gently flicked aside the flecks of snow from that thick brown hair of hers.

Each table at Mort's was festooned with a bowl of pickles and olives. "Which do you like better?" she asked me.

"Pickles. I can't stand olives."

"Oh."

"Why, is that a deal breaker?"

"Maybe."

We were still warming up and ordered coffee.

"Bet you five bucks Mort will be dead the next time we come back to Chicago," Leah said.

I pictured his carcass mounted on the wall behind the deli counter like Roy Rogers's horse.

"The next time, huh? So I guess I'm passing the test so far."

"Just don't blow it."

Perhaps it was the late afternoon glow of the streetlamps on Wabash Avenue, and the snow on Leah's hair and how she smiled while she pulled olives through her lips. Maybe it was how she joked around with the waitress like they'd known each other their whole lives. I did love Mort's Deli, and I was beginning to fall in love with Leah.

I didn't blow it, and neither did she. It went like that every Thanksgiving for a long, long time. We would drive from Minneapolis to Chicago, leave our kids at Grandma and Grandpa's house, and take the El down to the Loop, con a box of Frango mints at Marshall Field's, and shiver in the downtown wind until we stopped for a late afternoon snack at Mort's. We'd hear the sleet tapping the windows and the clank of silverware and plates. Leah would pick out olives from the bowl on the table and leave me the pickles, and with her cold hands dressed in mine, we would gaze at the neon glow in the fading afternoon light, both wondering whether Old Mort would survive another year, imagining the two of us living together forever.

Then one gray night it happened: Mort the Deli Guy ceased his fearless roar. Leah won my five dollars, and the place closed down. Her parents moved to Minneapolis, where they died within one year of each other.

And a few years after that, Leah experienced a mental health crisis.

DURING THAT FIRST WINTER TOGETHER in Duluth, Leah and I impersonated a pair of amorous icicles. I took her skating on a frozen, windy pond, and, wearing her puffy down jacket and earmuffs and white beret, she held her arms straight out and shot across the ice like a sailboat. We cross-country skied over at Lester Park, where we stopped and listened to the chickadees, the wind whistling through the spruce trees, the Lester River trickling through the rifts in the ice. One day I scrawled Leah's name in the snow with a long yellow pee stream. She was impressed, had never seen a guy do that, even in Chicago.

In late March, for Passover, I brought Leah to Phoenix to meet my mother and my brother David, his wife Lois, their kids, and Lois's extended family. Compared to the lifelong histrionics among Leah's own family of origin, a Seder at my mother's condo seemed to her refreshingly quaint and loving. After getting to know Leah, Lois said it was *besheyrt* that Leah and I met, a Yiddish word that more or less means "destined." Lois believed in that kind of stuff, like spirits of the departed visiting us. I hoped that my father, dead not even one year, somehow knew I finally met the right woman.

Leah and I talked about moving to the Twin Cities together that summer once she finished her master's degree. I liked Duluth fine, even though I was barely making a living and pissing away my life at age twenty-eight. "If I'm going to move to the Twin Cities," I told her, "you'll have to marry my ass."

To show her parents what a class act her daughter had taken up with, I had The Talk with them about our plans to move in together.

"Well, okay," her dad said awkwardly, and for once her mother shut up.

LEAH FOUND A SOCIAL WORK JOB at the county hospital and I took whatever work came along, and I don't know how we paid the bills. We rented our first apartment, a fourplex in an economically distressed neighborhood, for about three hundred bucks a month. Out front of the apartment building next door to ours, Leah noticed a well-mannered guy chain-smoking.

"He looks interesting," Leah said.

The building housed a group home and the man was Monte, who we later learned had schizophrenia. The more I tried to talk to Monte, the more he reminded me of my Uncle Milan, who my parents said had gotten shell-shocked during World War II and spent his remaining thirty years in a New Jersey rest home doing the Thorazine shuffle.[1]

A writer and his sullen wife lived across the hall from us, a cat lady upstairs from them, and a prostitute and her daughter above us. We'd hear the mom's heels clacking across the hardwood floors late at night with her guests. She was always friendly when we ran into her and allowed us to use her washer and dryer in the basement.

One night, Leah and her friend Jean arrived home late from the movies and banged on our apartment door, hollering, "Hurry up! Let us in! Let us in! There's a bunch of cops wearing SWAT jackets running around the neighbors' yards!"

We opened a window and watched the show until we saw an adrenaline-fueled officer cuffing the bad guy, hollering at him, "You're going to jail! You're going to jail!" Except the cop pronounced *jail* with two syllables: *Jay-uhl! Jay-uhl!* From then on, if either of us got pulled over for speeding we'd torment the other, "You're going to jay-uhl! You're going to jay-uhl!"

---

[1] My earliest childhood memory: a hot day in the parking lot of the state hospital outside Atlantic City, where Uncle Milan was getting treated, whatever that meant. I was about five years old. My big brother and I knew only to ask no questions. The sun was beating down on the parking lot, and we were boiling in the car waiting for my parents and grandparents to finish their visit. Later on, Uncle Milan would live in an Atlantic City rest home, which seemed to be a place where drugged-out veterans like him spent the day smoking and smiling dully at us boys.

We liked each other's goofy side. Leah told me she was a "partial vegetarian" and I said I was going to run a partial marathon to the bodega around the corner for a carton of milk. She said she liked my "Horowitz nose," never explaining what it meant except that I had one. I liked her baffling inventory of Yiddish-sounding words she invented, like *oyshkaveyshka, nushkanin,* and *patoochko.* She liked my love of the outdoors and the way I was close to my family in Arizona and friends in Pennsylvania. I called her an "NJG," for Nice Jewish Girl, so I became her NJB, the guy who religiously visited his father's grave when we vacationed in Phoenix.

One afternoon on a visit to my mother's condo, Leah and I grabbed a yellow legal pad and drove our rental car to a coffee shop to figure things out. Years later both my kids made big productions of getting engaged, but I don't remember what we wore or what we ate. It was a Village Inn diner, for Pete's sake. We drew up a list of the pros and cons of getting married. The pros must have had something to do with love and commitment and shared values and having fun and never needing to explain our jokes to each other. The cons had to do with my fear she'd want to move back to Chicago and her concerns about how little money I was making and that I'd leave my underpants and socks on the coffee table.

The pros outweighed the cons.

An hour later we called Leah's parents from a payphone and told them we had decided to get married. That evening during a shabbat dinner with my family we lit a pair of candles and my brother popped a bottle of champagne. And then, in July 1984, two years after my father died, I married the woman who told me she heard I had a big mouth.

CHAPTER 4

Nights in Tunisia

To: Jeff
May 27, 2015

*Ok, I know you love me, you know I fking love you. You know
I fking xeroxed the fking cards so if something like this fking
happened it would not take my fking time in Tunisia which
is costing a lot more than your fking time in Mpls., esp. when
I still need to make fking decisions about traveling to fking
Tunis and finding a fking hotel. Just fking forget it. Lauren is
now fking helping me. And you think I'm the one who is not
fking rational here?*

Based on what I could tell from her emails, Leah spent a day or
two in Jerusalem walking around the Old City, locating Great-Great-
Grandpa's tombstone on the Mount of Olives, touring Tel Aviv with an
acquaintance we'd met a few years earlier in the States. I'm not sure how
else she spent her time in Israel. Snapping pictures on her new iPhone.
Posting a hundred photos of flowers on Facebook. Bantering with the
hotel workers. Having a good time.

Not sleeping.

She wasn't sure which pills she should take or when she should take them. She may not have taken any meds at all. But somehow a week later she landed in Tunisia to volunteer on the nonprofit aid group's mission as planned—a testimony to her travel savvy, even when she was sleep-deprived and wired like a wind turbine. In Tunis she found her way to the training meetings with the North American group and the local field staff. In her emails she said she had been chatting up the hotel workers. Leah seemed to be more interested in hearing the voices of "the people" than the "elite stakeholders" associated with the nonprofit. I had the sense she saw herself on a quixotic mission on behalf of the commoners—in itself inspired and sincere, and probably enjoyable for her, although what windmill she was jousting was baffling to me.

It was, in hindsight, the first time I recognized the signs of grandiosity.

IT WAS SUNDAY MORNING Minnesota time, Sunday night in Tunisia, a week after my 2600-mile round-trip drive to the East Coast. By then Leah was sending a barrage of text messages and email not only to me, but copying her friends, our kids, and her psychologist. She was posting pictures of the meals she was eating, the flowers she was fancying, the oddities around town, and I couldn't tell if she was euphoric or losing her mind after sleeping so little. At one point she told me to call the pharmacy at Walgreens. "Ask the pharmacist what meds I'm supposed to be on and when I should take them. Tell them it's urgent. Say it's a dire emergency."

Our New York friend, Anita, called to ask me about strange emails and texts and IMs she too had been receiving from Leah. I said reading her messages was like watching an actor perform in two stage plays at once.

To: Jeff
May 28, 2015, 11:00 p.m.

I switched Lauren from Walgreens so she can work on Big Picture Issues while you work on meds. I've got her on iPad and you on iPhone, so am damn well not fking delusional or having "irrational thoughts" when I have her working on Big Picture, you working on meds, and my formerly suicidal Arabic, flute-playing poet working on transportation.

Who was Lauren, what Big Picture Issues was she working on, and when did she and Lauren become BFFs?

My formerly suicidal *who?*

I didn't know this Lauren's phone number, couldn't find it anywhere in the house. I made a couple calls, finally deduced who the woman was and her address in south Minneapolis.

Lauren, a few years older than I, pleasant, generous eyes, endearing smile. When she opened her door she seemed surprised to see me and said she was perplexed, too, because she really wasn't even a close friend of Leah. Said she couldn't make sense of Leah's messages either, had no idea what "the big issues" were she was supposed to be "working on."

"I wish I could help," Lauren said regretfully but, unlike me, unruffled.

I sat a while in my car, my bowels churning, a classic Jeffrey response to stress. Leah was five thousand miles away, sending too many pictures of too many flowers and weird texts and emails and IMs about suicidal poets and prescription chaos to people I didn't know.

If it was truly an emergency, a friend said, I should fly to Tunisia and bring her home.

As if. What could be worse in Leah's jacked-up brain than her overwrought prince of a husband riding up on a white steed and rescuing his damsel in distress?

Her "flute-playing poet" could take care of things. I trusted Leah. She was so capable and strong. So honest and savvy.

And, according to her email, so fking in love with me.

Of that, I was positive. Almost.

LEAH NEVER FOUND the new iPad but instead tapped away on her iPhone, emailing me a play-by-play account of how the nonprofit had failed to resolve a public health crisis but how she saved the life of one person, her room service guy, would-be poet, and new buddy, Tabek Taboubi. I tried picturing it: my compassionate, intelligent middle-aged American wife with a double master's degree in social work and public health, offering heartfelt advice to an underemployed Tunisian bellhop.

She explained to me that this Tabek Taboubi had worked in Iraq as a translator for the U.S. military and was thirty-seven years old and trying to save money for a bride service fee if he ever wanted to get married. "Maybe if we win the lottery we can sponsor him and bring him to the U.S. He's smart. He speaks four languages. Okay, maybe he's infatuated with me."

To: Jeff
May 28, 2015, 11:30 p.m.

To show you that I'm not having an affair, here's a text from
my room service friend who I talked to for hours. He told me

that he has a new view on life and isn't thinking about killing himself now.

"It's so nice to talk to, the way you talk I can feel it in every word you say, the way you move your lips with each letter, calm my sad soul. I know am crazy sometimes but not this time, something is here, what is that really I want to know . . . T.T."

I've helped him a little to have some hope and not continue to think of suicide, and get antidepressants and therapy.
And not to get all Jewy on you or anything, but "Whoever saves a life, it is considered as if he saved an entire world."
—Mishnah

Who was this woman suddenly quoting ancient Jewish texts?
But I never worried something was up between Leah and her Tunisian bellhop, twenty years her junior. It sounded just like Leah. She was the most generous person I knew.

THE CHAUNCEY GREENE wasn't so much a friend of Leah as a business "gonnegtion," as Meyer Wolfsheim told Nick Carraway in *The Great Gatsby*. He had soft hands, a gray bouffant, immaculate fingernails, and he carried himself tall with a rebar spine. The Chauncey Greene was on eight thousand boards of directors and had expertise on any subject you asked him about. His niece attended college in the Twin Cities, and we'd have her to our house for dinner because Leah was kindhearted and the young woman had severe anxiety.

I never did learn much about the gathering in Tunis, because all Leah wanted to do was rant about "the Chauncey Greene's condescending arrogance and some chain-smoking Dragon Lady bitch" who had joined her and the Chauncey Greene on a tour of the UNESCO World Heritage site at Kerkouane. I gathered from Leah that the woman was some random tourist from Houston, and beyond that I had no idea who she was or what she was doing there. And if it sounds like I didn't know what the hell was going on, it's because I didn't. But the Kerkouane Incident ended up shattering my life.

ANITA CALLED me again from New York, wanting to know if I knew what in the world was going on, and who were this Chauncey Greene and this Dragon Lady person Leah kept complaining about? Anita told me Leah was apparently in a crisis.

"Frankly," Anita said, "I'm quite concerned about her."

"Leah knew this Chauncey in Chicago," I explained. "The two of them and this other tourist were touring these UNESCO ruins. Leah had been up all night with her depressed Tunisian bellhop poet guy—"

"With *who?*"

"Her depressed Tunisian bellboy poet friend. She was texting and emailing me and I couldn't keep anything straight and there was the time zone difference and something about saving the bellhop from killing himself. They're in the town of Kerkouane—"

"The bellhop went with them? I don't understand."

"No. Listen. Leah, Chauncey Greene, and this other tourist. They were walking around the trinket shops and whatnot. Leah said she broke off from the other two. Told them she would be down the street and that she would meet them in twenty-five minutes. You know how Leah does stuff like that. She'll look around a museum gift shop so she doesn't have to pay to go in the museum while I'm outside girl-watching."

Anita laughed. Men!

"I mean, this is what I *think* happened. Leah didn't show up on time, or there was some miscommunication or I don't know what. Apparently, Chauncey Greene and this tourist found Leah wandering around and just *lit* into her. Literally screamed at her, according to Leah. *Ordered* her into the car. Chauncey kept yelling that he was *responsible* for her *safety*. You're picturing this, right? Leah getting yelled at by a doctor?"

"She must have hated that," Anita said.

"I mean, she's already completely strung out. On the other hand, this Chauncey Greene was the one who had arranged the trip and must have been worrying what the heck happened to Leah."

"Well, sure. He was probably concerned."

I told Anita how I had been getting all these texts and IMs from somewhere in Tunisia, every few minutes now. That Leah even *called* me at one point, crying, embarrassed for sobbing in front of these people.

"Anita," I said, "she was wailing on the phone, just hysterical, and angry about how, according to Leah, Chauncey Greene had been so *abusive,* the way he and this *bitch yelled* at her like that. The thing is, I don't know what to believe actually happened. The guy is a doctor, after all. And Leah was going on zero sleep. She had been up all night with this Tabek Taboubi—"

"With *who*?"

"The bellboy. The depressed poet. Heck, I don't know!"

"Frankly, this all sounds a little dangerous," Anita said.

"There's more. They're all at some other tourist site. Leah told me she stayed behind with the tour guide, sitting in the car, crying. Humiliated. Livid. Figuring Chauncey Greene and this other tourist are wondering what her deal was. Leah's on the phone with me, sobbing, asking me if she should lie to these people. If she should tell

39

them she was crying because our daughter broke off the engagement, for crissake."

"Well, I hope you said no."

"I said I didn't think it would be a good idea—wait, we just got a long email message. I'll call you back later."

> To: Jeff
> cc: Anita
> May 30, 2015
>
> *First, I wholeheartedly apologize for using the word "crisis" on the phone.*
>
> *I love you. Don't worry. There's no danger. I am just extremely upset and can't stop crying about how The Doctor and The Dragon Lady are treating me. I feel totally disrespected, not listened to, hurt, patronized, talked over, ignored, and bullied . . .*

Leah said she never got a chance to tell her side of the story, although I wasn't positive I understood what the story was, let alone her side of it.

A few minutes later, Leah emailed Anita and me and notified us she had been skipping doses of her meds. "I've been staying up late," she wrote, "talking, writing a lot, photographing, possibly because I'm feeling a bit manic."

Manic, huh? Yeah, a bit.

At the time I didn't really know what manic meant. I knew what a *maniac* was—a guy who drove eighty miles per hour in a school zone. If manic meant "obnoxious" or "self-centered" or "delusional" or "*meshugina*," I would have said Leah was right. If nothing else, she was finally admitting there was something wrong with her, and given the way she'd been yelling at me, I wanted the world to know.

HEY, MY WIFE ADMITTED SHE WAS FEELING A BIT MANIC

A couple of hours later, Chauncey Greene emailed me directly: "I'm concerned about Leah."

Chauncey's wife called me from Chicago to tell me she had no idea what was going on, but Chauncey was worried about Leah and so was she.

I thanked them both for caring. I let Leah know via email that Chauncey Greene had contacted me, and then his wife, and everyone was worried about her.

"Please tell me you're safe," I emailed her.

Leah replied via text that afternoon: "I feel let down and even somewhat betrayed by you. Why do I feel like I'm turning into something like the main character from *One Flew over the Cuckoo's Nest* or Kafka's *The Trial*?"

And a while later she continued her texting with venom: "Just don't you EVER fking tell me again that Chauncey Fking Greene is fking 'concerned' about me after he went fking disassociate and mortally wounded me emotionally while you wouldn't even CONFRONT the Good Fking Doctor on my behalf! And forget fking trying to 'help' me when I think this fking rage toward you has been building up over the last fking 30 years because of how I see your view of 'feminism' and what Leah 'needs' in terms of the good so-called doctor 'just being concerned' about poor, little five-year-old Leah because he fixes blown-up faces but is emotionally torturing his fking 'friend!' Your WORDS MATTER! Meanwhile, my blood fking sugar is dropping, and I think I've not been taking the morning meds in the fking morning and the night ones at night because I've been Fking TRAUMATIZED and the CRUX of the issue is you're more concerned about Chauncey Greene's fking feelings than mine! I just NEED YOUR FKING SUPPORT and you to PUT ME FKING FIRST! BRB."

Leah wrote "BRB" for "be right back," which was pretty funny after a rant like that.

But I wasn't laughing. Although I knew next to nothing about mental illness, I was witnessing in real time the onset of Leah's undiagnosed manic episode.

I also got my first whiff of a gaslighting.

Again and again I would ask myself that summer, "Was I really that big of a putz because I thanked Chauncey Greene for checking in with me about my wife's state of mind instead of scolding him for it?"

OVER THE NEXT FOUR MONTHS, the Kerkouane Incident and Jeff's Failure to Confront Chauncey Greene from Five Thousand Miles Away arose like the Loch Ness monster of mental health crises, over and over. At mercurial marriage counseling sessions. In diatribes to friends. To our children. To extended family. And nearly every day to me.

As Leah's undiagnosed mania aggrandized, Leah's Chauncey Greene Incident tirade became a rambling soliloquy: "See, I was in Tunisia—well, first I went to Israel—actually, first, I was laid off from my job and we went to New York for my daughter's *aufruf,* which is a Jewish tradition, and when I got to Brussels I didn't take my pills, and I wasn't getting enough sleep . . . " and eventually, as the harangue repeatedly bore through my skull, all I would hear was, "*Lorem ipsum dolor sit amet,* fucking arrogant fucking doctor and this *bitch,* and the *crux* of the issue is my asshole husband kissed this doctor's ass because he's rich and white and male and *he didn't stick up for me!*"

Et cetera, et cetera, a whorl of etched venom, a looped mix of rage and hurt:

Once Leah came home, it became a spiraling vituperation all that first summer and, after a major depression, a second manic episode the following summer, when the meltdowns and tirades and incidents and fiascoes increased in intensity.

Something insidious, something stark but still nameless was corroding Leah's brain. And as she and our marriage became unglued, so did my grasp of reality and my mental and physical health.

CHAPTER 5

Our House Is a
Very, Very, Very Fine House

During the summer of 2015, my sister-in-law Lois's older sister, Joni, underwent chemo treatments for stomach cancer. Like everyone else who knew Joni, Leah had been drawn to her vibrancy, warmth, and immeasurable compassion. Her fight with a malignant tumor was a horrible struggle, yet one she handled with grace and determination.

That year Leah mailed Joni "Thinking of You" notecards packed inside boxes with little tchotchkes—a fancy soap one month, a little bag of homemade bath salts the next. Leah heard few direct words of appreciation, but that was all right. Joni was sick for so long and lived far away. Leah never did those acts of kindness for the thanks. She and Joni had that in common. They were the two most thoughtful people I knew.

That was the heart of the Leah I knew, the one who emailed me this:

To: Jeff
Jun 24, 2015

So you know how Tabek Taboubi is my new friend and my

*new social work "project"? And he lives in Tunisia and is
poor and is suicidal, etc., etc.? When you go to Walgreens,
can you pick up a box of nicotine patches for him? Just think
of it as charity.*

Maybe it was charity. Maybe it was grandiosity. Maybe it was Leah being Leah.

As a peace offering of sorts, I bought the nicotine patches and stood in line at the post office for twenty minutes and mailed them to an address in Tunisia, wondering who would end up with them and how much they would go for on the black market—or if my kindhearted wife really was going to help break a suicidal bellhop's addiction to tobacco.

Yet such upright intentions were laced with uranium. With only three or four hours of sleep each night, her mind fluttered like hummingbird wings from idea to idea. She exclaimed to me that since returning from her trip she was full of "creative energy." Enrolling in her font class was only a first step in her resurgent career. She told me she was starting a consulting business, although what she was consulting about was a mystery to me. She insisted she could get all the work she wanted through her contacts and networking. She had credentials, she told me. She was building on her international expertise.

I couldn't keep up with any of it and mostly tried to stay out of her way to avoid a fight over my tepid skepticism.

Around six o'clock one evening she texted me from a Target store in St. Paul, asking me if she should buy me a presentable pair of new shorts to wear during our daughter's wedding weekend in Jamaica.

"No, thanks," I answered her.

Six hours later Leah texted me the fucking store was fucking closing but there was a fucking problem with her fucking Target credit card. At two in the morning she was still arguing with the store manager and trying to pay for whatever pointless *chazerai* she intended to buy. At eight o'clock the next morning she badgered me to go back with her to finish her shopping excursion.

I don't know what the deal was on the Target credit card. I don't know why Leah was in St. Paul in the first place and not at the Target near our house in Minneapolis. I don't know why I went back there with her that morning. I don't know why there were two packed shopping carts of merchandise awaiting her from the previous evening. I don't know why I examined the ugly Bing Crosby shorts she had picked out and why I waited around for another one hour, fifty-five minutes while she shopped for more crap. I don't know why I did a lot of things that summer, or during her manic episode the following year, and I certainly had no idea what Leah was doing or why.

To me she was expending her "creative energy" on a series of distractions or, more accurately, distractions from distractions, and few tasks were actually getting done.

"Leah, we need a list of stuff we have to do around the house and the errands we have to run and clothes we have to pack for the two wedding trips."

"I'll make the list."

"No, you're busy. I can make a spreadsheet with the things we need to do before Jamaica and a list for the trip to LA. It will only take me—"

"I said I'll make a goddamned list!"

Fine. Whatever. You know what, dear? As an alternative to taking on more projects and buying more crapola we don't need, you could just clean up the past month's six hundred pounds of mail and your eight hundred folders and the landfill of trash covering the entire dining room table.

But I was tired of arguing. Since the day she returned from Tunisia, Leah rehashed my defects, especially the Chauncey Greene Incident. *Why did you kiss Chauncey Greene's ass, Jeff? Why had you been so disrespectful, Jeff? Why had you not been more* supportive *of me, Jeff? Why, why, why?*

I dug through the rocks in my head for answers. I had two choices: I could duke it out with Leah in an endless war of words, or I could accept Leah's version of the Chauncey Greene Incident and wave a white flag.

I learned it didn't matter what I did. We'd end up in the same preposterous place:

"I Don't Understand Why You're Angry"

Me: I really thought Chauncey Greene was just concerned about you.

Leah: Poor little me. That is *so condescending*. If he weren't a rich *doctor* you would have stuck up for me.

Me: It wasn't a matter of sticking up for you or not.

Leah: *Words matter.* You didn't give a *shit* about how *I* felt. I was *mortally wounded*, and all you cared about was Chauncey Greene's feelings.

Me: What you were saying wasn't making any sense.

Leah: Take responsibility for your actions!

Me [*impatient*]: All I did was email him and thank him—

Leah: See? See? That is the *crux* of the issue.

Me: [*walking away*] Okay, we're not getting anywhere.

Leah: Oh, fine, walk away. That is *so* typical.

"Yes, I Completely See Why You're Angry"

Me: I can understand now how that must have been hard for you.

Leah: You didn't understand it at the time because all you cared about was yourself.

Me: You may be right about that.

Leah: So I'm right! See? See? The *crux* of the whole situation is that you could not admit I was *right!* You never want to admit you're wrong and I'm right. When it comes right down to it, your only concern is yourself.

Me [*impatient*]: You're right. My only concern is myself.

Leah: Don't get sarcastic. That is *so condescending. Words matter*. Tell me your *feelings*. Why can't you tell me your feelings? Because Zuckermans don't ever talk about their feelings!

Me: [*walking away*] Okay, we're not getting anywhere.

Leah: Oh, fine, walk away. That is *so* typical.

Well, poor me. It was all about *me*, Leah emailed me. "You have your fucking freelance business and you're making thirty-six thousand dollars a year, which isn't very much, and I'm going to make six figures in my consulting business and I'm getting appointments set up and I can't do all that and everything else around here."

And my response to her laundry list of grand responsibilities? "Roger to all that, Leah. Thank you."

LATE ONE EVENING, in a suburban parking lot, Leah spent a few hours emailing and texting people with her phone plugged into the cigarette lighter adapter, draining the car battery.

"It's not my fault that you didn't take care of the battery," Leah said when she called me. "All I ever ask you to do is take care of the cars. Is that too much to ask?"

She called AAA for a jump and found out a tow truck couldn't arrive until midnight.

"Gee, I'd be a real feminist if I drove down there and rescued you," I said.

She hung up on me, and I don't blame her. Sarcasm was no way to communicate the rage, fear, and self-doubt that were building inside me. A former girlfriend told me sarcasm is unresolved anger, defensiveness, and insecurity, to which I replied, "Yeah, like I'm ever sarcastic. Maybe you're the one with the problem." We broke up soon after that, of course. But never having dealt so intimately with a person acting like Leah, I did not have the wherewithal to voice my concerns more productively.

Leah did make it home safely that night. When I heard her walk in the back door, I lay in the dark pretending to sleep, horrified with myself for forcing her to fry in her own folly in a dark parking lot, pleased with myself for not pandering to her hissy fit.

And wondering what she was doing out in the suburbs that late in the first place.

A COUPLE DAYS LATER, my buddy Dr. J, my closest friend in the Twin Cities, dropped by my house. He was a few years younger than I, far more handsome and svelte, a transplanted Catholic from Pennsylvania with bright blue eyes and the calves of a fanatical bicyclist. He was finishing his doctorate in something or other and would invite me over for a study break and ask his wife to leave us alone so we could watch ballgames and hockey on the big TV in his basement and carry on like Wayne Campbell and Garth Algar.

"Hey," Dr. J said when he came to my front door. "You have time for a bottle of beer or two out on your deck?"

"Meet me out back."

He had biked over from his place, a few miles to the west in the suburbs. He looked a little rough from the ride over, but something else was going on.

"I think I'm getting divorced," Dr. J announced.

I was shocked. I was aware that for years his wife had dished up an annual Spousal Performance Review, which was one of the funniest things I'd ever heard and mocked him about relentlessly.

Now it wasn't so funny. I knew that the two of them were under a lot of stress. They had two teenage daughters, one of whom had health problems, and he was working a couple of jobs and pursuing a PhD. I had witnessed Dr. J's wife marching down to the basement in a snit, barely acknowledging me and growling a reminder at him about a kid's doctor's appointment or music lesson, which earned him a time-out or a demerit or detention. He barked back, his wife marched upstairs, he rolled his eyes as usual, and I figured she had her side of the story.

"I don't get it," I said. Sometimes I couldn't help myself. "You mean she's firing you from your marriage?"

"We were just with a counselor. My wife already made an appointment with an attorney."

Holy smokes. I was in more denial than Dr. J. If they were getting divorced, I guess it could happen to just about anyone . . . including Leah and me.

That was a helluva thought two weeks before we'd be flying to Jamaica for our daughter's wedding.

LEAH AND I weren't like Dr. J and his wife. For Pete's sake, we'd been married half our lives. We liked doing things together. Sure, sometimes on the invisible scoresheet I failed to Meet Expectations, and there was always Room for Improvement. But there was no getting fired at our house.

Still, I didn't want to end up like Dr. J, who often faulted himself for not putting enough effort into his marriage. Maybe I should start trying harder to get along with Leah.

So when an acquaintance of mine named Roberto and his wife Yolanda invited me to dinner in St. Paul in gratitude for some volunteering I'd done for his nonprofit, I asked Leah to join us.

"Will you come with me? Wednesday evening at seven thirty."

"Let me check my calendar. What time did you say?"

"Seven thirty."

"I'll be coming from the university. I'll have to meet you over there."

Immediately I regretted not saying five thirty to allow Leah two hours to hop in the shower.

I told Roberto we could both make it.

Around seven o'clock I got a call from Leah. She was stuck in the Little Mogadishu neighborhood of Minneapolis in the rain with another dead car battery and asked me to pick her up.

"Why did you run down the battery again?" I grumbled, the passive-aggressive tarantula crawling up my hind end.

"It's raining! Just come and pick me up. Don't be so unreasonable!"

I didn't know what to do. On the one hand, stopping for her on my way to dinner would take me only five minutes out of my way. I wanted her to come with me to dinner, in part because Roberto and Yolanda were expecting us, and in part because I was determined to try harder to get along with Leah.

On the other hand, what kind of doofus runs down her car battery twice in one week? There should have been consequences for her lousy decision making and time management. I was pissed because she caused her own problem and then yelled at me for being unreasonable. If I rescued her, it would have been an example of the classic Jewish joke about the difference between a schlemiel and a schlimazel: A schlemiel spills his soup on a schlimazel. Only a schlimazel would go out of his way to pick up the schlemiel who wore down her car battery.

But it was raining. My wife was in a jam. Married people help each other.

"So now we're going to be late as usual," I complained when she got in my car.

"So what if we're late? I had an emergency. If we're a few minutes late, who gives a shit?"

"It's impolite and arrogant! Why are you always late for everything?"

"Don't say always! Words matter. I'm not *always* late."

This was going to be a fun evening.

We arrived at the restaurant at a quarter to eight, and Roberto and Yolanda weren't there yet.

"See? You're all fucking pissed off about being late, and they're not even here."

"Quit draining your car battery while you're on your phone for two hours," I said, stupidly taking the bait.

Roberto and Yolanda finally sat down around eight o'clock. Leah and I managed a momentary détente, exchanged pleasantries, and ordered off the menu. She excused herself to go to the women's room.

They were a charming pair of immigrants, Roberto and Yolanda. They were younger than we were, both divorced, with a blended family, four daughters total. I'd met Yolanda only once before. You know how these awkward conversations go.

"So, Yolanda, how's that Brady Bunch deal of yours going with your two families?"

"Our kids do well together. They're pretty well adjusted to our situation."

"That's good."

Tortilla chips and salsa are delivered. I notice some lightning out the window. Was there something about a tornado watch?

"You know how sisters are. They argue all the time."

"Yeah. Our two kids used to fight a lot, too."

"Are they both girls?"

"No, a girl and a boy. Our daughter lives in New York and our son in Oregon."

The tortilla chips are good, we agree.

No sign of Leah.

"So do you two get along with your ex-spouses?"

"Yes and no."

Smiles.

"Roberto, what was the deal there with your first marriage? If it's any of my business."

"So how about those Minnesota Twins?"

We laugh.

Ten minutes later, Leah has not yet returned from the bathroom.

"You want more salsa?"

"Sure."

Twenty minutes later.

"So, Jeff, are you a Vikings fan?"

"No."

We ask for more tortilla chips.

A half hour after Leah left for the restroom, Yolanda asks me if she should check on her.

My wife? I think. *But we're having such a nice time.*

"Fine," I say. "Whatever. I'll text her."

Are you okay? I text.

I'm resting, she texts back.

Yolanda walks over to the women's room and returns a couple moments later.

"She's all right," Yolanda reports back.

Fifteen minutes later Leah emerges from the bathroom. Her face is puffy from crying. I'm just tired, she says. The four of us chat awkwardly for a few minutes, and the conversation comes to a dead end.

IT WAS POURING when we left the restaurant. Leah called AAA to meet us at her car for another jump. We beat the tow truck, and for some reason her car started and we canceled the tow. Leah and I drove home separately.

Maybe she's finally cracking, I hoped. Maybe she'll sleep for the next three days and wake up forgetting she had ever been to Tunisia.

At the end of the freeway exit ramp about a mile from our house I passed a beggar, dripping wet in the rain, holding a sign: Help needed God bless.

"Did you see that poor guy at the exit ramp?" I said to Leah when we got back to the house.

"Yeah. I'm going to make him some sandwiches."

"And bring them over right now? Uh, that's nice of you, but it's like ten-thirty and raining."

"I'll be right back."

I remember her getting home around midnight.

She remembers almost none of all this.

Roberto and Yolanda remember the evening because it was weird and sad.

I also remember wondering if Leah and I would survive as a couple, or if we were doomed, like Dr. J and his wife and Roberto and Yolanda and their ex-spouses.

OUR MARRIAGE was in crisis, Leah said, which was the one thing we agreed on. I was hoping her psychologist, Dr. Melnick, would grab Leah by the ears and tell her to get her shit together. But I wasn't invited to those sessions, and what went on there was apparently only Leah's business.

I suggested we try the free walk-in counseling clinic[1] in south Minneapolis. We had driven past the place a thousand times: a converted turn-of-the-century house staffed by short-term therapists working pro bono, serving for the most part the working poor with drug dependency and mental health issues.

Actually, *we* didn't have issues, according to Leah. *I* had issues. She deluged the counselor with the entire story, beginning with the Chauncey Greene Incident, but then she slammed the pause button and said, "Wait, first of all," hit the rewind button, explained how she and I met in Duluth, how we loved each other, how we were perfect for

---

[1] We're blessed to live in Minnesota, home of the 1961 Rose Bowl-winning Golden Gophers and the Therapy Capital of the Free World. See Walk-In Counseling Center, http://walkin.org/.

each other and had never had any problems. Then she switched gears, blathered on about how *great* she was doing, that she had so much *creative energy*, followed by a rant about her parents, her brother, my parents, my brother, a saga about screwing up her meds in Brussels, and a jeremiad about the tourist from Houston.

"And that Jeff doesn't understand that *words matter* and the *crux* of the issue is that Jeff is turning sixty-one years old this fall, the same age as his father when *he* died, and Jeff is just scared he's going to die—"

At which point the counselor interjected, "Whoa, hold on! *Hold on!*"

I sat there immobilized, waiting for Leah to do a Mike Tyson on me and bite off a chunk of my ear, and then I started weeping, dabbing my drippy eyes like a child.

"Oh, now you're crying!" Leah sneered. "Why? Because you pity yourself? Poor Jeffrey. See? That is the *crux* of the issue. It's all about *you*. What about *my* feelings?"

It went on like that for nearly an hour, until the counselor said we were out of time.

Leah wanted to know if we could have an additional session. She was so wound up that she would have spent all night at that place, talking the ears off a rotating shift of therapists.

"You can come back next week," the counselor said. "You might be assigned a different therapist. But I've made notes for our files."

I had a feeling the "notes" on the counselor's pad consisted of a grocery list and a doodle of a panic-stricken mouse about to get his tail cut off with a carving knife.

TAKE A DEEP BREATH, Jeff.

It was the Fourth of July. I loaded my bike onto my car and spent a couple hours cycling through the woods and prairies in a county park in the far western suburbs of Minneapolis. I'd worked hard all my life, had kept myself healthy since being diagnosed with celiac disease. All I wanted in my sixties and seventies was a peaceful retirement together with Leah and an occasional splurge on a slab of fresh halibut.

On my drive back to Minneapolis I hid out at a ballfield not far from Paisley Park in Chanhassen, watching some kids over on the swings with their parents. That got me reminiscing about spending Independence Days with my own family in Pittsburgh, and years later in the Twin Cities with Leah and Sarah and Joey when they were little. We took a snapshot of Sarah dressed in a red-white-and-blue clown suit that Leah had sewn, pulling little Joey with his painted nose in a wagon along a parade route over on Como Avenue, gaping at the men and women on stilts. We lived it up that day, indulging the kids with cotton candy and Bomb Pops because Leah's parents were too uptight to ever let her have fun.

When our kids were young we had little spending money, but later on, Leah and I both found good jobs with travel perks. Now Sarah was getting married and Joey was a teacher living in Portland and here I was on Independence Day, hiding from Leah's fury in a park a mile from Prince's mansion, about to leave town in a few days for Jamaica, and the two of us couldn't even go to Target together without igniting a Revolutionary War battle.

"It's liberating to get thirty-two years of anger off my chest," Leah told the crisis counselor.

She's been mad at me for that long? I wondered.

But it wasn't just me. I heard her for hours on the phone chewing out credit card companies and United Airlines, baying at the chain of command that she was a "communications professional," whatever that was, and offered to have them hire her as a consultant on customer relations. I hoped those poor souls on the other end of those calls were well paid. It must have been exhausting listening to Leah go on and on, and I suspect they'd been trained to never tell a ranting customer to just shut up. Worse for me was listening to her fuming to her friends and our children about her rants with the credit card companies and the airline, so I'd hear the same complaints over and over.

The thing is, I don't know what those managers should have said instead. I had no idea what to say or do, and I was living with it all day and all night. Later that summer, when I started attending support group meetings, I heard others' stories about getting pummeled by a family member's illness. You're supposed to choose your battles, but when you live with a person with a severe mental illness, you may be embroiled in a dozen verbal scrimmages a day, and you'll find yourself surrendering countless times, crushing your confidence in your own intuition.

The National Alliance on Mental Illness, or NAMI, the nation's leading grassroots education and advocacy organization, has 168,000 members. Talk to any of us who are family members and you'll get a hundred thousand stories about the exhausting moral and practical judgments we need to make every day.

Yet to say we must become captive to our loved ones' illnesses—a Stockholm-syndrome type of irrational love for our captors— overstates our family members' power over us and our impotence to make sane choices. Leah never held a gun to my head to force me to mail a box of nicotine patches to Tunisia or shop at Target at eight in the morning for a pair of shorts she wanted me to buy. I just needed months of therapy and years of support group meetings to help me better establish boundaries. In doing so, I learned to judge as neither noble nor contemptible my decisions or those of other spouses, parents, siblings, or friends in my shoes.

I held my ground on the shorts, though. They were really ugly.

A COUPLE of our closest friends, Emma and Shelley, invited a group of people to watch Fourth of July fireworks over the Mississippi River from their big viewing deck in downtown Minneapolis, so close to the explosions you could feel the heat.

"Not sure Leah and I will make it tonight," I texted Emma. "We decided to hold our own fireworks show in our living room."

"What do you mean? What's up?"

"Let's just say things are a tad tense around here."

But the heck with Leah. I texted her: "I intend to bike down to Emma and Shelley's condo." Riding the bike trail that evening along the railroad tracks from our house to downtown Minneapolis would be easier than dealing with the traffic jams, and anyway, Leah insisted she would get there on time and I should just go my fucking self.

She arrived by car a couple hours after I did, sparkling like always. I watched her do a splendid job of pretending to ignore me. I overheard her pontificating about her Target credit card fiasco, that she was going to write an article in the *New York Times* about it, that she was starting some kind of an LLC, or limited liability corporation—just blathering bombast from what I could tell.

I felt sad, a little embarrassed for her, for myself—except for the part where Leah had been grinding my face into a timid lather of self-doubt while proclaiming it was condescending of me to think I was responsible for her actions. That would lead to a screed about the Chauncey Greene Incident, about how I needed to take responsibility for the *pain* I caused her, and that I needed to deal with my own *feelings*, et cetera, et cetera.

At ten o'clock, the fireworks show began.

Ooh. Aah.

I hurried out alone right afterward to bike home through the gridlock in downtown Minneapolis. After turning off onto the bike trail,

I rode westward into the black Midwestern night. Again I had too much time to brood about our family, about how much I loved Leah, about how my normally funny, sweet wife was apparently losing her mind.

At the north end of Cedar Lake I stopped to breathe.

We'd spent an awful lot of hot summer nights together, going clear back to our honeymoon in southern Spain in 1984. Leah and I sweating buckets, listening through the walls of a six-dollar-a-night room to some poor guy coughing phlegm, sounding like a trombonist in a grade school band trying to play Stravinsky while the two of us giggled in the dark. In Sevilla we found a quieter *pensión*, made tender love one afternoon as a guitarist played Albéniz in the courtyard, walked under moonlight and gawked at young children out with their families for a midnight meal. Vacations in California, Florida, New England, the Puget Sound. A road trip around the deep South in 2014, a cotton field in northern Alabama at dusk, a cloud of dewy air, both of us struck by the beauty of the rolling Alabama landscape.

Now I was alone in the dark in Minneapolis, listening to the frogs croaking, the water licking the rocks on the shore of Cedar Lake, my sick belly rumbling, breathing the thick air. Feeling like a late-middle-aged man who had just watched fireworks entirely alone among a crowd of forty people on the balcony of his friends' condo in a nation of more than three hundred million Americans—not one of them his wife. Because the Leah he had known had suddenly drifted away like the smoke of spent fireworks.

Chapter 6

Wedding Bell Blues

"**J**amaica?" our friends smirked. "So your daughter is having a *destination* wedding!"

Uh-huh. The whole idea reeked of ostentation and privilege and guests' distress from forking over a fortune on airfare and hotel rooms, tempered only by unrelenting alcohol and weed.

None of that fit Leah's or my style. For our wedding in 1984 Leah bought two hundred bucks of Irish linen and paid a seamstress to sew her dress, and I bought a lightweight two-piece suit at Dayton's department store. The ceremony took place in the outdoor garden of a Skokie restaurant whose manager assured us, "The accent will be on the bagels." My childhood buddy Michael played a twelve-string guitar; other old friends held a chuppah above our heads that Leah had designed and sewn. For the reception we splurged on a klezmer dance band that played the traditional wedding dance song "Hava Nagila," and there is a photo of the two of us, frog-eyed and terror struck, hoisted high in the air on chairs by a few of our strongest friends as the rest of our guests circled around us in a joyous dance of the hora.

That was a long time ago, but for an old Jew like me, even if your daughter and her loving boyfriend were getting married at a *destination*, even if the accent would be on the non-kosher shellfish and a reggae band would play the wedding dance, and even if the mother of the bride was acting manic, there was nothing like celebrating a happy occasion with your family.

LEAH AND I had a predawn flight to catch from Minneapolis to Jamaica. She had a brainstorm: We would leave a day early and ride the light rail to Bloomington down by the airport, chillax in a cheap hotel all afternoon, find somewhere to eat dinner, board an airport shuttle around five in the morning, perhaps have time for a cup of coffee before the plane departed. Maybe throw some wild lovemaking in there at some point.

Smiley face.

She was five hours late getting out the door of our house, picked a fight with me at the 50th Street train station, and wandered around the Mall of America for hours while I ate a fifty-five-and-over dinner alone at a Denny's. She finally got to the motel at one in the morning after texting her friend Lauren all evening, slept one hour, and then called us a cab at four thirty to take us to the airport a couple miles away. After we checked our luggage I lost track of her at the TSA and flew to Jamaica without her, where I hung out in the airport for a few hours, walking in circles like a gerbil while getting angry texts from her about the fascist cops and an alternate flight from Miami she'd be taking, and telling me to stay put at the airport instead of heading to the beach resort to see my family.

Hmmm. Would anyone notice if the father of the bride skipped out on the whole event and chartered a fishing boat to Cuba?

I DIDN'T WANT to drag Joey into any of this. He had assumed I was exaggerating when I called his mother "uncontained." But later, when she saw Joey at the resort, Leah corralled him for a tirade about how she missed the plane because the TSA and airport cops stopped her at security.

"I just wanted to know if I could bring your old marijuana pipe on board and the *fucking* airport cops kept asking me what *meds* I was on, which was a fucking HIPAA *violation,* which I knew because I am a public health *professional,* and anyway it was none of their *fucking business* what meds I was on—"

"Mom, please don't swear so much—"

"I can *fucking* swear if I fucking want to. I *like* to swear—"

"It sounds like you had a rough flight—"

"'A rough flight'? That sounds condescending. And there's more."

Then she bellowed about the kerfuffle she got into with the fucking *flight attendant* on her way to Jamaica. "Can you *believe* I was escorted off the plane by the *captain?* Like I was some kind of fucking criminal or something? And I'm white and middle-class and educated and can you imagine, Joey, what would have happened if I were *black* or American *Indian?*"

Et cetera, like that, the whole first day.

The next morning at breakfast, Joey drew upon his training as a middle-school teacher and concocted a solution to the endless orations.

"Mom," he said to Leah.

"Stop interrupting me—"

"Mom, listen for one minute. I know how we can better talk to each other—"

"I am listening. I listen all the time, but you have to let me talk and not interrupt me—"

"Mom," Joey said patiently, "just listen. It's called a dyad. We use it with our students. The way it works is—"

"Daddy's and my communication problems are more complicated than—"

"Mom, *listen*. Listen! Will you just stop talking and listen?"

Leah shut her mouth at last. Joey had always worked magic with his mother.

"It's called a dyad. You set a timer, see, and you take turns talking. Each person gets one minute to talk. Or ninety seconds or two minutes, whatever you decide. And then no one gets to talk longer than—"

"That sounds *great*, Joey!" I exclaimed. "Leah, can we try that? The dyad timer? To help us with our communication issues?"

What a condescending crock of BS, I thought. Communication issues? One person around here is cracked wider than an oyster and I'm pretty sure it ain't me . . . at least yet.

Leah, Joey, and I tried it out. Leah would fiddle with the timer on her phone, press the start button, and then call "Time's up!" when the one or two or three minutes had expired. And it worked. Instead of yammering endlessly, Leah was now forced by the structure of the dyad to cut herself off after a couple moments, until the next time she spoke, and the time after that, and the time after that. And thus Joey and I survived the wedding weekend in 120-second increments.

AS FOR THE BRIDE, I tried to shield my daughter from the worst of her mother's madness that weekend. Sarah was stoic and relaxed and somehow managed to wear an invisible layer of armor underneath her swimsuit. Or maybe everyone but me was stoned.

Sarah and Seth had arranged a signing of the *ketubah,* the wedding contract, an hour before the ceremony. Based on an ancient Jewish marital rite, two witnesses sign the document, making the deal official (and the wedding ceremony itself moot). So with the hot tropical wind blowing in off the ocean, an honored handful of celebrants gathered for the signing in a quiet curtained room.

My brother David's wife Lois was one of the two witnesses at my wedding to Leah. Now their daughter Tova, a month older than Sarah and a niece whom I loved like a daughter, was there to sign her cousin's ketubah. Sarah and Seth's old friend officiated the certificate signing, offering some solemn words about love and marriage and Jewish tradition, and two old men, the fathers of the bride and groom, wept more proudly and joyfully than anyone.

From there we wound our way toward the oceanfront, where the seventy guests were being seated for the actual wedding ceremony. It was July, it was muggy, it had rained, and now the tropical flowers glistened. So did my wife, wearing a lavender sleeveless dress, her neck wrapped in a delicate pastel scarf, her face adorned with a little makeup and a smile, and with those red tints and thick brown curls laced by the light of the tropical sun, she sparkled like she did thirty years earlier at our own wedding.

She and I stood with the bride, waiting for the procession down the aisle to begin. Predictably, though, something woeful must have happened behind the scenes. Or maybe it was everything—the wedding, the stress, the after-effects of food poisoning on Sarah and Seth (we later found out), the ganja and the booze.

"Dad," Sarah muttered to me tearfully, "I can't *take* Mom! She's nuts!"

Sarah, adorned in a strapless white wedding gown, her eyes moist, her long brown tresses curled, standing slumped between her mother and me, minutes before her marriage ceremony.

I remember this anguished moment a few years later now, like watching myself in a horror movie. For my daughter's sake I somehow excavated a few morsels of strength and calm, vaguely aware I was stepping through a trapdoor into an abyss. Digging into the core of my heart for compassion for my sick wife and our unnerved daughter, I somehow found a shard of grace and love.

"Honey," I whispered into Sarah's ear. "I think something is wrong with Mom's brain. If she had cancer we would be there for her."

The guests were waiting for us.

"Sarah, try to be in the moment."

Then, as the sun dipped down over the Caribbean, Leah and I escorted our daughter slowly, serenely, past the gathered friends, past David and his family. Past them all we walked to the chuppah, under which the groom and our daughter's future awaited her.

And when in a centuries-old tradition Seth stomped the wedding glass with his right foot, I, with joy and terror, awaited the next calamity in our lives.

BACK IN MINNEAPOLIS, with only a few days to go before our flight to Los Angeles for Cousin Max's wedding, Leah was more consumed by creative energy than ever. She organized and then reorganized the bookshelves, the tools in the hardware drawer, and the box of spare change on our dresser. She tried to master a Mac operating system and said I wasn't much fucking help with that or with her mystery consulting business.

We decided to give the walk-in counseling clinic another try. We each had agendas: Leah set out to prove I was a sexist, self-centered, controlling asshole, and I set out to show the counselor Leah needed an exorcism.

"I read the previous notes in your file," the new counselor said. "As a reminder, to make progress it's best to talk about our feelings. Try avoiding accusatory 'you statements' and instead use 'I statements.'"[1]

"Can I go first?" I asked.

"Of course he wants to go first. This is what I mean by he never lets me talk—"

"It's Tuesday, Leah. We're leaving for our trip in three days. I noticed your unpacked suitcase is on the floor of the living room."

"That is so condescending. I said I'll be packed in time. I *feel* like he's trying to control me," and then she rambled on for ten minutes about just needing someone who would listen to her.

"I feel exhausted by all that," I said, when she was finally through.

"I feel like you're an asshole."

That went on for another forty-five minutes, and we ran out of time with nothing resolved. Again the therapist regretted the clinic was limited to crisis counseling and suggested we would benefit from ongoing work with a marriage therapist. I left the session doubting my sanity because none of these counselors seemed interested in diagnosing Leah as having lost her mind.

We went back a third time two days later. I was curious what would happen if I just sat there and said nothing. After Leah's forty-minute soliloquy, the counselor all but demanded Leah shut up and listen. In reaction, she burst from her chair, stormed out of the clinic, and ran to her car.

"Whoops," I said. "She left her purse."

The counselor gave me a look of sorrow, half pity, half astonishment,

---

[1] "An 'I' message or 'I' statement is a style of communication that focuses on the feelings or beliefs of the speaker rather than thoughts and characteristics that the speaker attributes to the listener." Avoid statements such as "You are driving me mad with your eight hundred unfinished projects." See "'I' Message," GoodTherapy Blog, February 2018, http://www.goodtherapy.org/blog/psychpedia/i-message.

a look that said the walk-in staff offers one-time counseling and the two of us needed a marital lobotomy.[2]

I chased after Leah out the front door of the clinic, called to her that she left her purse.

"Fuck you, asshole!" she screamed at me, and then she sped off in her Honda.

Hey, I thought, *the car battery worked.*

I MULLED backing out of the trip to Los Angeles, even though we'd lose a fortune on airfare and the hotel room we'd booked. And we would be the jerks who stuck a wedding party with the bill for uneaten dinners. But when I suggested to Leah we just bag the whole trip, she said, "Fine. Then I'll go without you."

Great. Dare I turn her loose on my extended family?

No. I had to take one for the team. I'd fly to LA with her and try to prevent a kamikaze hit on Cousin Max's wedding.

We managed to pack our suitcase in time for the Friday flight, but not without calamities before the plane even took off: the We Arrived Late to the Airport Incident; the Suitcase Is Too Heavy, Leah, Just Like I Told You Incident; and then the Now We Have to Run to the Gate Incident. For the most part I sucked it all up. But somewhere over Nevada there was the Spirit Airlines Credit Card Incident, which led to a monumental fight in the hotel and subsequent Leah Locked Me Out

---

[2] A couple of years later, when Leah was mired in depression and I was dwelling in my own mental health sub-basement, Leah suggested I get some one-on-one help at the same clinic. To my surprise, the therapist remembered me from my earlier sessions with Leah. "You must see hundreds of clients a year," I said. "We must have been really memorable." The counselor said, "Oh, you two were memorable, all right."

of Our Hotel Room Incident and then Jeff Listened to Bad Advice and
Sent a Pair of Cousins and a Security Guy Up to Our Room to Check
on Leah Catastrophe. Leah responded to that one with an uppercase,
six-hundred-thirty-word email diatribe, which I've edited. Subject line:
"You big FKG immature narcissist!"

> To: Jeff
> July 17, 2015
>
> *You're acting like a "begrudging, stubborn, childish
> Zuckerman!" YOU'RE ACTING LIKE A BIG BABY, won't
> continue the 60-second dyads, AND ARE OUT OF YOUR
> MIND.*
>
> *Plus, the situation is sooo bad that—you're gonna laugh at
> me—I don't feel physically or emotionally safe.*
>
> *Jeff, dear? It's not all about you. Too bad it's taken 31 years of
> marriage for you to get any insight into this.*
>
> *P.S. Even though I've refrained until now, the cat is now out of
> the bag, so FUCK YOU! FUCK, FUCK YOU*

For me to "get any insight" that I was out of *my* mind?

Her stupefying behavior was relentless. She was two hours late for
the groom's dinner. I reached a new low in couch surfing, ending up on
a cot in my nephew's hotel room for part of the night.

On Saturday morning my Cousin Merle, a licensed therapist from
New York City, reluctantly but lovingly wasted an hour of her vacation attempting to mediate a dialogue between two bickering crackpots.
Poor Cousin Merle, but at least we were meeting poolside in summery
southern California. I sat there dully confident an experienced clinician
like Merle would notice her Cousin Leah had gone off the deep end and

would yank a butterfly net out of her beach bag. But Merle seemed a bit too eager to give Leah the chance to snap off my head like a mousetrap while I melted in the sun like a slice of provolone.

(Months later Merle admitted she could tell Leah was manic, but the hotel pool was hardly the time and place to get into it, which I understood, especially from Merle's perspective. If I were in Merle's shoes, trying to survive a weekend with our extended family, I would have dived into the pool that morning and held my breath underwater until Leah wandered off and started applying for another fifty airline credit cards.)

By Sunday morning Leah and I agreed to change our vacation plans. She would visit her old hippie friends in Santa Barbara or wherever they lived because I couldn't give a rat's ass where she was going, and I would return home to Minnesota a day early. We had already spent a fortune that summer, and now there would be penalties for rebooking our flights. But I gave up caring about the money we were blowing on travel. I just wanted to sleep alone in my own bed.

CHAPTER 7

Just Because You're Paranoid

B ack home, I asked my friend Heshie Goldfarb to meet me for a late dinner—not that I could eat. Heshie was a quirky old Jew like me, with thinning hair and a high-pitched, rat-a-tat-tat cackle. We had been close friends since our boys were little, he and his wife Judy and Leah and I. Now I had to decide how much to blab about the bedlam at my house. Leah wasn't one to advertise her tribulations, particularly our marital *communication issues.*

We met on the outdoor patio of the French Meadow Café on Lyndale Avenue. After some silly chitter-chatter I finally cut to the chase. "Okay. So. Um. Um. See. So, um."

"That's easy for you to say."

"So, um," I tried again, "something is wrong with Leah."

"Is she sick?"

I scrunched my face. What do you say to that question . . . is Leah "sick"? I shook my head grimly, pointed my finger at my noodle, drawing circles in the air.

"What do you mean?" Heshie said. "She's . . . cuckoo?"

That's the word Heshie used. *Cuckoo.* It was the incorrect word, certainly not in the *DSM-V*.[1] But unofficially, yes, Heshie. She had been acting cuckoo. Like she was having a mental breakdown.

I popped my lid, the whole shmear. I felt like a heel telling Heshie the stories—the car battery calamities, the Target ado, the marijuana pipe at the TSA debacle, the argument with the flight attendant, the dyad timer, the Spirit Airlines credit card fight and its aftermath, and a dozen other fiascoes I won't get into. Good stories, in a way. Just weird enough that when you hear them for the first time and you're Heshie Goldfarb, of course you laugh, that crinkle-fried girlie giggle of his. I smiled, too, and sniggered at the inanity, which made me feel guilty because we were yukking it up over my wife's apparent nervous breakdown.

"Nervous breakdown," I heard myself saying. Maybe Leah was having some kind of nervous breakdown. That got me going, all right, and I did my best to keep Heshie from seeing how my eyes were flooding.

I wasn't done. I spilled the rest: the Chauncey Greene crisis, the email about her saving the depressed poet waiter in Tunisia from killing himself, about mailing the guy a box of nicotine patches.

"Wait, *what* depressed Tunisian bellhop? Nicotine patches?" I could tell Heshie was about to bust. "Jeffrey, what in the hell are you talking about?"

"In Kerkouane," I said. "This guy Tabek Taboubi. I mailed him a box of nicotine patches. Maybe he wasn't the waiter. The waiter was a guy in Tunis. Tabek Taboubi was the bellhop. Or maybe there were *two* depressed poets. The whole thing was so convoluted—"

When he heard all that, Heshie finally shrieked, a sonic boom of convulsive laughter that blew across the patio, sent an umbrella flying, a

[1] *The Diagnostic and Statistical Manual of the American Psychiatric Association,* the bible of mental illnesses.

fierce blast that would have thrown me from my chair if I weren't hanging on to the edge of the table for dear life.

Uh-huh, I thought, shaking my head. *What a pal. Ho-ho.*

Heshie was beside himself, wiping his eyes, tears dripping into his brown ale, squealing to me he was wetting his pants. Jumped up, said he had to run quick to take a leak. I'll be right back, Jeffrey, he said, waddling his penguin walk, laughing the whole way to the can.

Sheesh. Okay, so it was funny.

But the whole thing felt lousy. Heshie and I and our wives had known each other a long time. They cared about Leah, and I knew under the howling Heshie was astonished by how I described Leah's personality transformation.

It felt so disloyal telling these stories. As usual, I had made it sound like everything was Leah's fault, not mine, not that arrogant Chicago doctor and that tourist from Houston. I doubt Leah had blabbed to her friends about my personality "quirks," like how I'd probably spent four years of my life looking around the house for my wallet.

Eventually Heshie calmed down. He apologized for laughing, said he was truly sorry about what I had been going through, that it sounded horrible, that he and Judy loved the two of us, that the whole thing was a shock. Asked me if I was worried about my marriage.

Asked me if I was planning to move out or what.

It suddenly got quiet out there on the patio.

"Move out? Really?"

"I don't know, Jeffrey. I'm an architect. You need a therapist or a lawyer."

Heshie said he had a meeting with a client in the morning. Maybe he had heard enough.

"So," I said, "do I sound like an asshole?"

"You're not an asshole. There's something wrong with Leah,

my friend. There's something wrong with you, too, but we've always known that."

We laughed and paid the tab and headed out into the night. I checked my phone for the latest diatribe.

"Oh, my God, Heshie. Look. Look at this one."

It was a six-page text message, an eight-hundred-character rant, the Fidel Castro of texts.

Alas. I wish I had saved it for the historical record. All I can do is show from memory a word-cloud version of Leah's tirade to me that night:

Heshie read the message and looked aghast.

"Jeffrey, she's psychologically abusing you, my friend. I'd be a little scared if I were you. You better be careful."

Wait, what? Psychological abuse? Are you saying I am *an abused husband?*

No way. No way, man.

"Thanks for listening," I told Heshie, looking at him in the eyes. He was like a brother to me. "I'm glad you had a good laugh."

I smiled with him. It was sort of funny, in a way. I walked down the block to my car and got in and drove home, choking the steering wheel so tightly it screamed at me, too.

THE WORDS *psychological abuse* stung. For Pete's sake, my wife wasn't *abusive*. And I wasn't some weak-kneed toady, like henpecked Mr. Peterson on *The Bob Newhart Show*, the same actor who voiced Piglet in the Winnie the Pooh stories. That's who an abused husband is, right there. Piglet.

But I was rattled. When I arrived home I pulled my car into the garage out back in the alley. But instead of venturing into our split-entry house through the back door and dining room, I slipped in through the front door. There was no way I was going to sleep that night in bed with the sociopath who had texted me that rant. My son's old twin bed was downstairs in my office. I would be safe down there for a night, could deal with Leah's sick brain in the morning.

I lay in bed, fried as crisp as a Frito. *My wife is a sociopath*, I thought. *Or is she a psychopath? I always get them mixed up.*

Man, who cared? The point was that all of a sudden my wife had flipped out and she really had thought I was an asshole all along. That she hated me. *Hate.* What a word! People in normal marriages don't hate each other. Sure, they piss each other off constantly. But hate? Do couples who get divorced hate each other? My buddy Dr. J's wife flunked him on his annual Spousal Performance Review, but that was just a business decision, not hate!

Maybe Heshie was right, I thought. Psychological abuse. Maybe I'd stepped into *The Manchurian Candidate*, and the next thing I knew Leah would be flashing the queen of spades at me and I'd be taking the first train to Chicago and murdering the Chauncey Greene.

For God's sake, get a grip, Jeff. You're just paranoid. Your wife isn't a Russian spy; it's Leah we're talking about here.

Psychological abuse?

Suddenly, tossing and turning down there in the dark in my son's old bed, I fell into a pit of paranoia.

What if Leah hates me so much she wants to kill me? She won't shoot me. For one thing, there's no gun in the house. Leah with a gun? Get real, man. The woman couldn't load a water pistol, let alone fire a gun.

But she might stab me to death. We have those big kitchen knives. She could grab a knife, sneak downstairs after I fall asleep, slash my neck, and scream, "You weren't supportive *of me!* [Stab!] *That is the* crux *of the issue!"* [Stab! Stab!]

Boychik, I thought. *Listen to yourself. You're just panicking. What does Heshie know?*

On the other hand, I might be paranoid, but that doesn't mean Leah isn't going to murder me. I have to get out of the house. But it's midnight. Where am I supposed to go?

The loveseat in the screened-in deck. I can lock myself in with the latch on the screen door. Leah won't even know I'm out there.

I grabbed a thin blanket, tiptoed out the front door, shut it gently. I wasn't sure even if Leah was home, in bed, upstairs, drinking blood, or what. I shuffled through the dark path to the backyard, tiptoed up the wooden stairs leading to the deck. Quietly opened and gently closed the screen door, latched it shut. A cocker spaniel could have figured out how to get in there, especially one armed with a butcher's knife, but whatever. I'd figure it all out in the morning.

If I lived that long.

WHEN I WOKE UP, I figured I'd vamoose until the dust settled. First I needed to retrieve my keys and wallet from inside the house. I tried the back door. Locked. I went around to the front door. Also locked. Sheesh. Leah must have thought I had fallen asleep downstairs or assumed I never came home and locked all the doors before she went to bed.

Now what?

Between our bedroom and the deck is a chest-level window, which Leah had left unlocked. I could step on the loveseat and climb in the house through the window. If I were quiet, I wouldn't even wake her. I just needed to slither past and grab my keys and my wallet. She sleeps with earplugs, doesn't even hear the kitchen smoke detector go off when I burn a piece of toast. I just needed to hoist my way in through the window, grab my stuff, and skedaddle.

I gently slipped the window screen out of the frame, slid open the window, got one leg up and over the sill, then the other, softly lowered myself to the bedroom floor. Leah was still in bed, asleep. I snuck past her in the dark through the bedroom doorway, choked by the inanity of breaking into my own bedroom like a cartoon cat burglar. I spotted and grabbed my wallet off the coffee table.

Only needed to find my keys and blow out of there.

Not on the hook by the back door. Not on the dining room table, not on the kitchen counter. Not by the front door. Where were my keys? They couldn't be in our bedroom. I never went into the bedroom when I got home. The bathroom? *Where had I set my keys—*

"If you're looking for your keys, I hid them," Leah sneered.

Startled in my own house. Good God.

"Where did you put my keys, Leah? Leah, *where are my keys*?"

"I told you. I hid them."

"Where?"

"I'm not telling you."

"Fine, then I'll take your keys." They were on her desk.

"Oh, no, you don't!" Leah yelled at me, and she grabbed at the car-abiner that holds her keyrings.

"Leah, give me your keys!" I yelled back, and I grabbed at her wrist. "No!"

She refused to let go of her carabiner. I started wrestling her, and the two of us tumbled into the pantry, falling on top of the paper bags next to the mop bucket as Leah squeezed her keys in a death grip.

Don't hit her, I told myself.

"Ow!" she screamed.

Her house key visibly scraped the skin on her wrist. There was no blood, but I knew the jig was up. She started carrying on how she was going to call the cops on me and tell them I had physically assaulted her. I ran out the back door, Leah screaming at me from the deck, the neighbors surely hearing her. "You asshole! You *fucking asshole!*"

With shaking hands, I dug around underneath a rock by the garage entryway door for the hidden spare key, unlocked the door, grabbed my bike cable with a combination lock, got on my bicycle, and tore away from my psychopathic wife.

Panting, freaked out, I stopped a few blocks away and called my friend Emma, screaming incoherently into the phone.

"Calm down!" Emma said, maybe wondering if I was choking on a sock.

Me: [incomprehensible, shrieking]

"Jeff, listen to me. Just calm down." Emma understood the gist of it. "I'm at work. I want you to come over to our apartment at five o'clock. Will you be safe until then?"

"Sure," I said. Sure I was safe. I was sixty years old and had fallen into the pantry during a scuffle with my wife and I scraped her wrist a little and was riding around on my bicycle with nowhere to go and my marriage exploding before my eyes. Thank you, I said. Yes. See you at five o'clock.

I had time to kill before Emma would arrive home from work. I called my friend Marc, who lived in the same downtown apartment building overlooking the Mississippi River as Emma and Shelley.

"You mind if I stop by your place for a while?"

"Sure, come on up. The cats and I are just hanging out."

Biking around town in the midday heat was helping me burn off some anger, but my brain was swimming in fear of the unknown chaos I was heading into. For one thing, I was 95 percent sure Leah was the sick one in all this. But I could have handled it better. She wasn't really going to stab me last night. Cripes. Fighting over a set of keys with your wife? The whole thing sounded like some professional wrestling shenanigans. When did I become a Jewish Hulk Hogan? Why should anyone believe me?

My friends live in a fancy apartment building with a locked entryway where visitors buzz their way in past the security guy. A little waterfall in the grand foyer. Most guests who walk in don't look or smell like I did that day.

"Thanks for having me over," I told Marc when he answered his door. I loved the guy's face, like a continent where you wish you lived, an old-world Lebanese mustache, a sardonic smile, and laughing, expressive eyes. "Your condo looks great. Are you selling it?"

"No. Why do you ask?"

He had recently retired and had been making noise for years about moving to San Diego.

"It's so clean. I thought maybe you and a Realtor were staging it."

What I really wondered is how much a condo would cost in that building—plus I wondered why the guy even let me through the doorway once he got a whiff of me. I assumed he would spray the place with Lysol once I left.

"Jeff, how was Jamaica? How was Sarah's wedding?"

I could no longer hold it together. "Do you mind if I use your bathroom?"

I washed my hands, cried through the water as I splashed my face, sat on the commode and shit last night's dinner, and then washed my face a while longer. The guy's bathroom was so clean I avoided the hand towel and wiped the sink and my hands with a wad of tissues and flushed the toilet again.

"What's going on?" Marc asked me when I collapsed on a bar stool near his kitchen.

I barely knew where to begin. I gave him a quick version of the Kerkouane Incident, the TSA and wedding fiascoes, and the fight Leah and I had gotten into that morning.

"There you have it," I said. "You got any wine?"

"Help yourself, Jeff. Listen. It sounds like there's something wrong with Leah."

"I don't think I caught that. Say that again?"

"I've known you both a long time. From what you've told me, there's something wrong with Leah."

What a perfect thing for him to have said.

"How do you know it's not me?"

"Jeff, it isn't you."

I took a few deep breaths. "Is it okay if I sit here and cry into your Chablis until my other friends get home?"

"Yes, but now I'm going to have to fumigate the whole apartment."

I loved that guy's mustache smile. When it was time to go, he gave me the longest hug I'd gotten in months.

"I'm not gay, ya know," I said, and we both laughed.

As bad as I felt spilling my story to Marc, it felt particularly disgraceful tattling on Leah to Emma and Shelley. We had been couple-friends for twenty years. But Emma was like a sister to me, and I unloaded the whole shebang like a bucket of blood. I spared no detail of Leah's rage and the terror I felt, and I eventually curled into the fetal position in their living room.

"She has no insight," Emma said a little perilously, and then she said it again a few moments later, emphatically: "She has no insight."[2]

She and Shelley offered me their shower, presumably because I smelled like rotting meat. Emma said they'd put me up in their guest bedroom and lent me a clean T-shirt and pair of gym shorts to sleep in and said if Leah called them looking for me they'd keep quiet.

Not that I slept. I kept thinking how Leah had no idea where I was that night and must have been frantic. I felt terrible putting our friends in the middle of all this, asking them to lie on my behalf if she called. But Leah was oblivious to her monstrous behavior. She *lacked insight,* which I later learned is a measurable component of mental illness and refers to one's self-cognition that something is wrong.[3]

That is what Leah lacked, all right: self-cognition. Her mind was broken.

But absent any real knowledge about mental illness, I was trying to keep my balance while contorting myself like a circus performer. It took months to figure out what was wrong with Leah—and it took years for me to learn how to cope with her destructive mood disorder. I was

---

[2]   Ever an editor and composition teacher, I appreciated the succinct syntax of Emma's phrasing. That is, she didn't say, "She doesn't have any insight." That in my crisis I noticed Emma's graceful articulation of Leah's problem showed either my genetic predisposition for concise writing or that I had completely lost my mind. Or both.

[3]   See Frederick Cassidy, "Insight in Bipolar Disorder: Relationship to Episode Subtypes and System Dimensions," *Neuropsychiatric Disease and Treatment* 6, October 2010, https://www.ncbi.nlm.nih.gov/pmc/articles/PMC2951745/.

an American-born male fed the myth of self-reliance, prone to hiding behind a mask of sarcasm to avoid confrontation. I was quickly learning, though, that you can't BS yourself to survive something like this.

And you can't do it alone. You can't do it without the patience and open-mindedness of friends like Anita and Marc and Emma and Shelley and a couple dozen others who know who they are. Without the humanity and knowledge of our therapists, doctors, nurses, and pharmacists. Without our relatives and neighbors and rabbis. Without the interest of random strangers: a cashier I chatted up at Whole Foods, a server named Tiffany at a bar I used to go to in downtown Minneapolis. All their generosity and kindness, without judgment, toward me, toward Leah, and toward the two of us as a couple.

All of them hoping that, under the strata of manic energy and rage, Leah would have the insight to understand before it was too late that her mind and her marriage were spinning out of control.

LEAH WAS SCARED, all right. She contacted a dozen people, asking if they knew where I was that night. She texted a friend of mine in Colorado and copied me. "JZ freaked out, left the house at 10:00 am, refuses to talk to me, won't tell me where he is. Can you help me?"

I ignored her. Although unaware of it at the time, I was establishing a boundary, and for my own sanity I needed a break from Leah. Still, it felt hurtful and flat-out mean. That night at Emma and Shelley's was the first of many hiding out in a sea of guilt for lacerating Leah with the feeling I had abandoned her. Moreover, under the veneer of Leah's self-grandeur and rage, she had to know she was losing control of her mind. And if she didn't know, how sad was that? But given the way things were going, the protective wall I was building would have to be strong enough for me to endure the forthcoming storm surge.

CHAPTER 8

The Diagnosis

Maybe it was from getting badgered all summer by Leah. Maybe it was the exhaustion and contagion of Leah's still undiagnosed illness. Or maybe resistance was futile.

One night I cracked, too. I morphed into one of those wind-up walking monkey toys, except instead of crashing cymbals, I held a cleaning rag in one hand and a bucket of Mr. Clean in the other. I hoped that Leah, busily erecting another paper mountain on the dining room table, would be pleased I'd *taken some initiative* to wipe off the disgusting squalor. I began with the surface of the shelf on which the spare dish towels in the pantry were set. No one had wiped underneath the towels in years! There was dust on the outside of a box of Chex. Dust on the inside of a box of Chex. Dust on the household tools Leah had sorted and re-sorted a week or two ago. The dusty piles of pennies and nickels she had left spilled onto the hallway floor. Dust on the hands of the kitchen clock. Dust on my eyeglasses. Dust everywhere!

It was eleven thirty at night and I became a human car wash. No speck of dirt could escape me. Once finished wiping, I became Mop

Man the action figure. When was the last time anyone around here had mopped underneath the mop bucket? Or mopped the dustpan or dusted the mop, for that matter?

"Jeff! Jeff, stop! Stop for a minute!"

"Can't. Too much to clean. I just have a lot of creative energy!"

"Are you mocking me?"

"No way, José. Place just needs cleaning!"

"Okay, stop. I'm worried about you. I think I should call 911." She was still sore at me about calling security on her in Los Angeles, or maybe she was shocked to see what manic energy looks like.

"If you think that's best," I said breathlessly, "but I'll keep cleaning until the cops get here."

I finally did stop it. Somewhere in my sick head I had proven a point, although what point that was, and to whom I had proven it, I had no idea. Was I mocking Leah? Or was it a Freudian act of defiance and purification? The intensity of the frenetic cleaning was real, and the loss of control over the Force was unnerving.

That was the closest I ever felt to manic energy. I can't imagine weeks of that kind of loss of control. It's no wonder a bipolar manic episode can be followed by months of depression as the brain heals from an episode of mania.[1]

I haven't dusted the mop even once since then.

---

[1] "Our results indicate that volume decrease in frontal brain regions can be attributed to the incidence of manic episodes." See Christoph Abé et al., "Manic Episodes Are Related to Changes in Frontal Cortex: A Longitudinal Neuroimaging Study of Bipolar Disorder 1," *Brain* 138, no. 11 (November 2015). http://doi.org/10.1093/brain/awv266.

To: Dr. J
July 26, 2015

*Are you open to a Felix Unger–Oscar Madison Odd Couple
thing? I'm mostly kidding.*

When I couldn't cope with Leah's behavior at all, I ended up
in a tent somewhere or couch surfing, most often in my buddy Dr.
J's cellar. After eighteen years of marriage, the man had negotiated
a self-imposed banishment to his basement. To avoid the additional
cost of moving out during divorce negotiations, he set a mattress on
his laundry room floor, which left his spare couch in the downstairs
family room for me. I would let myself in Dr. J's back door and find
him and his forty-pound Persian house cat watching a ballgame on
TV. He was withdrawing from his wife's harangues through his daily meditation, weight lifting, thirty-mile rides on his stationary bike,
and a local craft IPA called Surly Furious. When a ballgame ended I'd
take a bump of bourbon and we'd play ping-pong, all of which sounds
like fun but only if you're, say, sixteen years old.

For sure, it was no long-term plan. For one thing, I was allergic to
Dr. J's cat, who thought I was a dick because I took too long to let her
out the back door so she could snarl at whatever critter was bugging
her in the night air. Moreover, I was trying to escape a marital feud, not
drown myself in someone else's.

I couldn't afford a hotel room, so most nights I slept at home in the
spare bed in my office, mostly to get away from Leah but also because
she was up all night bouncing off the walls. I stored my vitamins and
toiletries in the bathroom downstairs, so maybe my life wasn't all that
different from Dr. J's. I kept a suitcase packed with a week's worth of
clothes in case I needed to fly the coop and stowed my sleeping bag and

camping equipment in the trunk of the car. One day I withdrew a wad of fifty-dollar bills from the checking account at the credit union, which Leah probably forgot existed. I would gaze at FOR RENT signs in suburban apartment complexes, wondering how long I would last among all the other divorced dads before I drove to the airport, abandoned my car, and bought a one-way ticket to Palookaville.

I told few people where I was staying because (a) I didn't want Leah hunting me down and (b) I didn't want my friends to feel forced to lie about my whereabouts. But there was a downside to hiding. My friends were inundated with nasty red alerts Leah sent out via a Where's_My_Asshole_Husband? group email.

To: Heshie and Judy
cc: Jeff
July 28, 2015, 5:29 a.m.

You know that I'm a good person, right? And I would never even think about the possibility of stabbing Jeff (which I feel is his own paranoia) or "emotionally abuse" him. Do you actually believe that he would have stayed in our relationship 33 years (and in our marriage 31 years, as of tomorrow) if I was abusing him?

Fortunately, he's got a doctor's appointment. I hope it will make a difference in his mental health.

When I read that I felt guilty for betraying Leah's trust with our mutual friends. But I was irked by that crack about *my* mental health. Leah was telling everyone I was the sicko, which may have been true because I was deluded enough to think my pals might believe anything she was saying.

Obviously, I needed help.

I had to deal with my digestive system, feeling day after day like a rabid hyena was gnawing on my ileum. This wasn't a latent symptom of celiac disease but my body's Pavlovian reaction to anxiety and fear. I called Dr. Woody, our family practitioner whom Leah and I had been seeing for twenty-six years (probably a record in the managed-care era). Nearly my age, Dr. Woody was tall, brown-eyed, and still wore a Buster Brown haircut. To say he knew me intimately is an understatement. He knew my colorectal tract, knew my family history of heart disease, knew I had severe asthma attacks as a kid, and was the first to diagnose me with celiac disease a decade ago.

Instead of staring at the computer monitor during five-minute consultations, Dr. Woody bent the rules of the healthcare conglomerate and actually listened to patients. After I stopped eating gluten and got my GI system under control, I rarely saw him more than a couple times a year.

When I scheduled the appointment online for that late July morning, I had to indicate why I was coming in. So I typed something ambiguous like I had stomach "issues" and "other issues," cryptically suggesting the truth that I was coming unglued.

There must be a clinic protocol for a guy who walks in with his brains leaking out his nose. The nurse checked my blood pressure and pulse (Me: "Whew. I was afraid my wife ate my heart for breakfast.") and then handed me a laminated sheet for a self-assessment of my mental health.

Suddenly it all felt real, putting numbers on my anxiety.

When Dr. Woody entered the examination room and asked me what was up, I began blubbering to him. I described how weird Leah had been acting, that she had been yelling at me nonstop for two months, and how I was falling apart. "I haven't been eating, Dr. Woody. It feels like a gorilla is squeezing my chest. It feels like my whole body is a tube of toothpaste and my insides are squirting out the bottom of the tube. So to speak."

I knew what I meant, even if he didn't.

"Let me feel your gut."

While he was squeezing my belly I elaborated on Leah's rage, about how little she had been sleeping, about how she would talk and talk, how she couldn't focus, about her eight hundred projects, about how she blamed me for all our problems.

"You've known Leah for almost half her life," I whimpered. "It's so *unlike her.*" I finally lost it and started bawling, no different from a toddler getting a booster shot in his rear end.

"Jeff, hold on, pal. Hold on. Listen up. Listen to me."

Me [sobbing]: *Bwah haw haw haw.*

"I bet I know what's wrong with Leah. I'll be right back."

He left me alone in the exam room, presumably to deal with a patient who was actually sick. Maybe his diagnosis was I needed to grow a pair of balls. That lightened my mood momentarily. After all, the man had done my annual hernia check the past quarter century, and if anyone knew whether I had a pair of balls it was Dr. Woody. Or maybe his diagnosis was that Leah had married an imbecile. I wondered how many schlemiels like me walked in there every day. You go to your family doctor for strep throat, not to whine about your mental health.

"Here," Dr. Woody said a moment later when he returned to the exam room. He was grasping a piece of paper and handed it to me like a treasure map. "This explains what's wrong with Leah. It's called bipolar disorder, and she's having a manic episode. Check it out."

The paper said that during a manic episode, a person has a sustained and abnormally elevated, expansive, or irritable mood for at least one week, as well as at least three of the following symptoms:

- Grandiosity or an inflated sense of self.
- Little need for sleep.
- Feeling pressured to speak, talking loudly and rapidly.
- Easily distracted.
- Engaging in multiple tasks at one time—more than can be realistically accomplished in one day.
- Engaging in risky behavior like gambling or unprotected sex.
- Racing thoughts.

"Dr. Woody, that's it! That's Leah!"

"The good news is there's medicine to treat it. In the meantime, you *have* to take better care of yourself."

All we had to do was figure out how to get Leah in there for an evaluation.

AS I REFLECT on all of this, I'm stunned at how little I knew about mental illness. But why would I know anything? I recognized in vague terms that my Uncle Milan had schizophrenia and Leah had been on Prozac the past twenty years. But I never gave it much thought—specifically, I never connected her chronic depression to mental illness. She had a gratifying career and co-parented our two children. She had problems during the cold dark winters with seasonal affective disorder, but who in Minnesota doesn't? Hers was just worse, but it had never kept her from getting on with her life.

In Dr. Woody's office I understood for the first time that mental illness is a medical illness, meaning it can be treated by medical professionals.

This meant my wife could get better . . . and that my marriage could get better, too.

And what about me and my stomach issues? The problem wasn't gluten. Dr. Woody prescribed Ativan for my anxiety, said it should help my stomach. Said I should eat whatever I could. Don't worry about cholesterol, he said. Don't worry about anything. Just get food down your throat.

When the Ativan didn't help Dr. Woody put me on Zoloft, and finally a low dose of the antidepressant amitriptyline, which causes weird dreams, and which I still take. But I sleep well and my stomach is fine. Knock on wood.

OUR ANNIVERSARY was coming up.

During the genealogical hunt that led her to Great-Great-Grandpa's grave, Leah became more interested in my own background. She examined a box of old photos of mine in a closet and found a sepia-tinted picture taken in a photographer's studio in Yugoslavia around 1927. My Uncle Milan, about three years old, sat on my grandmother's lap. To one side was my father, the big brother, and to the other side was Olga, the big sister. My paternal grandfather was not in the photo; he had already sailed to America. I can imagine his family finding a photographer in Pakrac, the biggest city near their hamlet, or maybe Zagreb, where there were cousins.

Somehow the photo made it across the ocean. Somehow it survived ninety years. Somehow it ended up in a box in a closet in my house, and in my wife's hands. She took it to a specialty shop and had it enlarged and framed as a gift for me, the kindest thing Leah did for me that summer.

It might have been excess creative energy. More likely, it was just Leah being Leah.

And thus, despite all the tension, screaming, accusations, hiding, and anger, I told Dr. J that Leah and I decided for our anniversary to observe a truce.

"That's good to hear," Dr. J said. "I'm cheering for you two."

"I was reading an article about how the German and British troops at the Western Front sang carols to each other in the trenches on Christmas Eve in 1914."

"Great, I'll keep that in mind when I'm signing our divorce papers."

Though driving separately as usual, Leah and I agreed to meet across the river from downtown for a five o'clock matinee showing of *The End of the Tour*, an artsy film about the writing of *Infinite Jest*[2] by the late David[3] Foster[4] Wallace (speaking of pain, distress, and mental illness).[5] Traffic was bad, and I ditched my car in a parking lot a half-mile from the movie house and ran across the Hennepin Avenue Bridge to arrive on time.

There was no Leah, and after I'd run through the muggy July inferno, it was maddening to hang around the lobby waiting for her to show up for our very big deal anniversary date. I gave up and found a seat in the theater and fumed in the dark, wondering if she decided to blow me off or if she was too busy hopping in the shower to get there on time.

A half hour after the film started, I saw her marching down the aisle, peering through the dark to find me. Once she sat down, I could say with confidence after my visit to Dr. Woody, she *manically* started

---

[2] No, I never read it.

[3] This is just a footnote.

[4] So is this. Wallace used many footnotes.

[5] Soon after Wallace's suicide by hanging, David Remnick, in a stirring tribute, quoted a foreboding sentence from Wallace's short story "Brief Interviews with Hideous Men": "[None of his antidepressants] had delivered any significant relief from the pain and feelings of emotional isolation that rendered the depressed person's every waking hour an indescribable hell on earth." See D. T. Max, "The Unfinished: David Foster Wallace's Struggle to Surpass 'Infinite Jest,'" *The New Yorker* 85 (March 9, 2009). https://www.newyorker.com/magazine/2009/03/09/the-unfinished.

yapping loudly to get caught up on the plot. She wasn't just trying to annoy me, according to Dr. Woody's diagnosis. Leah's brain was broken, and there was literally no way to shut her up.

After the film we rode together in Leah's car to Restaurant Alma, less than a mile away. It was a splurge, the kind of pretentious place for yuppies willing to shell out twenty bucks for a wilted arugula leaf. But it was our anniversary and we were still married and she wanted to go there and I wasn't eating anything anyway so whatever.

Leah ordered a zucchini slider or some stupid thing while bubbling on about her meetings and consulting business, none of which was adding up to anything more substantive than a plate of celery sticks, and I finally chiseled through her monologue and mentioned my earlier doctor's appointment.

"Dr. Woody prescribed some meds for my stomach," I said. "He said I have anxiety and prescribed Ativan for me."

Leah merely replied how happy she was to hear that I was finally dealing with my mental illness. Before I could respond, she shoved her cell phone in my face and went on about the photos her friend had posted on Facebook, an *amazing* series of shots of the sunset. You *have* to look at these, she said.

"Can you believe how *good* these pictures are?" she exclaimed. "Look at them. Look! Why aren't you looking at them? Look at these goddamn pictures!"

My chest tightened. Started wheezing. Couldn't breathe. Felt queasy. Kept my wits about me. Figured it wasn't a heart attack, just some psychosomatic panic reaction to my *meshugina* wife and this fifty-dollar eggplant or whatever she'd ordered among all these nattering snobs.

"Dear, I don't feel well," I said, not angrily but desperately. "I can't breathe, Leah. I have to go right now."

I rushed out of the restaurant to her car, leaned over the trunk, stretched out my hands and arms, inhaled as deeply as I could. Exhaled. Inhaled, slowly exhaled. Tried to let the waves of anxiety rip through my arms and out my hands.

Inhaled, exhaled.

Inhaled, exhaled.

Leah paid our bill and drove me back downtown to fetch my Mazda. I sat there in my car and unwound, and a little while later I felt well enough to drive myself home.

That night I told Leah I was heading up north for a few days. I'll be back whenever, I said. Maybe Monday or Tuesday. I'm not sure when.

CHAPTER 9

Zuckerman Unglued

The next morning I called my fishing buddy Fender. He was a straight-talking recovering alcoholic whom I had known even longer than Leah. Fender grew up in a Finnish mining family on the Iron Range, as earthy as the soil he'd supposedly eaten in his impoverished childhood. Fender and his first wife had ditched each other, which was either a cause or effect of his drinking. Now he was happily married to his second wife, a nurse named Laura, and they adored each other. I updated him on what had been going on at my house. For years he had run a county social services agency and knew the mental health system inside and out.

"You should come up here," Fender told me. "I love you and Leah, Jeff."

That was Sober Fender. We'd had a falling-out when he was drinking. But all that 12-Step Higher Power stuff resonated with him, and in his late middle-age, with the love and support of Laura, he had embraced a spiritual wholeness I hadn't seen when we were younger. They'd bought a big house with a picture window looking out on a lake, a scene out of a travel magazine, with a finished basement apartment for visitors.

I drove four hours due north from the Twin Cities and bought the bait and fuel for Fender and Laura's fishing boat, and the three of us spent an afternoon angling for walleyes under a blue sky in God's country.

I filled them in on the entire story. "What do you think of that?"

"Yeah, well, you're pretty much fucked. You know, Jeff, Leah might never get better."

"Thanks," I said. That might sound sarcastic, but I was grateful for Fender's candor.

Laura was as honest and compassionate as Fender, without the sandpaper exterior. She and I shared a bottle of wine that night and told each other secrets. She had grown up in an abusive household, and the first time around had married a tyrant. "For your kids' sake," Laura said, "be glad they're out of the house during all this."

We were all up late, looking out at moonlight on the lake.

"Some nights Fender and I put on music and dance naked in the living room."

"Can you believe that?" Fender said, even blushing a little but with joy. He had nearly died in a car crash a long time ago and had gone for years unloved.

"I'm dazzled. I'm happy for you two. It's—"

"Jeff, why is that so surprising? That's how a normal marriage should work."

Fender just shrugged.

"It's just nice to see that you two are so in love with each other." I wasn't envious. I simply wanted some of that happiness again, too.

After a couple of days with them it was time to head out. I drove east through the scrub tamaracks and bogs of northern Minnesota and spent a few nights at Tettegouche State Park along Lake Superior. I set up my tent about fifty yards into the woods from the shore of the lake—beyond cell phone range and Leah's sniping. On hikes through the birch and aspen forests, I asked myself over and over what I should do. I was falling apart and needed to take care of myself. But if I left her now, wouldn't I be as reprehensible as Newt Gingrich, who supposedly left his wife Jackie for Calista while Jackie was dying of cancer?[1]

In the evenings I built a campfire, read a novel, and listened to the sounds of the vast lake and vague stirrings in the night air. A month from now summer would be over, and I essentially had no place to be.

Leah was my children's mother and my wife. I cared about her. For God's sake, I loved her. She was sick. Aren't those enough reasons to stay?

THE MINUTE I arrived home, Leah lit into me.

"You didn't buy the ground beef!"

There was a neighborhood block party that evening.

"I could have sworn you said you would buy it."

Good God, a Ground Beef Incident, I thought bitterly, picturing Fender and wife slow-dancing in the moonlight. If Leah was trying to make me feel guilty for leaving town for a few days, she was succeeding.

Swallowing my pride, the next day I called the local Jewish social services agency for help. I must have sounded like I was about to jump off a bridge because I was assigned the big-cheese therapist for an emergency appointment the next afternoon, a counselor named Jody. She was my age, maybe even older, with the motherly calm of someone who had heard it all. I dumped my heart out and Jody reassured me that, yes, it sounded like my wife's brain was broken and, yes, all I could do was take care of myself. She recommended I attend a NAMI support group for family members of loved ones with a mental illness.

---

[1] Not precisely true. See D'Angelo Gore, "The Gingrich Divorce Myth," FactCheck.org, https://www.factcheck.org/2011/12/the-gingrich-divorce-myth/.

I didn't hide any of this from Leah. I told her I went to a therapist, and that I planned to attend a support group the following day.

To: Jeff

August 8, 2015

I hope your therapist is able to conduct full psychiatric testing and have a psychiatrist (or Dr. Woody) evaluate whether any of your meds are having a negative effect on your thinking or behaviors (which have been very different—and odd—over the past couple of months).

I really am worried about you. Maybe when you go to your therapy group tonight, the facilitator could talk with you about other options, maybe even in-patient care on the psych unit at the hospital.

She was in denial herself. Right? Or was she projecting her fears about herself on me?

The first NAMI group I attended met in a church in a Twin Cities suburb. About ten people sat around a square cluster of tables in a classroom. The volunteer facilitator, Meredith, was a software engineer whose son had battled a mood disorder and had been in and out of hospitals numerous times. She set out pamphlets and chocolates and name tags. I was tempted to write *Hello, I'm . . . A Disaster*, but I was the new guy and might sound self-pitying around a group of people living with God-knows-what-heartache, so I just wrote *Jeff*.

I wasn't as stoic as most men my age, but I was battling my role model, my immigrant father, a sergeant in the South Pacific during World War II. There was a guy with something to complain about, not that he ever griped about anything. The last place he would have ended up would have been a shrink's couch or a support group, crying on a group of strangers' shoulders. Instead he played cards two or three nights a week, mostly with other Jewish war veterans, which in its own way was a mid-century support group—not that those men ever discussed their stupid feelings or, from what I knew, complained to each other about their wives.

Those were the postwar years, and now it was 2015 and we were ten strangers gathered in a support group at a church with some guy down the hall taking French horn lessons, which no one but me seemed to hear. Meredith directed us to go around the room one by one, summarizing in three minutes what was going on with our loved ones and what the hell we were doing there.

Three minutes?

"Well, you see, I'm here because my wife has been screaming at me for months now and people are telling me she has a mental illness and my counselor said I ought to come to this group and spill my guts because my diarrhea and stomachaches are getting worse and I can't sleep and I'm losing weight, which is not a recommended diet, ha-ha, and I have no long-term plan, I mean, I barely have a short-term plan. In fact, tonight I'm sleeping in a tent in Carver County to escape my wife's rage, and, boo-hoo, I'm sorry, you all. Boo-hoo. I'm sorry for taking too much time. I'm really sorry. Thank you for the tissues."

"That sounds really hard," Meredith said. "We're glad you're here." And she meant it, and once everyone gave an update on their situations, they came back to me and heard me carry on some more, and from then on I have gone to a couple of support groups two or three times a month, one of the best things I have done during this whole ordeal.

DR. WOODY had no firm plan for cajoling Leah to come to the clinic for her own mental health check-up. Because of HIPAA rules, he wasn't even supposed to be talking to me about Leah, even though she and I were married and I seemed headed for my own nervous breakdown if my wife didn't get her head examined. Moreover, had Dr. Woody contacted Leah and confronted her about his diagnosis, it would have been counterproductive: Leah would have felt accused, like we were ganging up on her, and she would have told us both to go to hell.

Still, he was our primary care doctor. I wondered if he could converse with Leah's psychologist directly about what I had told him and he had concluded.

In short, without Leah's written permission, the answer was no.

He suggested that Leah and I make an appointment with a family therapist[2] in the same clinic so Leah would think I was at least trying to get us help and he would be able to track how she was doing.

Or something like that.

It didn't really work, although Leah was pleased with me for finally *taking some initiative.* She thought it would be helpful if we found someone who could work with us on our *communication problems.* Which to Leah meant she could once again prattle on for fifty minutes to some poor schmo about the Chauncey Greene Incident and the asshole she had married thirty-one years earlier. Leah, driving separately to the appointment, arrived late, which I figured I could use as a weapon once she started in about all my faults, which was a hell of a thought when you're going into marriage counseling, walking in there with a scorecard rather than an open mind to get an objective handle on what's what.

---

[2]   Psst: Most insurance companies will not cover *marriage* therapy, but they will cover individual or *family* therapy. It's critical to find out how the therapist plans to code and submit your bill.

The young blond woman with whom we met reminded me of Glinda the Good Witch of the North from *The Wizard of Oz*. I crossed my fingers, hoping she would tell Leah she needed a brain transplant.

"What brings us here today?" Glinda said, like a Perkins waitress, and I immediately despised her.

Leah's latest oration included her diagnosis of my mental health problem: Leah determined that I was afraid I would die in three months because I would be sixty-one years old, and my father, who smoked three packs of cigarettes a day, died at that age. I kept hoping thin-lipped Glinda would smile knowingly and order Leah at long last to shut the hell up and just tap her heels together three times, and suddenly Leah and I would be somewhere over the rainbow making love in the afternoon as the vestiges of the three-month tornado disappeared over the horizon, ruining someone else's lives instead of our own.

It didn't work that way.

Glinda assigned us an insipid homework task to work on our *communication problems* and talk about our goddamn feelings. As we left the appointment, I kept looking for nonverbal cues from Glinda signaling to me that she could tell my wife was clearly a few slices shy of a loaf.

But I got nothin' from the woman, and as Leah and I drove away in our separate cars, my *feeling* was that this Glinda could shove her communication problems up her nose if she couldn't figure out a way to get my wife and me the help we actually needed.

MY GOD, I had to figure this thing out. I loved my wife, and she was sick. But I needed help, too, which wasn't going to come from the Good Witch of the North. I called the social services agency again, and in mid-August I was assigned a longer-term counselor named Arlene.

I took notes in my journal as Arlene spoke: "You can't help Leah. You don't know how to best live with her. You agitate her. Your relationship has gone awry because she's not well."

She called ours not a marriage problem but a mental health problem and said it's hard not to get sucked into it. "Don't do anything drastic. You may have to rent a place for a while."

I told her she was right. I couldn't keep hiding in Dr. J's basement forever because Leah would figure out where he lives and show up and take us both out with a steak knife.

"You need a safe space," Therapist Arlene said.

Maybe I could just hide out under the desk in this nice person's carpeted office until Leah got better.

An acquaintance told me he knew someone who rented out a house through Airbnb. Said it was available that week, and if I told the owners my sob story they would give me a good deal. "They'll probably charge you just the cleaning fee. I'm pretty sure the place is empty this week."

Thus, I holed up for a few days in a palace in a tony Minneapolis neighborhood. I didn't want to mess up the nice bedsheets the owners provided and instead slept in my sleeping bag atop the duvet, hoping the landlord would cut me some slack on the cleaning fee. I was worried about my finances and took on extra freelance work and ate little more than a box of Cheerios. My paranoia was thick and I parked a couple of blocks away, irrationally imagining Leah driving up and down every street in the Twin Cities on the lookout for my silver Mazda. I assumed she would send out another blast email to her expanded My_Husband_Is_an_Asshole Listserv, but I didn't tell a soul where I was. I didn't want to put anyone, even my closest friends, in a rough spot by having to lie on my behalf.

On Saturday afternoon I walked morosely all around Lake Harriet. Leah and I had taken our kids there countless times when they were young. I yearned to be like one of those handsome couples pushing baby strollers on the footpath or guiding a sailboat across the waves, with windblown hair and glimmering smiles, the kinds of people exuding adherence to a Mediterranean diet, oral hygiene, and constant in-the-moonlight sex.

DR. WOODY AND I finally figured out a way to get Leah to come to see him so he could discuss her mental health. It was ingenious: I would tell Leah I needed her to come with me to see Dr. Woody about *my* mental health.

It was a set-up, somewhat unethical. But in my view the moral compass was altered when someone I loved could not see her sickness. Ultimately, it was Leah's decision whether to get the help she needed. But in the realm of mental illness treatment, nothing is black and white. In dozens of support group meetings I've attended, we family members have gyrated around questions of our loved ones' responsibility for their actions when their sicknesses interfere with their decision making. I can't speak for my doctor or the people in my group. Knee-deep at the time in Leah's still-undiagnosed mental illness, I can present only what I did, with Dr. Woody's help, to maintain the human bond between two best friends and lovers.

Dr. Woody scheduled an appointment for me—and Leah—at one-thirty on a Wednesday afternoon. Leah and I drove separately, and for once she was on time. The two of us were led to the examination room. There was no preliminary chit-chat with the nurse; Dr. Woody saw us immediately and got right down to business. He told us he cared about us, that he had been our doctor for twenty-six years, and that he wanted to know what was going on with us.

"With *us*?" Leah exclaimed. "*I'm* fine. *He's* the one with the mental health problem."

"Let me hear what's been going on," Dr. Woody replied calmly.

He asked for it, he got it. Leah launched into her half-hour list of grievances, less profane than her typical rants, but the usual essential bullet points. She was so *glad*, of course, that Dr. Woody was treating me for my depression.

"Actually, my situational anxiety—"

"Don't interrupt me. You see? You *see*, Dr. Woody? This is exactly what he does," et cetera, et cetera.

I was elated that our doctor was getting a full-frontal view of Leah's rage. All Dr. Woody had to do now was corral her and prescribe a month of downers.

She went on and on, and it seemed like we were going in circles for an hour. Who gets that kind of one-on-one attention from a primary care doctor?

"Don't worry about the time," Dr. Woody said.

The appointment lasted ninety minutes. Dr. Woody directed most of his questions to Leah rather than to me, and inside I silently gloated. *Ha, ha, Leah. You're the sick one around here, not me.* She calmed down enough to hear out Dr. Woody and agreed to come in for a follow-up appointment.

That was all right with me. It was a start. It took six years to end World War II. We weren't going to fix Leah and our marriage that afternoon.

Leah and I walked away from the exam room together and headed to the lobby. By the time we got to the clinic door she once again lost control and started yelling at me.

"Fuck you, you fucking asshole!" she screamed as she ran toward her car.

That's okay. I still think Dr. Woody deserves the Nobel Prize in medicine.

I later found out he had come in to the clinic on his day off.

ONE MORNING after I stayed overnight at Dr. J's place I walked to a nearby doughnut shop for coffee. This was no way to live. In the mid-1970s I rented a tiny spare room in the back of Macel's Beauty Shop in Auburndale, Florida. The refrigerator stood at the foot of my cot and I washed my dishes in the bathroom sink. I was idealistic and stupid back then, but it was good enough forty years ago, and I wondered what made me think I was such a hotshot now. But didn't I at least deserve a kitchen sink? I did a back-of-the-envelope calculation of how much it would cost to live on my own each month if I moved out.

Rent	$1,000
Groceries	350
Utilities	300
Insurance & car	150
Health care	500
Fun	4
	$2304

I couldn't keep spending money on fast food, couldn't keep bugging friends, couldn't move into a cheap motel, couldn't do that to our kids, couldn't walk the gangplank into a legal separation. I had only my 401(k) rollover to live on if it came to that, and from what I read Leah would get half of that. With only a few irrational options and no good ones, I kept living at home and hoped Glinda the Good Witch of the North would get Leah the hell committed.

"How is the hard work on your communication problems going?" Glinda began each session.

"Well, Glinda, the other day I made an egregious *communication error* in a restaurant before the waiter even brought us the water and Leah lit into me and ran out the door. I stood behind her car while she kept backing up, and if I hadn't jumped out of the way she would have run me over."

"That's not how it happened," Leah said.

I rolled my eyes and zipped my mouth, as usual. What was the point of arguing or discussing whether Leah had tried to run me over?

On that day Leah at least showed up. Still habitually and spitefully late for everything, she sometimes arrived ten minutes late and Glinda canceled the entire appointment for both of us. When Leah did eventually get there, she would be bursting with snarky superiority about how *great* she was doing, how *her* life was going, about her *creative energy* and how her *El-El-Cee* consulting business was taking off, like she had any idea what an LLC even is. She bragged about making great progress on her projects, which was such utter poppycock it jabbed my heart with a pitchfork, but she had great confidence that things were improving because I was finally getting help.

I DIDN'T EXACTLY MOVE OUT. Amid the fights and further fiascoes, we were trying to live together and love one another and carry on our lives. So when an old friend of Leah's asked if she and I would join her and her boyfriend on a Friday sailboat cruise on the St. Croix River, Leah jumped at the chance.

"It'll be great!" Leah said to me. "We can drive out to Stillwater, and I won't talk the whole way, and we'll just have a nice time with Jean and Kenny."

Wow, a summer night on a sailboat. I'd never done that. But would I have to know how to jib or job or whatever it's called?

"Jean said we only have to bring some picnic food, and she and Kenny will take care of the rest. It'll be so much fun!"

During a manic episode a person's entire set of emotions is intensified. Leah, for example, was exuberant about her El-El-Cee. She was feeling euphorically creative. She was ebullient about weeding the garden. She was convinced our love for each other would get us past our communication issues, and she was positive we would have a fantastic time with Jean and Kenny if we just relaxed and avoided arguments.

What the heck. I was game for an adventure. And, at Glinda's insistence, I was responsible for half the "hard work on our communication problems."

Jean's sailboat was docked at a river marina that looked to me like the harbor of a Mediterranean city, like a scene out of a Waspy travel magazine with ads for bleached white activewear and recipes for lobster bisque. The boat had two sails and a mile of rope and nouns and verbs straight out of *Moby Dick*. Best of all, the sailboat was thirty or forty feet long, and Jean gave me permission to hide out on the bow while she and Kenny did all the work (and Leah yakked with them instead of me).

Alas, the wind was calm, so once we motored from the marina to the river, the boat just sat there in the middle of the St. Croix. But who cared? Leah and I were doing something together, or at least we were adrift in the same forty-foot boat, eating cold cuts and drinking wine, with a pink sunset on the Minnesota horizon. What a pleasant way to spend an August evening . . . my first with Leah in months.

AND THEN.

Two nights later, Leah suggested we should have a late dinner on our deck. This would be real progress, she said. We could cut up a melon, make a nice salad. Grill some salmon. We could talk. Just a quiet August evening together. If I thought she was talking too much I could set the dyad timer, she said.

"Set the timer."

You're kidding me. In my mind, timing our exchanges meant we were getting nowhere fast. But I was supposed to be *supportive* and stop blaming Leah for our *communication problems* because it was up to me, too, to work on our marriage, et cetera, et cetera. Which is to say, Leah's looped sermons about how I didn't even try, how I just criticized her *because, Jeff, you never want to talk about your feelings, which is the crux of the problem because you're just like all the other Zuckermans* lorem ipsum dolor.

Yet I liked eating on our deck with Leah. A couple summers earlier we had hired a carpenter to screen in a section so we could finally enjoy a summer night without inhaling a lungful of mosquitoes. I had tacked a string of lights to the ceiling and enjoyed the aura they cast—that is until a bulb blew, which was another looped jeremiad: If I had saved the fucking receipt last January when I bought the bulbs on after-Christmas clearance I could try to *return* them *but now you have to throw all the wires in the garbage can* et cetera.

Leah was right, of course. I was just another environmental menace because I was a tightwad and insisted on buying cheap strings of bulbs, burnt out just like my stupid life, and if I had any sense I would forget dinner on the deck and microwave a bowl of popcorn and sulk in bed.

Get ahold of yourself, I thought. *Enjoy the wine and night air with your wife.* So what if the bulbs don't work? That's what the candles are for. Leah had bought candles, all right, a maniacal number of candles. Candles all over the place, enough candles to burn down the goddamn deck. And sconces. She'd bought sconces for the goddamn candles, more sconces than Hogwarts Castle, so if any readers need any candles or sconces, let me know. They're out in the garage if I haven't thrown them in the garbage yet.

Calm down, man. You can do this.

It was already midnight because Leah had dinked around saying she was going to get dinner started and as usual there were a dozen distractions and for all I knew the salmon had to hop in the shower before we broiled it. I ended up cooking dinner and I was in a lousy mood and my stomach was churning after stuffing it with watermelon and dread. We hadn't even begun The Talk yet, which somehow became something we would start at midnight. First we had to figure out how long to set the dyad timer, always a fight in itself. Sometimes we'd agree on four minutes, or only two minutes, or sometimes, when I was unnerved, for ninety seconds, and then there would be an argument about that, over the amount of time it took for Leah to fiddle around with the timer on her phone, if she should set the timer for ninety seconds or for one minute and thirty seconds, and I'd say let's use the kitchen timer, it's easier, and then she'd set the timer on her cell phone to time the fight about how long it took to set the timer. Then I'd say forget the timer, just talk, and she'd say we had *agreed* on using the timer, it's the only thing that works, and why do *you* get to decide, and we'd have a ninety-second fight about that. Or if one of us exceeded the allotted time, that would be another argument, because did you have to stop mid-sentence if the timer went off? Or could you at least finish your sentence? If you went overtime you had to take that amount of time off the next time you talked, which would mean more diddling the timer on the cell phone. Or if you didn't use the full ninety seconds could you choose to add time to your next turn? Is that how we should do it? Because I used only eighty seconds last time so I get to add ten seconds next time.

Which led to another fight about the rules. Who even gets to make the rules on how you get to talk? Because the *crux* of the matter is that I was so controlling and that only since Leah had started going to therapy had she figured out the problem was that I was a fucking male ("Please don't swear." "I'll fucking swear if I want to. Why do you get to make the rules?") and I was a Zuckerman et cetera, et cetera, so I sat there mute, and Leah sneered, "You see? You *see*? You're not talking, you're sulking just like your mother and you're sitting there and just pouting like that time she came to the old house"—*ding!* Two minutes were up.

Then I'd take the bait, talk myself into circles, go on about "I" statements, that we weren't using I statements the way we were supposed to and she was going on and on about the same old things and driving me crazy—

"That isn't an I statement."

"You just interrupted me."

"Oh, I'm the one not using I statements? You did it again. You said 'you.' Use I statements."

"I was interrupted by you."

"Talk about your feelings."

"I feel interrupted."

I imagined this conversation as a monologue written by M. C. Escher, two people talking not just in circles but in an inane verbal Möbius strip.

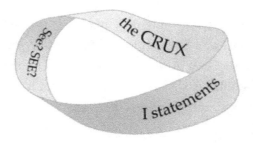

We had been out there for two hours that night—two hours—and to what end? To what end? Leah, as usual, insisted we were finally making *progress*, which I recognized in her eyes meant she was winning, although winning what, I had no idea. I just knew she was manic and maybe she didn't need any sleep, but I was exhausted. My God, it was two o'clock in the morning and from what I could tell Leah could have lasted a month out there on the deck talking in two-minute increments.

"Enough!" I finally yelled, and I ran inside to go to bed.

But that was just the prelude, because that was the night of the Shower Stall Incident, the night I unraveled in the bottom of the shower stall, a memory I packed away for months, the *feelings* locked and sealed in a cranny in my brain until the following year when my therapist extracted the Shower Stall Incident from my psyche using a Veterans Administration–approved trauma-recovery therapy called EMDR.

I'll get to that later.

CHAPTER 10

Calling All Cars

I needed additional help, to say the least. For advice I called Hennepin County's crisis intervention unit, called COPE, for County Outreach for Psychiatric Emergencies. When the crisis counselor asked for my name and my wife's name I hesitated, but I was done protecting Leah. On the phone I sensed it would do no good to rant like a maniac myself, and I kept calm, described what had been going on the past couple of months, stuck to the facts, told the counselor the stories, about Dr. Woody's diagnosis, about the insanity on the deck until two in the morning. I could hear the woman clicking away notes on her computer.

That went on for fifteen minutes, and the phone counselor sounded aghast. But, she said, unless Leah was a danger to herself or anyone else or had actually bludgeoned me to death, there wasn't a whole lot the county crisis folks could do to help.

But call back if things get worse, she told me. And in the meantime take care of yourself, she said.

I hoped that was her way of telling me to move to a cave in the Andes Mountains.

UNGLUED

ON THE LAST DAY OF AUGUST, Leah attacked me for the final time.

It was midafternoon, after another ten-round verbal prizefight in our bedroom. Terrified by her relentless, almost corporeal barrage of scolding, curses, and shrieks but still unwilling to whack her one across the kisser, I ran for my life into the upstairs bathroom. I tried locking her out, but Leah was too quick and the only thing I could do was duck down crazily inside the dry bathtub and lie there cowering. This time Leah's berating went on uncontrolled for twenty minutes—her eyeballs popping out, every psychotic morsel of her anger with me, my family, her parents, and the world pouring forth in a torrent of madness.

My God, I wanted to punch her, but I couldn't. All I could do was lie with my back against the sides of the tub, so terrified by this possessed woman and overwhelmed by the flood of her rage that part of me drifted off into a kind of out-of-body experience, like I was shutting out her abuse under a protective tortoise shell.

It went on and on, for such is a manic episode, her mind tapping into an inner well of neural energy. When I finally sprang free, Leah chased me again back into our bedroom, haranguing me, somehow pinning me down on the carpet. She knelt with all her weight on my wrists, gushed up a wad of drool and dribbled it down at my face, screaming and laughing hysterically while pinching the skin on my upper chest like a pair of pliers. *Whatever you do,* I thought, *you cannot hit your wife. You have to take it.* And against the out-of-control adrenaline-fueled energy that I was battling, I somehow managed to squirm out from underneath her.

"Goddammit!" I screamed at Leah. "I'm calling 911!"

"Go ahead! Call! I'll tell them *you* attacked me *first* with a set of keys!"

Wow. Okay.

She couldn't stop me from dialing. But I didn't call the police; I called the county crisis line.

They could hear Leah yelling at me, screaming what a fucking bastard I was and how I should go *lorem impsum dolor* myself.

She had lost all control, and I was thrilled. Because of my call a few days earlier after the Shower Stall Incident, Leah was already "in the system," and at long last I could force the issue.

"We'll send the police out right away," the counselor said.

I guess someone finally figured out this Leah woman was a danger to others—well, to me—as well as herself.

I hung up, ran out of the house, and cradled myself in an Adirondack chair in my front yard, wheezing, tenderly rubbing the crimson pinch marks on my chest, waiting for the cops. I wondered which neighbors had heard all the yelling, and if Leah would still be there when they showed up, and if I would somehow end up getting arrested.

The police arrived quickly, a testament to the importance of getting your loved one into the system—at least to the extent you have a system and it works like ours did. There was no siren, but when a cop car stops on our block, people are watching. How embarrassing. I trotted over to the squad car and told the officers what was going on. Why they or anyone else believed me, the husband, is a mystery. Was it because I showed them the red welts on my chest?

I watched the two officers walk up to the front door. Leah made a big production of welcoming them into the house. She's smart, my wife. She can sure put on a show. But listening through the open living-room window I could hear the mania in her voice, hear her acting like the whole thing was just a *big misunderstanding*, that yes, Officer, we have been having *our communication problems*, et cetera, et cetera, but we are seeing a marriage therapist and we are making *excellent progress*, and, hey, *he* was the one who scratched my wrist with a set of *keys*. You should be talking to *him*, not me, because see-this-whole-thing-started-see-I-went-to-Tunisia-actually-back-up-it-started-on-my-way-to-Israel-*don't-interrupt-me*-because-if-you-really-want-to-hear-what-happened *lorem ipsum amet,* et cetera.

Me, thinking: *You're going to jay-uhl, Leah. You're going to jay-uhl.*

After about ten minutes of her rant the cops exited the house, calmed me down a bit, said, "Good luck, Bub," and drove away.

A few moments later I gathered some clean clothes and my meds and I drove away, too.

I was embarrassed that, because I couldn't handle my wife, I had to call the police to my house. I imagined the two officers laughing about how that scrawny old dude lifted his T-shirt and showed them a mark on his titty where the wife pinched him. Luckily, the two cops were capable and kind. But the more I've become embroiled in the mental health system, and the more I've watched the news, the more I've seen that the police are the de facto mental health "system" in this country—too often with deadly results. Maybe the cops who came to our house had received de-escalation training like officers receive in St. Paul. Maybe these two cops had a heart. Or maybe Leah and I were just lucky to be a pair of middle-class whites.

AFTER THE COPS SHOWED UP, my friend Heshie called, asked me if I knew my wife had emailed a dozen people exclaiming what an *asshole!* I was.

No surprise. I had been getting ten or fifteen such email messages a day, often copied to a dozen people, some I barely knew. Her California crowd. My cousins. Her poet friend in Chicago, the Mickey Marks. Ten or fifteen IMs, text messages, Facebook messages, calendar updates, calendar invitations. Sometimes that many a morning, that many an hour. Relentless notifications keeping pace with the swirling synapses in Leah's hypermanic head.

"Just a second," I said to Heshie, dismally. "Did Leah type 'you *are* an asshole' or '*you* are an asshole'?"

"I think it was more like you are an *asshole*. Hey, who's this Mickey Marks, anyway?"

"Some depressed poet she knows in Chicago."

All evening long, more text messages. She said she'd found herself a hotel room and it was none of my fucking business where she was. Payback for calling the cops to the house, payback for my selfish nights of camping in my luxury tent and eating instant oatmeal for dinner, payback for crashing on Dr. J's basement couch with his cat.

My stomach was in knots, but I knew I had to get some food. I drove to a supermarket and walked inside, feeling lost. I was ashamed for running up the sympathy tab with my Twin Cities friends and decided to phone my old Pittsburgh friend Beth while I shopped for something edible. When she answered, she heard in my voice I was cracking up. I let her know what had been going on since I'd seen her and her husband in the spring, a protracted tale of woe that took me past the fruit section, the deli counter, the dairy section, back down through the soda pop aisle, to the cashier, and then back out to the car.

"You gotta be kidding me," Beth kept saying. "Oh, Jeff."

And then Beth told me her story—everyone has one—about her sister's old boyfriend, a guy who had a mental breakdown and no one could figure it out. They thought maybe he had a brain injury, just a complete personality change, sad as hell. Her sister couldn't stand this guy anymore, a tragic story . . .

By the time Beth was done talking, this friend of forty-five years, I was getting choked up, missing her, missing my old life, missing my old wife, because I was trapped in my Mazda in a supermarket parking lot wiping a glob of yogurt out of my mustache, killing time because I couldn't keep living in my house for fear of getting eaten alive by my rabid spouse. I mean, my God, Beth, can you believe this?

"I love you, Jeff," Beth said. "Take care of yourself."

And for the five hundredth time that summer I could barely breathe, could barely swallow any warm raspberry yogurt, felt myself gagging on the plastic spoon I pocketed at the deli case.

Off I drove to my hideout in Dr. J's basement. At a red light I looked at a text message from Leah inviting me to join her for a madcap night of middle-aged purple-rain sexylove in a downtown Minneapolis hotel room *(okay, so that's where she is)*, a *nice* hotel room, she texted me, because *you've been spending so much money so I can, too*. It was an offer, she texted me, to cast aside our *communication problems* for one enchanted evening.

Per the *DSM-V*: "Obsessive hypersexual behaviors." Sure, I'd like to spend the night wrapped in my wife's arms and bosom and hair, tucked tightly in clean 8,000-thread-count Egyptian cotton sheets instead of my sleeping bag that's starting to smell like a Persian cat hairball.

The answer was no.

Instead, I drove home.

HOW ODD. No messages all day.

By midday Tuesday, Leah's digital footprint was a phantom. Amidst her paper fortress on the dining room table was her laptop, with both her email accounts and Facebook page wide open. I snuck into her online world, synched to her mobile device attached these days like a tumor to her paw.

The thing is this: After months of her screaming at me, about me, and about the world, I was getting a tad, you know, worried? Like, okay. Where . . . the frick . . . was my wife?

Leah's online calendar showed no scheduled appointments that morning, but she had a font class to attend late that afternoon at the community college. I was unsure if she would need to stop by the house for her books or for any homework she had avoided all week while instead working on her twelve thousand other projects.

All communication from Leah had ceased around eight o'clock that morning. By midafternoon, still no messages. No anything. Our children had not heard from her, either.

The house was silent, except for the ticking of the little plastic clock on the coffee table.

Three o'clock that afternoon. Nothing. Four o'clock. No text messages. No Facebook posts. On the synched accounts on her computer, no outgoing email messages from her cell phone.

I decided to look for her over at the community college, a ten-minute drive from our house. If she wanted to get pissed off at me for once again feeling like I had to rescue her, *just like fucking Chauncey Greene*, so be it. I was really worried.

I knew which building her class met in but not which room. I could figure it out somehow. If she was there, okay. If not . . .

CHAPTER 11

Pop Goes the Weasel

I didn't recognize the phone number when I looked at my phone. "This is Lori, a nurse in the psychiatric emergency room at Hennepin County Medical Center. I'm looking for Jeffrey Zuckerman."

HCMC was the same hospital where Leah had been a social worker in the 1980s. The same hospital where she'd birthed our two children.

"Yes, this is me. This is I." I knew immediately. "The husband."

"Your wife is safe now. We need you to come down here."

How astonishing was the call when I received it. I felt no relief that, rather than floating face down in the Mississippi River, my spouse was in good hands. What was shocking was the intensity of my vindictiveness. Proof, at long last, I was right! She was *out of her fucking mind all along.*

Or at least that's what I thought right at that moment.

AS SOON AS I GAINED ENTRY through the locked door of the adult psychiatric ER, I saw Leah sitting wigged-out in the unit's outer lobby. The first things I noticed were her eyes, popping out of her head like a pair of Slinkys. She was wearing a hospital wristband and a white hospital bathrobe over a set of maroon scrubs. Normally her long curly hair was braided or, when she took an hour to blow it dry and please me, it hung sensuously halfway down her back and through my loins. Today her hair looked electrified, beyond Angela Davis Afro-radical-chic. I knew that crazed hairdo because Leah would occasionally poof it like that at home to amuse me and then beg me to let her cut off her hair once and for all.

Leah introduced me to the other patient in the psych ER lobby, a morose black woman who looked scared out of her wits. "I will *speak on her behalf*," Leah said to an approaching ER nurse, "because as you can clearly see with your own two eyeballs, this woman is African American and another victim in this *patriarchal farce*."

Leah—or her doppelgänger—was cuckoo, all right, in full-on denial anything was wrong with her, briefly calm and then revved like a launchpad rocket, smoke and flames shooting from her crazed eyes, demanding, "Jeff, call our lawyer *immediately*."[1]

"Leah, he's an *estate* attorney—"

"Yes, call him up and tell him I am being held against my will in this fucking hospital so just call him up and tell him to get his ass *down* here. And call the goddamn rabbi."

She was conjoined with the psych ER goblins, enraged, humiliated, and nose-diving into the red-hot coals of a bipolar manic tempest, about to get locked up for God knows how long for having a brain chemistry as thoroughly scrambled as her morning eggs.

---

[1] I did call our lawyer and, at Leah's insistence, an attorney friend who works specifically on mental health cases. She served us well, but we spent a ton of money by hiring her and likely would have been just as well represented by a court-appointed attorney. I am sure there are times it makes sense to seek outside counsel. This was not one of them.

"Take my goddamn picture," she ordered me.

Cameras are prohibited anywhere around a psych unit—understandably so, for privacy—but Leah demanded I shoot a photo of her while I was loitering in the psych ER waiting room and had access to my own phone, and I wasn't about to disobey her.

Later on I was glad I snapped the photo. Inside that woman's head, whoever I was looking at, was Leah, the nice Jewish girl I had married, the loving mother of our children, the woman with the silly sense of humor. Leah, the secular Jew with the electromagnetic hair shooting from her scalp like a tumbleweed, staring at me straight-faced, a resigned Christ-like gaze in her eyes, her mouth a mocking frown of divine gravitas as she held up to her face a maroon hard-covered Holy Bible just like she was hawking a box of Wheaties.

I smiled, for the first time in days.

PEOPLE IN MY SUPPORT GROUP often describe their frustration with their loved ones' misperceptions of reality, figuratively insisting the grass in the front yard is orange with such vehemence that a spouse no longer believes it is green. Leah forgets a lot of details, so this is only what I was able to glean, and I do not know if it is completely accurate.

She stayed at a Minneapolis hotel on Monday, the night of the romantic interlude I had turned down. Whether or not sleeping occurred, I don't know. Around dawn, she wandered the downtown skyways doing who-knows-what fanciful sociological research. Or maybe she was just hungry.

She got lost a block or two away from the hotel trying to find her way back to her room and somehow ended up on the ninth floor of an office building. ("It was the *right fucking building*, and for some reason they locked the fucking door.") A security guard confronted her, asked her what she was doing there. A fracas occurred. Technically, a misdemeanor fifth-degree assault. ("I barely even fucking touched him.") Officers of the law were involved. Plastic handcuffs were applied. ("*I'm suing them for assault and battery.* Look at these marks on *my fucking wrists.*") An ambulance was called to the scene of the incident. A medication was injected. The alleged perp, my honeybuns, was escorted to the psych ER at HCMC about seven blocks away. An evaluation was undertaken. The husband was notified.

Or something like that.

LEAH WAS ADMITTED on a Tuesday. On Wednesday morning I had to track down her suitcase and other belongings, including our Honda Fit. I called the hotel receptionist, who told me they had her suitcase and some other stuff in storage, but he had no idea where our car was. When I showed up at the hotel the front desk guy acted casual, like things like that happened all the time, guests disappearing overnight. It took me a couple hours and phone calls to find our car parked illegally at a meter a few blocks from the hotel. No parking ticket, just some manic gal's plastic salad shell on the roof of the car the whole time, couple empty brewskis on the front seat.

Oh, and for your information, Leah told me, she brought the beers from the house and for whatever reason decided to eat her salad in the car. So don't say *I was fucking drinking and driving.*

THIS WAS THE drill each time Leah was hospitalized, and it'll be something like this for you.

The elevator will disgorge you in a deserted back alley of the hospital, down the hall from a beige locked metal door. You'll press a buzzer, wait, press it again, wait, and press it again. Someone on the intercom will eventually answer and ask who you are and who you're there to see. You'll say the name of your family member or friend, and, if your patient wants you around, the staff will remotely unlock the outer door. (The signage sucks. Watch for a light the size of an apple seed turn from red to green.)

The little alcove before the locked inner door will be lined with metal lockers where you deposit your cell phone, purse or backpack, and any would-be weapons of self-destruction, such as a purse strap, mirror, plastic bag, or AR-15. You're being watched. Buzz again and a nurse will electronically unlock the second door, through which you enter the general unit of the psych ward.

The TV will be on. Patients will be walking around or drugged or hanging out or attending beauty shop class or art class or group therapy or swearing at the staff or wasting the day not much different from you or me when we're sick and, I believe, healing. The staff members at the front desk will be staring at computers, or doing paperwork, or getting ready to check the patients' blood pressure, or dealing with patients' anxieties or anger. What the staff members will not be interested in is who you are or what in God's name you're doing there when on a nice autumn day like this you could be outside playing golf.

There will be few other visitors besides you.

The severely ill patients like Leah who need a higher level of care and security will be housed in the psychiatric intensive care unit. At HCMC, it's down past the nurses' station in the general unit. You will need to ask for an escort because there is no going back and forth between the two wards.

It's not a time to be shy. Ask questions. And no matter what happens, don't take anything personally. Your loved one or friend is sick and scared and afraid and literally beyond reason.

No one really explained any of this to me, or much of anything at all, before I saw Leah for the first time on the psych ward.

"SO HOW'S SHE DOING?" I asked Lori, the supervising nurse.

"Well, she's a little amped . . . "

A little amped? Ha, ha!

When I saw Leah she was dripping fury, oozing mania like sweat. She was relentlessly angry at me—for her being held there, for visiting her, for not visiting her, for having told a couple friends she was there, for not getting her released, for my being a control freak, for my wanting her to be there, for calling the cops on her to our house, for how the cops who brought her to the hospital had treated her and left bruises on her wrists, for what a fucking jail it was, for how these condescending assholes didn't give a shit about her rights, how she needed her goddamn phone, how no one was fucking telling her what was going on, how they were all a bunch of low-paid condescending bastard fascists who didn't care about anything but controlling the patients because they were on a *fucking power trip* just like *the Chauncey Fucking Greene.*

Leah's assigned social worker gave me a heads-up about my wife's legal status. She was on a seventy-two-hour hold, I was told, meaning she was required to remain in the locked ward for three days. The clock started ticking on Wednesday, and weekends and holidays don't count. Thus, the earliest she could be released was the following Monday.

Whatever, I thought. I'd heard the horror stories in my support group. Three days, five days, what difference would it make? Come next week they'd give her the heave-ho, and I'd be back living in my tent.

I knew enough to shut up and listen and trust the staff and to advocate for Leah's health and safety and, selfishly, my own well-being. There would be a pair of court hearings to determine how long Leah needed to stay beyond the initial seventy-two hours. Given the difficulty of their jobs, I was grateful the staff members were patient with me and were trying to calm me down as I alternated between weeping and becoming unglued during my initial meetings with staff.

On my way out, Nurse Lori told me I needed to take care of myself and the staff would take care of my wife. "It's best you not come here to visit her. You might set her off if she sees you."

A COUNTY COURT REPRESENTATIVE named Al was assigned to Leah's case. I was clueless about the process and called my fishing buddy Fender, the social worker, who tried to explain it in plain English.

"See, this guy Al's job is to gather evidence to represent the county's interest to make sure a patient is being held in the 'least restrictive environment.' To hold someone against his or her will in a locked psychiatric ward, the court has to issue an order based on the evidence at hand—including the psychiatrist's recommendation."

"What about the husband who's completely freaking out that they're gonna release his wife before she's ready?"

"Theoretically, the family member's account can be a factor. On the other hand, they might not give a shit. Listen," Fender said, "when you talk to these people, try not to get emotional. Just give them the facts. Be specific about how she's been behaving and how abnormal she's been acting. Do your kids know anything?"

"They know a lot."

"This Al person might contact them, too."

Great. Not only was I going to have to rat out Leah—my kids might have to squeal on their own mother.

"It's for Leah's own good, Jeff," Fender said. "Just remember that. She's really sick."

I emailed Sarah, Joey, and my brother David a long update. I explained that a guy named Al might call any of us, and any information, along with police, medical, and social worker accounts, would be on the record and thus accessible to Leah.

I didn't go into detail about just how off-the-wall Leah was talking and acting in the hospital. She still had ideas about the consulting business she was supposedly running, her El-El-Cee. She wanted me to talk to her font class teacher and let him know she couldn't make it to class but she would be keeping up with the work. She told me about the urgent email messages she needed to write. She needed me to bring all her papers from home, all the folders of work she was doing. All of it.

"All of it?"

"Just *bring it in*. And bring me some *fucking flowers* from the garden!"

Which I did. I cut a bouquet of black-eyed Susans, and Leah set the flowers in plastic cups of water in the common area for the other patients to enjoy. I brought more flowers the next day, and the next, even after whatever I said had enraged her and she threw me out after a couple of minutes and the staff scolded me and told me not to come back because I was just upsetting Leah.

Ah! So that's why I hardly ever saw any other visitors.

I was learning on the fly, fighting the stereotypes of the severely mentally ill and their caretakers. I, for one, could never do the jobs of the nurses or mental health staff. A mental health worker told me that during one of Leah's first nights there, she was still so wired she paced the hallways late into the night, badgered the staff for access to her cell phone because she had her *business* to run, screamed at the staff, ranted even worse than at our house, acted almost psychotically beyond the need for sleep. When the worker told me the staff had to give Leah an injection of Haldol to settle her down, I broke up crying, picturing my poor wife so out of control she needed to be pinned down like an animal and get a needle jammed in her ass.

Although Leah has no memory of that night, her overall impressions of the psych ward are a lot harsher than mine. Of course they are. A few years later, Melody Moezzi's account of her own "imprisonment" in a psychiatric institution resonated thoroughly with Leah:

> The power dynamic that exists at Ashwood, and at countless other deceptively innocuous-sounding facilities like it, is insurmountable. The "providers" are in charge. The "consumers" are subservient. It's like a mini-dictatorship. [They should] hear us out, check their facts and treat us with basic human dignity and respect.[2]

In contrast, I never saw Leah's time in the psych ward in such brutal terms. Then again, I was so strung out by her behavior and so incapable of corralling it myself that I'm sure I gave the staff the benefit of the doubt while Leah was hospitalized. I admired how her assigned psychiatrist, Dr. Patek, the nurses, and the mental health workers seemed to take none of the patients' wrath personally; they knew that patients were there because they were sick and needed healing.

And I found out why there's a bench outside the door to the locked ward. It's not for family members when they're waiting to be let in. It's for people like me to sit down and sob once we've visited our loved ones.

---

[2] Melody Moezzi, *Haldol and Hyacinths* (New York: Penguin, 2013), p. 235.

Unlike the staff, I did take everything personally.

And unlike Leah, I was allowed to go home.

PATIENTS HAVE ACCESS to a community landline on a wall phone across from the nurses' station for local calls, affording them no privacy and, with its six-inch stiff metal receiver cord, no chance of using it as a suicide device. I noticed how little the patients used the phone, suggesting they had few people to call in the first place. When Sarah, Joey, and I tried calling Leah, we were flummoxed by how many times the wall phone would ring before a patient would pick it up, and by the number of times whoever picked it up would get distracted and leave the phone dangling for the next twenty minutes.

The caller ID on outgoing calls from the hospital was disguised, ending in 0000. My stomach would ache whenever I saw that Leah was trying to call me, a half-dozen times a day, starting as early as seven thirty in the morning. Each time I answered she launched into a speech about being held prisoner, about suing the cops for cuffing her, about some *shit* that went on during the night, how they *wouldn't let her have her fucking cell phone*, how she wanted to know when the *fuck* I would get down there with the stuff she needed for her business and if I made those calls for her and who was taking care of the yard and if I'd raked any leaves and if I'd cleaned the house yet and who *else* I had told without her *fucking* permission that she was in the hospital and that she wanted me to bring her flowers.

"Good morning. How am I?" I answered sarcastically, igniting another diatribe from Leah about how all I cared about was *my fucking self.*

Yet I continued to brace myself and picked up the phone dutifully that first week when Leah called me. How could I not? She was alone in a locked psychiatric ICU. A nurse told me that whether Leah was capable of knowing it or not, my wife was more terrified than I of the mania that besieged her and she had no one—no one—in her life but her self-pitying husband and our woebegone offspring on each coast. If not me, who else would she scream at?

But that disguised phone number, the rapid-fire invectives, it all eventually kicked me in the stomach and began to create a mild traumatic pain, and I finally quit answering her calls.

"*Why didn't you pick up the fucking phone?*" she would snap at me.

"Good morning, dear."

A N D   T H E N there was the sweet side.

Leah's manic episode blew the lid off her internal pressure cooker, detonating her emotions like lava bombs. I'd seen her illness bring out the worst in her all summer, and now her best. Her kindness and compassion percolated mercifully, particularly in her interactions with the other patients.

From the get-go Leah made several new "friends" as the severely ill cycled through the intensive care psych ward. Some patients had been hospitalized before Leah arrived and were recovering in the ICU only until they improved enough to graduate into the magic kingdom of the general psych unit. Others were longer-term convalescents, like Leah, there for days or weeks, depending on the outcome of their court order and the availability of beds.

When I would visit her, Leah would be amped like a game-show emcee, eager to introduce me to her fellow patients. At times she was slightly hypersexualized, wound around me like an octopus; every emotion was exaggerated. I suppose she got a bang out of showing off her silver fox of a sweetheart—until a couple minutes later when she'd go ballistic and throw me out of there.

In her self-perceived role as the ward's de facto patient representative, Leah's forbearance and interest in the other patients was grandiose albeit sincere. She advocated for them with the hospital staff from a place deep in her heart, which wrenched my soul. In gratitude to Leah for her kindness, a spectacularly immature and manipulative young patient named Daniella began calling Leah "Mommy." During her hourly meltdowns, Daniella experienced severe mood shifts and lobbed the N-word at a black patient. Despite her tantrums and hokum, Daniella's hysterics were sad to behold; you never knew a patient's diagnosis, and I admired Leah for her ardor and humor about the inanity of living on a psych ward.

"You missed a good one last night," Leah would grin if there had been a violent and weird outburst involving hurled missiles or the cops. I'd always loved her sardonic side, bemused and calm. When she wasn't screaming at me, I felt moments of relief that I hadn't completely lost Leah—whoever she was under her patient scrubs.

But her determination to overstep her assigned role as psychiatric patient, a modern-day Randle McMurphy, clearly exasperated the staff: the more strong-willed Leah was, the less stable she was in the eyes of the staff, and the less capable of functioning beyond the ICU. Plus, compared to the trained mental health workers, Leah had no idea what she was doing. She refused to kowtow to the staff's demands and perceived she was on a noble struggle for patient rights and human dignity.

Years later I'm not sure Leah was all that wrong about psych wards. Someone at NAMI told me the problem with the mental health system is there isn't one. In the 1960s, when President Kennedy and others decided to deinstitutionalize the mentally ill, no one had a long-term plan or the funding to treat them. I sure as heck wasn't capable of giving Leah the care she needed. Family members I've met lament through broken hearts and red eyes their inadequacy as caregivers, the shortage of hospital beds, the absence of effective treatment options, and their realistic fears their loved ones will end up homeless. There has to be a less dehumanizing way to remedy the needs of the mentally ill, but I don't know what it is.

In any case, although Leah's ego might have been boosted by Daniella and other patients, this "Mommy" business got a little weird even for Leah (and I sure wasn't interested in being Daniella's Daddy). But it didn't matter. The minute the patients were discharged from the ward you never knew what happened to them.

THE ACCUSATIONS, anger, and indigestion got to me. I wanted to be supportive of Leah, but I still had no idea what that actually meant. I was physically and emotionally exhausted from keeping up the house, running back and forth to the hospital, driving around the downtown construction, hunting for a parking spot, winding my way through the maze of hallways to the psych ward, talking to doctors, trying to be optimistic, and remaining calm when she screamed at me.

She was sick. And if I didn't start taking care of myself, I would be too.

But for how long could I continue to lean on my friends for support? I consciously tried to spread my grief carefully lest my Jeffrey Downer lament erode the goodwill of my friends. With no family members in Minnesota, I called David in Arizona and told him it was time for him to come help take care of his little brother, on my dime. The minute I picked him up at the airport I began breathing a bit deeper, at long last.

David knew I was falling apart. Because of her emails and behavior, Leah's mania was no secret—with him, our cousins, many friends, Leah's own people, passing acquaintances. Her hospitalization added a thick layer of sludge to the morass.

At my invitation, David accompanied me downtown to attend a meeting with Leah and her medical team. She knew David was in town, and she went back and forth about whether to see him in the hospital. At times she accused him of being in on the conspiracy to keep her penned in. At times she was eager to see the brother-in-law she loved. And at times, I surmised, she was maniacally smug about the situation, like he and the rest of the so-called sane world should just *see* how these condescending quacks were treating her because, see, *they're* the crazy ones, not her.

The case meeting was tense. Leah, still manic, often interrupted Dr. Patek and other staff members, correcting all their errors of thinking and logic, disputing their assessments of her mental health, ripping into them for their condescension and power trips, for misunderstanding her creativity as a *professional graphic designer* and social worker *herself*. My brother—the best man at our wedding—sat there stunned. I hadn't over-stated her mania; if anything, I'd grown so accustomed to her anger and grandiosity that I'd lost perspective on how bad it was.

"Why did you tell Lois I'm here?" she sneered.

"I didn't," David said. I was sure Lois knew.

"You promise you won't tell her?"

Dr. Patek looked at David. How could he not tell his wife that Leah was in the hospital?

"If it will help you get better, Leah," he said, choking back tears, "I won't tell her."

I was maddened by the scene playing out as just another manip-ulative sham: my sicko wife, powerless to leave the hospital but some-how controlling not only me but the doctors, the nurses, and now my own brother.

"So when am I going to get released?" Leah all but shouted.

Nearly two weeks into Leah's hospitalization, Dr. Patek made no promises.

THE STIGMA of mental illness was pestering me. If your neighbor slips on the ice and bangs his head on the ground and ends up with a traumatic brain injury, you bring over the tuna casserole. Who's not willing to walk another neighbor's dog when she's getting treated for back surgery? Who judges the fellow with Lou Gehrig's disease, the woman with Parkinson's?

I was done playing charades.

I started with my next-door neighbors, Barb and Hal. They're a little older than are Leah and I, like us with grown kids out of the house. Barb, a native Iowan, sweet-natured and calm. Hal can be as gruff as bark on an ash tree but has a warm, funny side when he's in a good mood every few months.

"So here's the deal," I told them over coffee at their dining room table. "You may have noticed things have been a little weird over at our house lately."

"Well, ya," Barb said. "We've been hearing some stuff. We kinda wondered."

"The thing is," I blubbered, "Leah's been diagnosed with a mental illness. She's got the bipolar disorder."

Cripes, I could barely even say it out loud. I'd spent the summer so royally barbequed, my public emotions packed away so deeply, that as I sat in my long-time neighbors' house and cracked my heart open a bit, the tears started again. Just shut up, Jeff, and shovel your walk in the winter and grow your raspberries every summer and share them with the neighbors. Don't bring down these people with your mess of a life. Good neighbors don't do that.

"Well," Barb said, "ya know, our Sam's got that too. When he was in high school—"

Their son Sam is in his late thirties now.

"Oh, man," Hal laughed. "You never heard those fights we had?"

"He's still dealing with it," Barb said. "Sam. He can get so depressed. I don't think he's been manic for a while, but—"

"It absolutely sucks," Hal said. "I'm really sorry to hear that."

But Sam has gotten better, they assured me.

"Wait, so he's gotten better?"

Even if Sam hadn't improved, I was glad they said he had. I needed hope.

And that's how it went as I spilled the truth to my neighbors. Everyone knew someone with something or other. Everyone felt bad for me, especially bad for Leah. Everyone cared about us both. Everyone asked what they could do to help.

It's hard to explain just how listening to my story with grace and without judgment was exactly the help I needed.

HOPELESS AND OVERWHELMED, I invited my brother to attend a Friday night synagogue service with me. David declined. We'd been observant in childhood and when our children were young, but he withdrew from congregational life once his kids grew older. Leah and I maintained a spiritual home at our temple—spiritual in the broadest sense, meaning we enjoyed a group of friends to gossip with, found comfort in Jewish traditions and ethos, and figured we would have someone to conduct and attend our funerals.

A traditional Jewish Shabbat service includes the *Mi'sh'beyrach* prayer, when the names of those in need of healing are read aloud and we ask God for a speedy recovery and, in this country, adequate health insurance. The night I attended when David was in town, I couldn't decide if the right thing to do was recite a public prayer of healing for my wife or give the poor woman some dignity and shut my mouth and sit there and silently weep. This was the synagogue where Leah and I had dropped the kids off for Sunday School for fifteen years, where we celebrated their bar and bat mitzvahs with a hundred or more of our friends and relatives.

Now, many years later, the kids and our previous rabbi long gone, I could barely even make small talk with any congregants. Instead, among two hundred other worshippers, I felt completely alone, searching the empty seats in vain for the ghosts of my family.

That's when I stood up and asked God to heal my wife and take care of me, because after two weeks in the hospital, nothing else seemed to be doing any good.

LEAH TOLD ME the mental health staff agreed to let her hold a Rosh Hashanah service to celebrate the Jewish new year inside a conference room in the ward. I asked her what she wanted David and me to bring to the hospital. Leah barked orders at me and, I imagined, scolded the naïve staff of county-employed do-gooders, demanding I bring the prayer books, yarmulkes, and a seasonal round challah bread.

"With raisins," she said. "And wine. But they probably won't let you bring wine so just bring grape juice. And candlesticks and candles. Oh, and bring a bottle of hair conditioner. I'm all out."

"Leah, they're not going to let me bring candles and candlesticks into the ward."

"Who the fuck cares? It's a religious service. Just bring them."

"I can't bring candles."

"There's going to be like eight people here so bring everything we have and get down here."

I wasn't about to drive all over town trying to locate a challah an hour before the start of the holiday. But I managed to find a bag of a half-dozen potato rolls at the Whole Foods, along with a bottle of grape juice and hair conditioner. I grabbed our pair of holiday prayer books and eight yarmulkes, threw everything into a paper shopping bag, and headed downtown.

David and I entered the hospital through the night visitors' entrance, navigated the maze of corridors, buzzed the staff to let us in, and stowed our cell phones in a locker.

"What's in the bag?" Leah's nurse asked when we entered the ward.

Leah was awaiting us eagerly. "It's our materials for our goddamned Jewish religious service," she explained.

She was pissed I didn't bother with candles. Her mind racing, she told the staff we needed a flashlight, that Jews mark the start of the holiday with a traditional lighting of the flashlight.

"What about this?"

"It's a bottle of hair conditioner," Leah said, a bit snarky.

"Is it part of the service?"

"What do *you* think?" Like these idiots didn't even know anything about Judaism.

The staff led us into the conference room for our service and warily forked over a flashlight, which we placed in the center of the table with the potato rolls and juice and cups and bottle of hair conditioner. Joining Leah, David, and me were a couple of other patients, a pair of guys named Johnny and Stanley. Johnny brought along a broken guitar he liked to pretend to strum.

Johnny's father, Leah insisted to David and me, was rich and owned the Minnesota Twins.

"That's right," Johnny said. He said he lived in a six-floor apartment building across the street from Target Field.

"Which floor?"

"All six," Johnny said.

"The Pohlad family owns the Twins," I said quietly to Leah.

"No they don't!"

Johnny had the first few words of a Hebrew prayer tattooed on his arm. Leah said he had attended the same Reform synagogue where our kids had been enrolled in preschool.

I had no idea what was real.

Our other worshipper, Stanley, was a solemn, soft-spoken African-American man I'd chatted with during other visits to the ward. According to Leah, Stanley had some Jewish blood and was interested in exploring his Jewish roots. David played along, squirming, a liberal Jew in the broadest sense, supporting his maniacal sister-in-law, his bemused but despairing little brother, and especially Stanley. We had no idea what his story was. But the incalculable appreciation and earnestness he exuded overshadowed the event's burlesque. Here he was, groomed and gathered on this holy day, a yarmulke atop his head, with Leah, her fellow patients, her husband, and her husband's brother. I sensed it was as near a family gathering as Stanley had engaged in for a long time, and I found his sincerity so touching that I felt like sobbing.

Leah took charge of the service, ordering us to open our prayer books, leading us in Hebrew and in English as we chanted the traditional lighting of the flashlight and the blessing over the grape juice and then the potato rolls and hair conditioner. Apparently Johnny had in fact grown up Jewish. He strummed his imaginary guitar strings while singing some of the words, at times to made-up tunes. Oddest of all, Stanley sang along too, in Hebrew and in English, about a quarter beat behind the rest of us. He wasn't so much mouthing the words but parroting them. He was intent on learning about Judaism, on enveloping himself in these extraordinarily holy rituals in this extraordinarily weird place.

After maybe ten minutes we concluded by singing the *Adon Olam*, a traditional closing song.

"Okay, I'm tired," Leah said. "The service is over. You can go now. Wait, leave the rest of the potato rolls. Kiss me goodnight. Now leave."

No doubt the whole thing sounds like a mania-fueled mockery. In a comical way, it was Leah being Leah—silly, even a little snide.

But it was so much more than that. She was a secular, questioning Jew who was clinging to an annual ritual, a joyful celebration of life and family in the most unlikely of places. Among these strangers, peeking out from under an unbearable blanket of manic egoism, was Leah's fundamental generosity of spirit, of compassion, of kindness.

Back out through the locked doors, David and I staggered down the maze of hospital corridors, quiet and exhausted, drained by what we had just participated in.

Many times over the next eight days that led up to the holy day of atonement, Yom Kippur, I prayed to God for Leah's recovery from her disorder and forgiveness for my bitter desperation.

THE NEXT MORNING, on Rosh Hashanah, David and I loaded a pair of bicycles onto the back of my car, drove south, and spent the day pedaling on Minnesota's best paved bikeway, a former railroad bed that winds its way seventy miles through the woods and farmlands of southeastern Minnesota. I embraced the early autumn woodlands and the Root River wilderness with the person I'd loved for the past sixty years, the guy who had helped raise me and taught me most of what I knew as a child and had been there for me as best he could from sixteen hundred miles away during that summer's horror show.

I traditionally cast off a stone each Rosh Hashanah in a private tashlich[3] service, not only for my people's collective sins but, when

---

[3]   *Tashlich* (n.): From the Hebrew, trans. "to cast." A New Year's custom dating back to the prophet Nehemiah. Casting off our past year of sins by lobbing a stone or, in modern times, Goldfish crackers into a moving body of water.

applicable, for my own lousy year, and I pray to God to help me be less of a selfish lout in the year to come.

So, nearing the end of a thirty-mile ride, I asked David if he would stop for a few last moments of peace and quiet before the depressing car trip back to real life in Minneapolis. Almost no one goes biking during the middle of the week except the occasional geezers like us enjoying nature and stalling heart disease. The bike trail at that point is about a hundred feet above the Root River, which flows from its source in the farmlands of Mower County eastward to its mouth at the Mississippi River. When you look up you see eagles and hawks soaring against the hill-country cliffs, and if you look down, below the cottonwoods and oaks that line the bank, you might see kids in rubber rafts or fly fishermen casting for trout.

We pulled over on the trail. I parked my bike in the tawny early autumn grass, stood still and closed my eyes, intent on hearing the breeze and the robins, the crickets and the river tickling the rocks and shoreline, intent on cradling the rays of the September sun. I felt my lungs inhaling the country air, felt the presence of my hushed big brother, of life around me, the spot on Earth where I now stood nearing the end of my sixtieth year. Mostly on that quiet afternoon I wanted time to pray, for my wife's healing, for my own health, for a better year to come than this shit show I had endured the past few months.

With that, I cast off a rock the size of my heart far down the bank out into the river below and heard it splash. And then David and I headed back to my car for the trip home to Minneapolis.

DURING THE EIGHT DAYS between Rosh Hashanah and Yom Kippur, as the meds clicked, the windmills spinning in Leah's head finally decelerated. The hospital staff thought Leah was doing well enough to graduate from the ICU to the less restrictive albeit locked general unit.

"I guess it's time for me to grow up," I told my brother. "You should head home."

I bought him a return flight and bade him farewell at the airport and sent him back to Arizona.

"Doing well enough" in the psych ward means, in part, obeying the rules, which Leah had combatted so persistently the first couple of weeks in the hospital while the meds did their thing. In the general psych unit she gained a few privileges, like wearing her street clothes instead of scrubs and, under staff supervision, taking a walk around the block with a group of other patients and riding in a hospital van to an outing at Minnehaha Park. Those were sunny days, and I was happy for Leah after she had been cooped up for three weeks in an airless psychiatric ward watching life pass her by through a set of plate-glass windows.

And I was worried sick the hospital staff and courts would spring her before she was ready. *Spring* was her word, like a crook in a gangster flick who'd busted out of the slammer, like she was about to pull a fast one and obliterate my own safehouse.

I never got a straight story from anyone about when they would be discharging her. I didn't want to bug her social worker who, if you were lucky, took a day to return a call.

I get it. The staff is overworked, and who would want to talk all day to a quacking husband torn between his fear of his wife's manic wrath and his desire for his wife to get well and come home? Although the psychiatrist and courts are interested in the family members' perspectives, the care team, not the family, decides when the patient no longer needs a restricted environment and can be discharged.

A FEW DAYS before her release, Leah asked me to bring a clean blouse and skirt to the hospital. She had talked her way into a one-evening pass to attend Kol Nidre services, the beginning of Yom Kippur, the holiest day of the Jewish calendar. On this Day of Atonement we Jews aren't even supposed to drink water, and we self-flagellate for our collective and personal sins, like screaming at our spouses when they pin us down in our bathtubs.[4]

I wondered how far she could push the Jewish card with the doctors and nurses. But the hospital staff, understandably ignorant of a cultural but atheistic Jew like Leah, was relentless in their pursuit of ethnic and religious equality. And more to the point, they thought she was stabilizing, even if I remained skeptical.

Rather than worship at our own temple, Leah insisted we attend a small congregation in south Minneapolis. We had known the part-time rabbi there for a long time, a brilliant and kind woman, and the lay cantor, a friend of Leah's who looked like Mr. Clean and sang like Art Garfunkel.

Maybe Leah's mood actually was improving. She wasn't as wound up as I anticipated with this first taste of freedom in weeks. Part of me feared the whole thing was a scam and she might pull a Shawshank and demand I hightail it to Mexico with her. But there were no theatrics during the twenty-minute drive to the synagogue.

When we arrived we found seats toward the back of the crowded congregation, next to an aisle in case we needed to make a quick

---

[4] For starters: "For the sin which we have committed before You under duress or willingly. And for the sin which we have committed before You with an utterance of the lips. And for the sin which we have committed before You through speech. And for the sin which we have committed before You in passing judgment." Traditionally, Judaism has 613 commandments. Given what was going on through my head and what came out of my mouth, I had a lot of atoning to do. See "The Text of Al Chet," High Holidays, Chabad.org, https://www.chabad.org/library/article_cdo/aid/6577/jewish/Text-of-Al-Chet.htm.

getaway. We were acquainted with very few worshippers, and Leah exchanged only a nod and small wave with Mr. Clean.

My head was in a thousand places at once, a comorbid sense of relief, gratitude, repentance, encouragement in Leah's improvement, and terror that she might still bolt. God only knows what she was thinking. But not even fifteen minutes into the service, she whispered to me that she had a headache and said she wanted to leave and go back to the hospital, which was fine with me.

I don't recall waving farewell to Mr. Clean. I do remember this: On the way back downtown, she asked me to stop at a Ben and Jerry's for ice cream. I didn't bother checking the Talmud to see if it's okay for a person on leave from the psych ward to break a fast on Yom Kippur and eat Chocolate Fudge Brownie at an ice cream franchise started by a couple of Jewish guys.

"Of course I'll stop," I said.

Over the ensuing days, Leah continued to improve. Late one afternoon, twenty-five days after being admitted to the hospital, she was well enough to be discharged. She demanded I drive us straight from HCMC to an alumni event at the University of Minnesota, where we saw several of her former colleagues and nibbled hors d'oeuvres, and at long last we drove home together.

The next day Leah and I began gluing back together her life . . . and our long, fractured marriage.

Down

CHAPTER 12

Recovery

By mid-October, with the aid of the pharmaceutical cocktail she had been prescribed, Leah's mania petered out, and the two of us set about healing our marriage. Leah continued seeing her therapist, Dr. Melnick, and I my own, albeit with less urgency. Under the terms of the court order after her release from the hospital, Leah had enrolled in a partial day-treatment program at Abbott Northwestern Hospital in Minneapolis. She would attend classes on topics in mental illness and participate in group therapy. She was also assigned a county-contracted case manager named Monica who, in accordance with the six-month stay of commitment,[1] would

---

[1] "A stay of commitment means that the court will not enforce the commitment as long as the person participates voluntarily in a treatment plan. If he or she does not follow the rules of this treatment plan (for example, staying clean if there is a drug problem, taking medication or attending groups), then the court-ordered commitment begins." (Understanding the Minnesota Civil Commitment Process [NAMI: 2016], https://namimn.org/wp-content/uploads/sites/188/2018/03/civilcommitmentbookletfinal-2016.pdf.). The civil commitment process is overwhelming. I was lucky that my friend Fender in the human services field guided me through all this. It's not the time to be shy: you have to ask the social workers and the case manager questions if you don't know what's going on.

meet with Leah monthly and monitor her progress.

Although embarrassing to Leah, from our family's perspective, a case manager's supervision was a relief. We had no desire to drown in any downstream bureaucratic or bipolar maelstroms without someone tossing us a life preserver; less selfishly, my kids and I hoped the county mental health system's involvement would ensure Leah had the medical, social, and psychological support she needed to get healthy and prevent a relapse into mania.

Of the little Leah remembered about the events of that summer, most of her memories were cockeyed. Something I read helped me de-personalize it:

> Memory and cognition problems are at their worst during manic episodes. Patients operating at high speeds due to mania have a hard time encoding new information into their memories and also show difficulty accessing memories.[2]

In other words, during a manic episode a person's mind is working so rapidly that memories never form in the first place. The ensuing amnesia heals the psyche of someone who has experienced a manic episode.

Too bad amnesia isn't contagious. My head needed healing as well from the emotional Tilt-a-Whirl I'd been riding. I was heartened one day when Leah wanted to go on a bike ride with me. We stopped at a park bench and I nearly gasped when she said, "I'm going to look into flights for a trip back to Tunisia."

---

[2] Dennis Thompson, Jr., "Bipolar Disorder and Memory Loss," *Bipolar Disorder, Everyday Health*, updated July 2010. https://www.everydayhealth.com/bipolar-disorder/bipolar-disorder-and-memory-loss.aspx.

After all that we have been through, I thought, *she still doesn't get it. What am I supposed to do now? Be supportive of that?*

Following the advice from the books I'd read, I decided to *respond* to what she said, not *react*. Instead of screaming at Leah, I merely said I thought we should take things one day at a time.

At my next NAMI support group meeting I mentioned Leah's terrible idea about going back to Tunisia. One woman said that when her husband said something asinine, she drank a glass of water. "It works every time," she said. "As long as I'm drinking a glass of water, I'm not getting sucked into a stupid argument."

A fellow I eventually befriended and nicknamed Jack Lemmon offered us all some good advice (the guy looked and talked just like the late actor Jack Lemmon). His wife of thirty-five years had severe depression coupled with alcoholism, and he had attended and learned a lot in his Al-Anon meetings. "In Al-Anon," Jack said, "they talk about the three C's: I didn't cause it, I can't control it, I can't cure it. I have to remember that all the time."

Someone else in our group mentioned the serenity prayer, asking for the ability to accept the things we couldn't change, to take it one day at a time or, in a crisis, one hour at a time. Don't do anything drastic. You don't have to decide anything today.

"If after six months or more little has changed," Julie Fast and John Preston write, "that is when you have to make decisions about your own life. Do you stay or go?"[3]

Let's see, it was October. Six months from now would be March 2016. Man, that sounded like a long way off.

---

[3] Julie Fast and John Preston, *Loving Someone with Bipolar Disorder: Understanding and Helping Your Partner*, 2d ed. (Oakland: New Harbinger, 2012), 191.

I WROTE in my journal:

OCTOBER 18, 2015

Leah may be getting depressed.

She fell asleep at 7:30 p.m. She's gaining weight. Something is wrong with her knees and hands. Not sure what else, but I can't fix her.

In the hospital Leah was prescribed Zyprexa, a mood stabilizer that brought her back to Earth. The list of side effects from any of those medications is spine-tingling, and I avoided the personal horror stories on whack-job antimedication websites about developing a second head or causing a rash all over your car fenders or spontaneously combusting like those drummers in *Spinal Tap*.

Or, if you're like Leah, gaining a lot of weight. Late one night we panicked when her feet blew up like volleyballs and her knuckles ached so badly she couldn't bend her fingers. Leah agreed to let me drive her to a hospital emergency room out in the suburbs, a clinic covered by our insurance with a nearby all-night Burger King where I could buy a cup of Sprite to calm my gut.

The ER doc and nurses were concerned, too, and for the rest of the night they ran a battery of cardio tests on Leah to rule out Really Bad Things. At daybreak the doctors decided to take her off Zyprexa and sent her away on an intergalactic odyssey to find the right medication.

It didn't take long for her to sink rapidly into a stygian depression. She had trouble getting out of bed. She needed extra sleep. She stopped eating. She began shutting down.

After the summer of rage the house became eerily quiet, with Leah shutting the bedroom door soon after dinner and arising only well into the morning. She had struggled with seasonal affective disorder for years and still had her fluorescent light box, but she doubted it had done any good. And it was only October, not the middle of winter. She began spending afternoons in bed and gave me too much time to mope.

Leah's doctors and nurses talked in terms of *baseline mood*—that is, someone's "normal" self compared to how he or she behaves during an episode. In fact, as the illness progressed, both Leah and I began losing track of what "normal" even meant, which is one of the sadder aspects of depression. You and your friends and your loved one end up asking yourselves if you would even recognize "normal," fearing a manic or depressed state is the new normal.

But we never gave up hope. And for a few days, including my birthday in October 2015, Leah's mood was close to baseline—spirited, funny, and audacious.

WHEN LEAH WAS MANIC she purchased a Groupon for archery lessons at Average Joe's, an indoor shooting range in a far northern suburb of the Twin Cities.

It wasn't a nutty idea like the others. It was a different nutty idea.

"I'm good at bow and arrow," Leah bragged when she bought the Groupon, referring to summer camp mastery fifty years earlier.

What the heck. Leah had already paid for two hours of bowing and arrowing, which included a free glass of pop and a short lesson. This would be a birthday adventure, the kind of thing normal couples do—although for a paranoid city boy like me it was also an expedition to Michele Bachmann country, unfamiliar territory crawling with paranoid right-wing survivalists who hid surplus mortar shells in their underground bunkers.

More to the point, I still worried that Leah would lose her shit and aim an arrow at an invisible apple atop my head. But I needed to get over my lingering fear and anger, especially as the remnants of Leah's mania vanished.

Technically Leah was a veteran archer, but Average Joe himself gave us a lesson anyway. He patiently showed us two urban boneheads the right way to hold the bow and aim the arrows at the bullseye targets twenty yards away. Told us the rules about shouting "Clear!" when it was time to gather up our arrows so no one got killed. Demonstrated the way to pull the string and let the arrow fly.

Leah impressed me; she was a tenacious archer. I did well, too. A half hour of bows and arrows later the birthday boy had scored even more points than Leah and we were bored and her arm muscles ached and we told Average Joe we'd had enough archery for one day.

"Maybe it's more fun shooting arrows at an elk," I told Leah. "But thanks for setting up the archery lesson on my birthday."

"We should play billiards next time. I was pretty good at it in rec therapy in the hospital."

Back in Minneapolis we stopped for dinner at an Irish pub ("It's okay. The pharmacist said I could have one glass of wine"), and we laughed while imitating the *boing!* and *thwup!* sounds from the archery range. Someone had left a newspaper on the seat of our booth. I checked the sports section and Leah checked the local news and obituaries.

"Here's one," she said. "Would you have married me if my name were Ketzia Lipschitz?" She liked to do that, find a weird name of a dead person from the old country.

"I had a cousin named Hyman Bensky," I said. "Super nice guy. He went by Hymie. You could have been Mrs. Hyman Bensky."

"I'm going to change my name to Ketzia Lipschitz."

She'd gotten her sense of humor back, the best birthday gift I could imagine.

After dinner we walked to the Film Society down on Main Street, the site of the anniversary fiasco that summer, to see *Veronica*, a heist picture filmed in a single, ninety-minute shoot. My heart leapt as Leah and I held hands through the film, which resembled the past four months of her life: one compressed, nonstop movie take that ended only under Leah's sedation in a psychiatric ward.

On an unusually warm October evening, we strolled hand in hand along the Mississippi River back to the car. I was hopeful for the two of us, happily ignoring the cold, dark night of the coming Upper Midwest winter.

DURING THE SUMMER I had been too strung out and exhausted to write very much in my journal. I regret that. Usually I have a bad short-term memory. Emails and texts helped fill in some gaps, but I wish I had a more complete record of my thoughts and feelings those months. I took notes in my journal when I met with counselors, but much of what I wrote looks like the penmanship of a kangaroo.

As things calmed down, I began to write more frequently.

OCTOBER 26, 2015

It's been downhill since my birthday. Leah is dealing with depression, and I'm dealing with my hostility about her illness. It's easier to live with depression than mania. But I'm sad for Leah, a new phase of all this. She is talking about going to Tunisia again.

NOVEMBER 10

Leah is in the depth of depression. I've never seen her like this.
How much is chemical or seasonal or psychological?
I can't bring up my bitterness about her manic behavior.

One woman in our support group said a blanket apology isn't
as fulfilling as an acknowledgment of individual harmful acts,
like the Bathtub Incident. In my group we ended up laughing
about the cops visiting the house after she squeezed my
boobie. The sheer absurdity of our lives.

I was using my journal to try to make sense of the inexplicable.
The most noticeable phrase, though, was "the sheer absurdity of our
lives." Somehow it was comforting to use a word like *absurd*. It gave
me a way to assess my life and our marriage with more humor and less
bitterness. It also gave me a historical account of the bipolar ride I had
become hitched to.

While manic, Leah had signed up to attend a professional conference in Chicago in the fall. *You need to be supportive*, she had implored
me at the time. She would see her former colleagues at the conference
(dear God, please, not Chauncey Greene), rub a few elbows, hand out
her business card, sell herself as a consultant.

And leave me the hell alone for a weekend. "Go for it!" I begged
her at the time.

Now, four months later, Leah had plummeted into depression; she
was emotionally raw, physically weak, and melancholy. In Chicago she'd
have to be "up" for a few days both around her old crowd and during the
keynote address, resisting the urge to slither on the floor like a comatose
boiled noodle.

Yet even in her sadness Leah exuded the strength of character I
had always admired. I'll be okay, she said. She had already spent the

money on a Greyhound bus ticket and for the conference. She planned to stay the first night at the conference hotel and then with her high school friend the Liz NoParking and her husband, the Nick Something.

I'd met this Liz NoParking a few times. I don't recall Leah or anyone else calling her anything but Liz NoParking. It was a play on her last name, something like Noporchnik. She had a toothy smile, and unlike Leah, was a jock, a Chicago Bears season ticket holder who on a linebacker blitz could probably grind up my ass like a walnut. I hadn't met this Nick husband but assumed he playfully threw telephone poles at little guys like me. A while back I told Liz NoParking I had grown up in Pittsburgh, that I had attended the Immaculate Reception game as a stadium vendor.[4]

"That's awesome!" Liz NoParking had squealed. "I can get you a seat when the Bears play the Steelers!"

It would be a whole awesome weekend thing, Liz said: tailgating, all kinds of awesome fun with a corybantic pack of drunken Chicago Bears fans.

"Sounds awesome, Liz," I said. "No, thanks."

Leah had been spending twelve, maybe sixteen hours a day in bed, recovering from her months of mania. I envisioned her trying to find her way from the bus depot to the conference, and then from there to Liz NoParking's house, and then back to the bus station, and then back to Minnesota—all without ending up in the hospital.

But I was resigned. I would drop off Leah at the Greyhound station downtown, drive to my house, mainline a few hundred kilos of mescaline, and loop the Doors for three days on my stereo. Or, better, take a bath, fix myself a sandwich, and spend the time sleeping in peace.

---

[4]   I didn't actually see the Immaculate Reception because everyone in front of me was jumping twelve feet in the air.

And if Leah did make it to the conference? I pictured her inhaling a couple quick glasses of wine at cocktail hour, flirting with a potted fichus tree, spinning around in her bed, and waking up with a headache that would blow the roof off the Marriott.

I WASN'T THAT FAR OFF. Leah called me a few times during the weekend, exhausted and embarrassed by the awkwardness of seeing her Minnesota crowd at the conference, the people who a few weeks before had trembled from her grandiosity. (Whew. No Chauncey Greene.) She didn't last long at the conference, wasn't sure why she was there. She might bag the whole thing, Leah said, just hide at the Liz NoParking's house.

On Sunday morning Leah called me sobbing about her lost weekend and her lack of sleep. She said she had spent most of the time in the guest bedroom and that the Liz NoParking had *no understanding at all* of depression. Leah said she needed to come home. She needed sleep. The meds were screwing her up. Do you love me? Will you meet me at the bus station? Please tell me you love me!

"And *who the fuck is Jay Cutler?*" she wept, not angrily, just dismally aware of how lost she was in the world.

"The Bears' quarterback. And of course I love you," I said. Whoever *you* are, dear.

For the record: the Vikings beat the Bears, 23–20. Sorry, Liz NoParking. But thanks for putting up Leah for the weekend.

AFTER SHE RETURNED from Chicago, Leah and I met with her new psychiatric nurse practitioner, Ms. Fine, at a clinic near the Mall of America in Bloomington. This was my first time in Bloomington since the middle-of-the-night debacle before we flew to Jamaica for our daughter's wedding and Leah's run-in with the airport cops. Returning to places where Leah and I had our brouhahas set my stomach roiling, like when you run into a former girlfriend walking arm-in-arm with the stud she dumped you for.

But I would dutifully drive her there to give this Ms. Fine the straight dope in case Leah tried to bluff her way through a phony self-assessment. Over the past couple of weeks Leah had lost her appetite; now she felt faint from malnourishment. When we arrived at the clinic parking lot, she barely managed to stagger to Ms. Fine's office on the second floor. I was afraid for Leah, worried she would deflate like a balloon in the clinic lobby and die of exhaustion and malnutrition.

Why a psychiatric nurse practitioner? Health insurance, of course. We would learn over the coming years that locating and keeping a top-notch psychiatrist was as difficult and random as finding the right cocktail of meds. Psychopharmacology was a game of Whac-a-Mole: any drug that addressed one symptom seemed to entail a new side effect.

Ms. Fine, a bit younger than us, had a friendly, earnest face. She diligently studied Leah's vital signs and listened to her weakly expel a few yes–no answers. To my incongruous relief, Ms. Fine was alarmed by Leah's level of malnourishment.

"You're severely dehydrated. You need to get your medication adjusted. I want you to go to the hospital and get yourself admitted."

Leah was crestfallen, looking like she was about to crumble into a pile of cinders. "I'm not going back to the psychiatric ward," she muttered, shattering my heart in a wave of compassion. "Can't you just put me back on Prozac?"

"I think there's too much risk of it setting off a manic episode. You need to go to the ER and let them decide."

If she refused, I figured, Ms. Fine would call the county case manager and let her deal with it.

EACH BREATH of Leah's was labored as we walked back to the car. She had lost control in a different way than during the summer, like her entire being was dissolving. She acquiesced and let me drive her to Abbott Northwestern Hospital, where she'd done the three-week partial-day program upon her release from HCMC.

She spent five days in Abbott's psychiatric unit. I couldn't figure out why, with no indication of suicidal thoughts, Leah needed to be segregated in a locked ward for her depression. She had agreed to be admitted to the hospital voluntarily. She knew she was sick, too weak to swallow a spoonful of mashed potatoes, let alone kill herself. I heard few answers, but then again, I asked few questions. My wife was crushed by the weight of a post-manic pharmaceutical boulder, and I was beyond trying to figure out how the mental health system might save her.

One jolt, though: In the common area of the psych ward we saw a nurse wheeling an acquaintance of ours through the room. Jill was about Leah's age, with lively blue eyes and an endearing smile. Although I didn't know Jill well, I had enjoyed our gregarious interactions. Now, hunched in a wheelchair, Jill was hollow-eyed, vacant, her jaw drooping lethargically. *Geez,* I wondered. *Had she just been to electro-shock therapy or what?* When Leah and Jill saw each other, there was awkward embarrassment: What's a nice gal like you doing in a place like this?

Neither Jill, nor Leah, nor I said much to each other. The fog of mental illness stigma is as thick as mud, even there in the psych ward. But over the next couple of years, Jill, her husband Rob, Leah, and I eventually "came out" to each other. Jill and her gentle husband would become two of my guiding lights, although my heart still aches for them as they continue to ride the roller coaster of Jill's chronic depression.

IN LATE DECEMBER Joey came home to Minneapolis from Oregon during a winter break from teaching. I was glad to have someone to spell me in my caregiving role, and he was eager to see his old posse. Leah pulled herself out of bed long enough to attend a small Chanukah party at our friends Heshie and Judy's house, but she spent much of the evening lying on their couch in the living room while the rest of us ate dinner and celebrated the holiday.

New Year's Eve 2015. *Auld lang syne.* In English, "times gone by."

I took a scrap of paper into the bathroom and scribbled down the year. I held the paper while Joey lit a match and set it on fire. We watched it burn for a couple seconds until I dropped it into the toilet, listened to the sizzle, and gave it a flush.

I'll take a cup o' kindness yet.

CHAPTER 13

What Does Depression Bleed?

Depression bleeds relationships through suspicion, the lack of confidence and self-respect, the inability to enjoy life, to walk or talk or think normally, the exhaustion, the night terrors, the day terrors. There is nothing good to be said for it except that it gives you the experience of how it must be to be old, to be old and sick, to be dying; to be slow of mind; to be lacking in grace, polish, and coordination; to be ugly; to have no belief in the possibilities of life, the pleasures of sex, the exquisiteness of music, or the ability to make yourself and others laugh.

—Kay Redfield Jamison

Over the winter and spring I learned what Leah's depression bleeds. She loses interest in reading, cooking, having friends over, snowshoeing, hiking in the woods, taking walks around the Minneapolis Chain of Lakes. In sewing, painting, visiting art museums, attending concerts and plays. In using her computer, talking on the phone, finding a job, volunteering, gardening, having sex, watering the grass. She loses her taste for spicy food and derives no pleasure from a bouquet of flowers.

She has no interest in changing the sheets on the bed, deciding what to eat for dinner, going through the mail, paying bills, cleaning the house, brushing her teeth, showering, washing her hair, arising from bed, swearing, pointing out my faults and inadequacies. She suffers horrible sweating episodes, which, according to an endocrinologist, a neurologist, and a gynecologist, are unrelated to menopause and are idiopathic and incurable (although, with no evidence, her neurologist thinks these are related to the meds Leah is taking). She becomes more isolated when she is depressed, and the more depressed she is, the more isolated.

Since first experiencing bipolar depression, Leah says she feels neither sadness nor happiness, neither anger nor joy. She feels no pleasure at all, a condition known as anhedonia,[1] a component of several mental illnesses and Woody Allen's original title for the movie *Annie Hall*.

She says she feels nothing.

In short, like 6.7 percent of all American adults in 2016, like 8.5 percent of all women, according to the National Institute of Mental Health, Leah was clinically depressed. *One out of twelve women.* Nearly two thirds of those with a major depressive episode are severely impaired by their depression.

That was Leah. That statistic was my wife.

I had never thought much about that kind of paralyzing depression until I lived with and loved a woman experiencing it. No matter what travails and self-imposed miseries I have endured during my sixty-five years on the planet, not one morning have I been unable or unwilling to get out of bed. Even my Uncle Milan, drugged with Thorazine for his schizophrenia, arose from bed in the morning, but he was a cigarette addict and had been told to smoke outside.

---

[1] See "Anhedonia: What to Do When You've Lost Your Joy," *Depression Alliance*, http://www.depressionalliance.org/anhedonia/.

"Leah," I would tell my wife when I had nothing left to say, "I would rather be me than you." When I said that I experienced a stew of love laced with guilt, grief, frustration, anger, compassion, and sorrow. Those abject words changed nothing.

AS WINTER WORE ON in Minneapolis, I wore out. I continued my freelance editing work, shoveled the snow, bought the food, cooked the meals, washed the dishes, watered the plants, vacuumed the floors, dusted the shelves, scrubbed the shower, paid the bills, calculated the taxes, whacked off—anything a single mom or dad does most every day of the year. So, boo-hoo on me, I'd remind myself, insulting my piggish self-pity, leading to even more guilt.

To take care of myself I spent as much time as possible with friends, attended movies alone or with my friend Heshie, called my children and brother and cousins, or had a bump of bourbon with Dr. J while watching the Pittsburgh Penguins chase the Stanley Cup on the big TV in his basement. For exercise I smacked a hockey puck against the boards on an otherwise empty skating rink, went off into the woods to cross-country ski or snowshoe, and did my best to stanch the blood pouring from my heart for my wife.

I continued to attend a couple of NAMI support groups each month to learn how spouses and partners in similar straits coped with their loved ones' depression. One woman whose attendance I appreciated, Melody, showed up to remind herself that her own partner had improved over time and to give the rest of us hope.

"Don't forget," Melody said, "when you're depressed, it takes all your energy just to get out of bed."

"That's right," said the facilitator, Tasha. She had not only a husband with a mental illness but a son who had been diagnosed with bipolar disorder, and she had battled depression herself. "If someone had cancer you wouldn't blame her for being sick in bed."

It was a good point. A person in bed with the flu, a fever of 102, parched throat, drippy nose, coughing and aching—he's sick, we think. *Stay home and rest!* A person with a mental illness? *Get your act together,* we think.

In other words, I thought, *tsk-tsk for being such a self-centered twit, Jeff.*

"Well," Melody responded, "we're only human. Resentment is normal."

That resonated with me. Although not a Catholic and certainly not a nun, I castigated myself too often for falling short of Mother Teresa's example. Not only did I not wash the feet of the poor or share my dentures with the toothless—I pissed and moaned about having to clean the frying pan after sautéing tilapia in canola oil.

"We're all coping with our loved ones' illnesses as best we can," Melody said. "Be kind to yourself. You wake up each morning and ask yourself, 'How can I try to do a better job today?' And at the end of the day, you hope you did as good a job as you could. That's all we're accountable for."

"You have to set boundaries," said Tom the Harley guy. "Our loved ones can't dominate our lives. You have to take care of yourself."

"We can only endure so much," Skin and Bones Mike said. "That's whether caring for an aging parent, an unhealthy spouse, or a chronically ill child."

"Endure?" Tasha remarked. "That's harsh. I don't *endure* my husband's or son's mental illness. I love them and give them the support they need. *Endure* sounds like, I don't know, when you can't endure one more day of winter and you fly off to Miami Beach for a week. I mean, we can't just endure a family member."

I had kept quiet but finally said, "I get what they're saying, Tasha. I don't know how it is if you have a child with a chronic illness. You can't just up and leave him. But I gotta get out of that morgue I'm living in or I'm going to go crazy, too."

Right about then, a young woman in our group named Sally spoke up. For five years she had been living with and loving an army veteran boyfriend, a guy with PTSD, rapid-cycling bipolar disorder, and outbursts of rage (although he never acted violently toward her). I know I wouldn't have taken a swing at this Sally. She looked like the boxer Laila Ali and could have kicked anyone's ass in that room, especially mine. I admired her courage for sticking with the boyfriend, who was hardly the only veteran whose partner *endured* the PTSD their loved ones suffered.

"My therapist pointed out the difference between *caretaking* and *caregiving*," Sally told us. "Caretaking crosses boundaries, and we end up resentful because we're trying to fix someone else instead of taking care of ourselves. Care*giving* puts the onus on someone else. We're there to support someone while they figure out how to deal with their lives."

I can't fix Leah, I reminded myself. I can only take care of myself.

By the way, Sally stopped attending our support group. Some spouses and partners improved and their loved ones stopped coming. Some spouses in a support group returned after a six-month absence for a tune-up when they were falling apart. Some spouses got divorced and you never saw them again. Some stopped coming because their loved ones took their own lives. Some spouses burned out and left their loved ones, moved away, or lost hope and wilted.

Some spouses, like me, hung in there . . . season after season, year after year.

A N D   W H A T does living with someone living with depression bleed?

One Saturday morning that January, fifteen below, twenty-five below wind chill, I started dreading that I was catching Leah's depression.

I had ants in my pants and knew I had to get out of the house, which felt as depressing as a mortuary. I could picture myself in a dark grey suit, tidying the living room, setting out a Kleenex box and switching the table lamp to low, slamming shut a coffin lid on myself, awaiting the bereaved to arrive to mourn my death from self-pity.

In Minnesota we call that cabin fever; you start losing your mind, and if you can't make it to Bermuda you at least need a long walk. I decided to hike through the snow a mile or so and warm up at a coffee shop. What I really wanted was a seedy old-man bar, the kind of place where you would peer through the smoke and find Hemingway bent over a glass of claret, embers aglow in the fireplace along with the ashes of a writer's failed first draft, burnt like toast, nothing to eat but hard cheese and stale bread, a cozy place with a brick wall where a man can brood, can strain in the dark to read a faded Jack London book.

My God, that was cabin fever, all right. Forget a coffee shop. I needed a beach somewhere warm, away from my wife's depression, as contagious as the measles, trapping me like a chipmunk in a cage. But Leah needed me at home, and I needed to be there or I would drown in abandonment guilt.

So through the snow I crunched, half shivering, nose running, my beard frosted like a lemon sno-cone. Trudged all the way along the bike trail past Cedar Lake, ice thick as a casket, over to where you can sneak through a chain-link fence and cross the Burlington-Northern tracks by the Fiat dealer. Hauled myself along in my heavy winter coat, clomped across the parking lot of a strip mall, finally got to a Panera Bread.

"How's it going?" the perky counter gal, nametag Tonya, asked me.

She gazed right through the permafrost on my beard. *I'll b-b-b-be f-f-f-fine, Tonya*, I thought, *after I thaw my fingers inside a cup of boiling water*.

"I'm awesome," I mumbled, ordering a cup of coffee. "See, it's not like my wife has cancer. If my wife had cancer, now that would suck."

"Have a good one," Tonya said when she rung me up.

Man, I had some reflecting to do. I had to *journal*, had to get all this morose wisdom down on paper, all these inane insights about living in the winter with someone living with depression.

I sipped my coffee and stared absently out the window toward the parking lot, pondering our dog, who I had brought to the PetSmart next door on the last day of his life a few Christmas Eves ago. There's gloominess for you: you're sitting by yourself in a coffee shop at a strip mall, excreting self-pity like a fetid landfill, and you look out a window and recall your dog dying on Christmas Eve.

Just then a maroon sedan the size of a houseboat pulled to a stop outside the door to the Panera. A Mercury Grand Marquis, the kind of car Leah's father used to drive, a tank built thick to deflect any compact cars or hapless pedestrians in the path of a doddering *alte kocker*. The driver left the car running and emerged from the vehicle, a tall guy in a topcoat and felt hat, and I watched him clop through the thick slush around the front of the car. He looked a little older than I, and I watched him pivot around the front of the car to the passenger's side, sliding around and grabbing the grille with his gloved hands for dear life, shuffling to the other side of this houseboat to open the passenger door to let someone out.

Then, for the next five minutes, I watched this fellow in the felt hat assist a much older man in the passenger seat. Must have been his father or grandfather. I mean, this guy getting out of the car was old. Biblically old. The guy in the topcoat—I'll call him Sonny Boy—swung open the car door and stood shivering on the curb and waited for the old man to step or fall out. I watched as the old guy lifted his right leg out of the car, and then, a few minutes later, his left leg. I thought of those science films in grade school of an eaglet breaking through the eggshell, a single crack one day, couple more cracks the next, and, by day three, the beak. After I'd gotten a refill of coffee the old man, with Sonny Boy's help, managed to hoist himself out on the sidewalk. I watched him put his hand under Sonny Boy's arm, and then the two of them, like a pair of penguins, slow-danced across the ice to the doorway of the Panera like marathon dancers holding each other up in the 1920s.

I think the counter staff recognized them, or maybe they too had watched these two guys through the front window. The older man's smile warmed the whole place up like a bonfire, so happy he looked to have made it to the Panera that Saturday morning. He must have looked forward all week to sliding across the ice with Sonny Boy for a brioche and cup of black coffee at a Panera Bread.

I gazed back out the window at that Mercury, still idling, blinkers flashing, icy exhaust puffing away in that frozen air. I sat there in the Panera and, jolting myself, months of emotion leaked out and I began to whimper. I was so happy for that old man and for his elation about breakfast and gratitude for living another day, so admiring of the generous patience of his escort Sonny Boy . . . and I, bitter and bereft, quietly wept, lost and alone in a vinyl booth at Panera, grieving the bleary marathon of my marriage to my once young wife, who now a mile and a lifetime away lay gloomily in the dark in our bed under a comforter, utterly joyless, utterly alone.

That's what depression bleeds, right there.

CHAPTER 14

Self-Care

A friend said I needed help—yeah, no shit—and recommended I see a new therapist, a woman named Crystal Oakley. She had a private practice and reminded me vaguely of the actress Lauren Graham from *Parenthood* and *Gilmore Girls*, and we hit it off fine.

I was spending more than a hundred bucks out of pocket and figured why hold back. I told Crystal the backstory about Leah's illness and our marriage and her anhedonia and how I watched Sonny Boy help the old guy at the Panera. I said I knew I was thinking unrealistically, like I could save her like some superhero action figure husband, and I felt unglued.

"What do you think?" I said to Crystal. "You think I'm a codependent nutjob?"

"What do I think, Jeff? I think you better take better care of yourself or you'll get as sick as Leah. And then how will you take care of her? Have you thought about getting out of town for a while?"

"I can't leave town right now. If anything, I should be a better person, like Sonny Boy."

"You don't know anything about that guy! He might have pissed and moaned for a month about taking that old man out for breakfast."

Crystal asked me what would happen if I left Leah alone for a few days, if someone could make sure she was all right.

"She doesn't want anyone coming over to the house."

"Are you afraid she'll starve to death if you leave town? Or kill herself?"

"She's too sick to kill herself."

"Well, she's an adult. Ask her if she can handle your going away a few days. She gets to make choices."

When I came home I was a snake and told Leah that my new therapist demanded I take a vacation.

"I called Joey," I told Leah. "He said I should come visit him in Portland. But I need you to be honest and tell me if you'll be okay here by yourself."

"I'll be okay, I guess."

I wasn't entirely convinced by that answer, but, as Crystal said, Leah had the right to choose whether to be honest with me. (And how *condescending* I would have been if I had discounted her response.) I cajoled Leah into getting dressed and accompanying me to the super-market to buy groceries for her while I was out of town. She hadn't been to a store of any kind in weeks, to a grocery store in months. When we arrived at the market, in her fog Leah struggled to remember how it even worked—that you took a shopping cart from the front of the store, headed toward the fresh fruits and vegetables, the aisle with canned soup, then to the frozen food section.

"My brain is broken," she murmured, one of dozens of times she would utter those words over the course of her illness.

She was like a refugee from North Korea suddenly finding herself at an Old Country Buffet, overwhelmed by the choices. Nothing looked good. There were too many kinds of peanut butter. She liked the idea of macaroni and cheese, but it would be too hard to cook. Fresh food would rot. She couldn't think how anyone could possibly plan a meal. It was too difficult to think, too much to process.

"I can just eat hot dogs and granola."

Sheesh. Even her food was depressing. I was impatient waiting for her to decide, and we left the store with a half-dozen frozen burritos and a couple cans of soup, what I anticipated we would buy in the first place.

When, during the next appointment, I blew off steam to Therapist Crystal, she said I should reinforce anything positive, that I had no inkling how hard it was for Leah to get out of bed. "But you're human. Don't feel guilty."

"I don't know if she'll eat while I'm gone. Can a person live on burritos?"

"Respect what she said. She told you to take a vacation. Go visit your son. Unless you think she might hurt herself . . . "

"No, she wouldn't do that. She's too weak to try it. I've heard the danger zone is when they're coming out of a depression."

THUS, I flew to Portland to stay with Joey and his two roommates at their apartment. Their washing machine had gotten plugged up and smelled like sewage. I wondered if a bat was hiding in their bathroom, shedding hair and tiny turds in the sink and tub. But I loved those boys. The three of them had grown up together in Minnesota and through high school played music in a rock-and-roll band. They all landed in Oregon post-college and were learning how to be adults. One of them worked at Nike. Heshie's son was an artist applying to grad school. Joey was a band director at a junior high school and invited me to observe one of his classes. I had a thrill watching my son's enthusiasm and patience in front of a classroom of adolescent musicians blowing their noses through their trombones.

Well, Leah and I did something right, I thought proudly.

One morning I reveled in a warm, wet springtime hike through Tryon Creek Nature Park in Lake Oswego. Compared to the bleak sludge of a lingering Minnesota winter, the forest looked green as a cucumber. On the weekend Joey drove me to Cannon Beach on the Pacific Ocean for some father-and-son hiking through the mist of the nearby rainforest.

"I can't believe how beautiful this state is," I said to Joey. "I wish we had done more stuff outdoors with you and Sarah when you two were young."

"You like camping alone."

"You were too busy playing drums and dropping acid with your goofy friends."

"We didn't drop acid. Did you?"

"No. Even if I did I wouldn't tell you. Speaking of acid, did you see that movie called *Wild*? I think they filmed part of it here."

"No. What's it about?"

"See, this writer—she's from Minneapolis—she was sexually abused, and her mother dies, and she becomes a drug addict, and she ends up hiking the Pacific Crest Trail—"

"Sounds uplifting," Joey said.

He didn't want to hear it. We were trying to live in the moment and avoid the topic, yet his mom's illness lingered in the heavy Oregon air. Later we walked together on the beach, and I savored the sound of the Pacific waves crashing into the shore on a foggy and nippy Oregon afternoon.

"You remember the Stapler Incident?" I asked Joey. It was one of the weirder things that had gone on in Jamaica. "It's sort of funny, if you think about it now."

"The Stapler Incident! She was the *only one* who could staple those pages together properly," Joey said. "No one else could do it right except Mom. 'Stop! Joey! You're not stapling the pages together correctly!' Man, did she get upset about that."

"Well, there's a manic episode for you."

"You know, sometimes it's like she has a mental illness or something," Joey said, and we laughed. It was gratifying how a harrowing incident like that, at the time so painful, was metamorphosing into the absurd.

Although we were processing Leah's mania, during the silence we were both still crying on the inside. That was his mother and my wife, for God's sake, and his heart was broken. What the heck happened to his mom?

On my last day in Portland, Joey and his roommates invited a half-dozen of their friends to Sunday Soup Night, a weekly tradition at their apartment. The laughter of those young people was rejuvenating. They were all intelligent, funny, and sensitive, and they reminded me of my old life back in Pennsylvania right after college, minus the intelligence and sensitivity.

I had been warned that one young man there, named Moses, of all things, was a mess. His girlfriend had taken her own life a few months earlier. I didn't pry about his girlfriend, but he knew enough about Leah to know I was having a hard time dealing with her illness.

"You know, Jeff," he said, "if you obsess about the past you're depressed. If you worry about the future you're anxious. If you're in the present you're happy."

He had studied Buddhism at Lewis and Clark College and looked a little like John Lennon.

Alas, I checked the calendar. It was 2016, not 1968. I had to go home the next day.

CHAPTER 15

And What Do May Flowers Bring?

With spring approaching, Leah's depression refused to lift. It had been six months since I had read that we spouses should assess our situations every half year and decide if we should hang around or bolt. I reasoned that as long as Leah was doing everything she could to get better, I wasn't going anywhere. She needed me. And I loved her.

I had also learned the limits of my role as husband. It was up to Leah and her medical team, not me, to figure out how to fix her. She took her prescribed meds and saw her psychologist, but whatever mystical pathways into the subconscious anyone was unraveling remained a mystery. She had minimal contact with friends. She withdrew from connections on social media; she said she had forgotten how to even log in to her accounts.

One concern for my children and me was the expiration of Leah's six-month stay of commitment and the monthly visit with the case manager, Monica. Leah was considered "stable" now by the county mental health system. I understood the reality: Monica had a caseload of forty clients, some no doubt in more dire shape than Leah. In essence,

Monica had provided only a monthly wellness check for Leah and an illusory lifeline to the social safety net for my family.

Convinced only a bonk on Leah's noodle could effect such a drastic personality change, an acquaintance urged her to see her oddball but competent neurologist for neuropsych testing and an MRI. Dr. Migraine had treated Leah in the past for her headaches (and given me one because of the way she would stare at her computer monitor while Leah was talking to her).

"The tests might indicate a neurological problem," Dr. Migraine told us, "but they could actually be measuring symptoms of depression." Leah, whose parents both experienced dementia in their later years, had several years earlier undergone a full battery of baseline neurological tests and found nothing alarming.

Still, Dr. Migraine followed up and scheduled a brain scan.

"I have some good news and some bad news," I reported to our children a couple weeks later. "The good news is the MRI indicated there's no abnormality. The bad news is the MRI indicated there's no abnormality."

LEAH HAD EXPERIENCED many years of the winter blues, but until the previous summer her internal switch had never gone haywire when the daylight hours lengthened in the Upper Midwest. All I needed for my hobgoblins to curdle my blood was one whiff of a warm evening on our deck and a glance at the bedroom window through which I had crawled to fetch my keys the previous summer when my world was shattering.

"I'm scared," I told Leah. "I'm afraid you'll go manic again this summer."

"I can hardly even imagine that," she uttered weakly.

No kidding. The woman could barely toast a bagel without collapsing. She had gained insight into her illness since the previous summer, and I tried to reassure myself my fear was irrational. But I was reading books about the cyclical nature of bipolar disorder and heard horror stories about seasonal triggers. Maybe subconsciously I hoped she would stay safely mired in her subterranean depression rather than swing back into her previous summer's maniacal energy and creativity.

Even the word *creativity* evoked shards of anger at Leah's endless, inane *creative* detritus that ended up littering our house like a recycling center, a *creative* wreckage I was still cleaning up.

Suspicious of my own damaged judgment, I met periodically with Crystal for support and encouragement—and to whine. I whined about feeling like I was living in a catacomb. I whined about the nonstop Haydn and Schubert sonatas playing all day on the radio, befogging our house with musical nimbus clouds. I whined that when the radio was turned off all I heard was the clock in the living room tick-tick-ticking away like the minutes of my life. I whined because my wife was sick and all I cared about was myself, and I whined about all my whining.

"My God," Crystal said, "just change the radio station!"

Wow, I wrote in my notebook, *change the radio station. Crystal said I can do that.*

That afternoon I swallowed my cowardice and confronted Leah with two imperatives.

"That's it! No more weepy cello music! I'm turning on the jazz station. And I'm opening the living room window to get some fresh air in here!"

When I told a friend about it, she exclaimed, "Are you *kidding* me? You needed your counselor's permission for *that?*"

"Yeah. At a hundred thirty bucks an hour."

The inanity appalls me. I had lost any perspective on the extent to which my own needs were consumed by Leah's illness. Yet I understand how intent on playing the Super Husband I'd been, performing heroic feats of mental and physical fortitude thinking I could help my sick wife get better.

And if you love your spouse, you won't believe the crazy stuff you'll end up doing, too.

"THE BEST THING my husband ever did," a NAMI support group cofacilitator, Marlys, told us, "was DBT. He did DBT for a whole year and it really changed him."

DBT. I had trouble remembering what the D stood for. *Diabolical* behavioral therapy? No, it's *dialectical* behavioral therapy. Nearly all of Leah's therapists and doctors recommended Leah enroll in a DBT program, the apparent go-to therapy for people with mood disorders.

The keys to DBT, I learned, are mindfulness, interpersonal effectiveness, and learning to control intense emotions and to manage distress. I've heard that everyone, not just those with mental illnesses, would be a little healthier with DBT. It's been shown to be particularly helpful treating people with borderline personality disorder, an illness in which people have difficulty regulating their emotions and thoughts, act impulsively, and often end up in ruined relationships.

For it to succeed, DBT requires someone to engage in a half-year or yearlong program of weekly individual counseling, group therapy, skills development, and homework assignments.

"It's a lot of work," Marlys warned our group. "But it sure helped my husband. I think it saved his life."[1]

When Leah started her DBT program that April, I saw what Marlys

---

[1] On at least one occasion, Marlys's husband threatened to take his own life. She reported that one year of DBT did wonders for her husband's depression.

meant. Leah brought home a binder of worksheets that looked as thick as the federal tax code.

I was skeptical that this DBT business would cure Leah's depression, dubious that Leah would have the energy to even open the notebook. The daughter of an atheist design engineer and a strict empiricist herself, Leah wasn't one for meditative hocus-pocus. But at least insurance covered it. Her one-on-one counselor was well versed in mental illness, and Leah would be getting out of the house twice a week with someone not named Jeffrey Zuckerman.

Once again, because it is all about me, I was in favor of it because *I* would be getting some relief too. The counselors would be keeping their eyes on Leah if she started going manic or, God forbid, her depression deepened and she became suicidal.

ONE OTHER GIANT LEAP for Leah-kind: with prodding from me and her psychologist, she started attending a NAMI support group for those living with a mental illness. The group met weekly down the hall in the same Minneapolis church as my monthly partners' and spouses' gatherings. I told Leah we could drive there together, that she would be with people who "got it," many of whom were making inroads into improved health. She would learn about community resources and be reminded that, yes, she was a good person, albeit one with a lousy medical illness. And, I thought with humility, she would have a place to bitch about her husband's imperfections.

That first time Leah accompanied me to the church was the saddest thing I'd witnessed yet. I'd been to these groups now a couple dozen times and had gotten over the awkwardness. Falling to pieces the previous summer during Leah's undiagnosed mania, I felt at the time like a self-absorbed ass, sobbing and confused, resorting to humor as a defense mechanism: "Enough about me. Let's talk about me."

Now, when I pulled up to the church and stared at Leah in the passenger seat, she looked vacant, near tears. Despite all my fear and anger during her manic episode, a year later I was reminded that at Leah's core was her devotion to her family, her love of adventure, her profound desire to continue her professional career in public health. Depression sucked for us both. On a good day I could ruefully embrace the joy and optimism of a year earlier when we had gathered for the aufruf on Long Island, her determination to lose just a few pounds for Sarah's wedding, the glow in the photos along the oceanfront that July day . . . and all that was lost. Instead I could feel the pit in my wife's stomach, the one we all experience the first day of junior high school. *Will I have to talk? Will the other kids like me? Will they judge me? Will they think I'm crazy?*

"I know this is hard," I said to Leah, gently.

It was a moment of unmitigated love for my wife, of friendship and admiration and sorrow and loss. The mother of my children looked as petrified and vulnerable as a child. She was about to admit to the world—and to herself—that she was a fifty-eight-year-old woman struggling with the intractable effects of a mental illness.

I held Leah's hand as we walked into the church. She was weeping openly and completely, the first time I had seen her cry since she fell into her emotional vacuum more than six months prior.

"Leah, dear, you can do this," I reassured her.

Two hours later, the car ride home was silent. The woman I cherished was wading alone in her inner gulf of grief. I was anguished for Leah but heartened that at least she had attended a group.

"It will get easier," I said.

That's called hope, the essential nutrient we nourish in each other during our support group meetings.

LEAH FOUND a new psychiatrist. We would again be starting from scratch, although her new doctor had access to Leah's medical records from her hospitalization. The psychiatrist resembled Karen Carpenter, an underrated singer, in my view, albeit one whose life came to a tragic end related to an implacable eating disorder. I noticed among the framed degrees on the office wall that "Dr. Carpenter" had received medical training from, among other places, the U.S. Army. Perhaps Leah's case was small potatoes compared to those of war veterans, but Dr. Carpenter didn't treat Leah that way. Right off the bat I could tell Dr. Carpenter cared about my wife. In a managed-care world in which too little of our health care is managed and too few insurance companies care, I was struck by Dr. Carpenter's willingness to meet with us for well over an hour. She actually listened to what Leah had to say, even when we were scheduled for twenty-minute appointments, and she stated unequivocally her belief that Leah would get healthy.[2]

One important note regarding "our" appointments: In previous years I had rarely accompanied Leah to doctors' consultations when she was treated for physical ailments. But Leah asked me to join her for these psychiatric appointments. She was aware that her self-described broken brain would prevent her from articulating the state of her mental health or remembering past events or follow-up instructions from her doctor. It was awkward to mansplain on Leah's behalf and discomfiting to share my perceptions of her moods. My post-mania anger burbled just beneath the surface of anything I said—and especially anything that sounded *condescending*.

But I was diligent in my note-taking and helped Leah and myself keep track of the pharmaceutical buffet she continued to ingest. Over

---

[2]   After our first couple of appointments, I mailed a note to the hospital administration expressing my gratitude for the care Dr. Carpenter was providing Leah. Isn't it the least we can do?

time I lost any shame for asking a lot of questions. I did my best not to speak for Leah, and I tried to stay objective in my reporting to Dr. Carpenter about Leah's health. Whatever I said, my only intention was to help Leah get well.

FROM AN EMAIL UPDATE to our children:

APRIL 11, 2016

Mom was feeling a little less down this morning on our way to Dr. Carpenter's office. We talked about gardening and volunteering this summer.

With a bit of reluctance, but mostly with confidence, Dr. Carpenter is going to add Prozac to the mix of meds Mom is on. Yes, Prozac, like all antidepressants, can be dangerous and cause mania, but if Mom stays on the Seroquel it will likely counterbalance any danger. It helps her sleep, which is I guess the most important thing of all.

It could take 5 weeks to see an effect. The doctor assured me Mom is going to get better.

With each failure and subsequent new med, I feared we were running out of options. "Don't worry," Leah's doctors would assure us, "new medicines are being developed all the time."

That was Big Pharma's message, as well, in their whimsical advertisements showing comely middle-aged women plucking daisy petals thanks to the latest panacea for bipolar purgatory. My grade of C in high school chemistry hardly prepared me to understand the bullshit spewed by marketing hacks eager to peddle the chemists' latest concoctions that might repair my wife's neurotransmitters and serotonin levels. Each time Leah started a new medication we were told it would take a month or two to see a change in Leah's health—or to make no impact, or to make her mood even worse. Discouraged and cynical about the drug companies, I wondered if astrology was no less a scam than psychopharmacology. Maybe instead of swallowing all those pills Leah just needed to wait until the moon was in the Seventh House and Jupiter aligned with Mars, and then she would find peace, and love would steer the stars.

But I had no choice except to trust her doctors . . . especially Dr. Carpenter.

SIGNS OF LIFE in the Upper Midwest: daffodils, azaleas, and, at long last, Leah arising from bed. We designated three of her friends as our "emergency contacts," people we could alert if Leah felt suicidal or if signs of mania reappeared. I emailed them all and mentioned that, on a walk through the woods near Cedar Lake, Leah said to me, "Just now for a minute I didn't feel so bad."

She also said to me, "*When* I get better."

Keep hope alive . . . keep hope alive.

But the reality of Leah's melancholy and the fallout from mania remained. I worried about money. I worried she wasn't consuming enough calories and liquids. I worried that I was falling apart riding in circles on her bipolar Ferris wheel.

Leah reminded me we had a plan. If I started hearing a time-bomb ticking, I had doctors and emergency documents to disarm it.

One night in mid-May we splurged on tickets to a Broadway touring group's production of *The Book of Mormon*. A friend who had first-hand experience with the Latter-Day Saints and had worked in theater told me I should go. "It's hilarious. The music is great."

She was right. The production seemed to wiggle back and forth across the boundaries of comedy, offensiveness, and poignancy. It was funny and loud, and the music and dancing were dazzling.

I should have known better. Leah hated it.

On the way home I picked a big fight with her. "How could you hate it? It was bright! It was funny! It was joyful! You are *incapable* of experiencing joy!"

I was in a horrible mood. I parked the car in our garage and spent the next hour walking around the neighborhood. I walked all the way down to the lifeguard stand on the beach at Cedar Lake, climbed up into the chair, sat there, and fumed until well after midnight.

"I don't know why I bothered trying," I wrote in my journal the next day. "I need nurturing. I can't just be the nurturer. Crystal said, 'If you become hostage to her mental illness, you are going down.' How do I love her and not be held hostage by her disorder?"

I decided to blow town again and escape the empty sighs I could hear inside the envelope of Leah's depression. I stowed my camping gear in my car and headed to a state park in western Minnesota. If Leah needed me, I was two hours away.

The campsite I chose was too close to a bright streetlight and a generator running all night by the bathroom. I would have been better off in my own backyard, but severe depression penetrates walls and blankets neighborhoods like pea soup, and besides, there's nothing like cooking weenies over a campfire to sustain your soul.

When I called Leah from the campground to check in, something remarkable happened.

"I must be getting better," she said. "I cried the whole time I was with my DBT counselor today."

She cried. What wonderful news! Was she starting to feel her emotions again?

ON A CAMPING TRIP you have time to think.

Here is part of how I became me. After my grandfather Marko left for America, it took more than a decade and the coming Nazi invasion for my people to leave their tiny village in Yugoslavia. My father came to this country in 1938. My Uncle Milan and my Bubbee Rose came soon after. My dad's older sister Olga and I don't know how many other relatives stayed behind and were murdered by either the Nazis or Ustaše fascists. I don't know the details because no one ever found out what happened to anyone and no one ever talked about it.

Once my father gained citizenship, he enlisted in the U.S. Army and was shipped off to the Philippines. My grandfather Marko and a thousand other European Jews became egg farmers in South Jersey. After the war my parents married and worked all the time and never complained. My other grandmother, Bubbee Sophie, became a widow when she was young and moved back and forth between my New York relatives and our house in Pittsburgh. When I was in sixth grade she passed away. My bereaved parents came home from work that day and covered the mirrors in black cloth like their grandparents had done.[3] I asked if it was okay if I went outside to play, and my dad said go ahead.

In 1973, when I was a college freshman, Marko dropped dead chasing after a fire on his farm, and shell-shocked Uncle Milan and my grandmother became my dad's obligation. Uncle Milan stayed in the New Jersey rest home until he died. Bubbee Rose moved into our Pittsburgh house, and my mother would yell at her for being a nervous little old lady.

---

[3]   I learned we're supposed to mourn rather than care how we look. Hasidic Jews offer an alternative reason: after a death in the family, evil spirits visit the home, and their reflections may be visible in a mirror. See "Why Are the Mirrors Covered in a House of Mourning?" Questions & Answers, Chabad.org, https://www.chabad.org/library/article_cdo/aid/2969340/jewish/Why-Are-the-Mirrors-Covered-in-a-House-of-Mourning.htm.

I loved both grandmothers, the farmer grandmother because she was sweet and talked English poorly and said funny true things about my mother behind her back. I loved the New York grandmother because she knitted me a gold sweater I keep in my closet to this day and bought me chocolate truffles and took me to the Statue of Liberty and was always yelling and crying hysterically in Yiddish, which my cousins and I found scary and comical. I loved my grandfather Marko most, because he had a tractor and played checkers with me and the mandolin and the zither.

My father had two heart attacks, the first when he was only thirty-eight years old and I was only four. That was a lot of death and displacement and calamities for one family. My brother and I know for a fact my father never went to a therapist. He was resilient without ever saying the word. He worked and volunteered and played poker and went bowling with his friends. Every Saturday my family would get together with my mother's crabby aunts and uncles in the Squirrel Hill neighborhood of Pittsburgh, and I'm sure there were a lot of other things my father would rather have been doing on a summer afternoon than listen to a bunch of my mother's relatives gossiping. But family mattered to my father, maybe because his had been all but obliterated that century.

But that's conjecture because no one complained, ever, and certainly never discussed their feelings. My brother and I were taught not by words but by example. Don't look back. Work hard. Appreciate what you've got. Be a *mensch* and do the right thing.

Leah and I promised to love each other in sickness and in health. I'm sure if I had gotten sick Leah would have stuck by me. But in contrast to my parents, as the one-year mark approached since our marriage became unglued, I despised her illness and myself for complaining so much and handling it so poorly. All I wanted to do was head for South America and hide away in a cabin for the rest of my life like the Sundance Kid.

One day I was talking to my rabbi about my parents and I started to sob out of resentment because my parents showed me how to love and mourn but never taught me how to grieve, and I couldn't save myself or my wife from drowning in a psychological swamp.

"It sounds like your parents were imperfect," my rabbi said with a slight smile.

My parents' odyssey ended in Arizona, my father's at age sixty-one, my mother at ninety-five. My children have seen me weep over their graves, which I figure is the least I can do for my parents, even when it's 115 degrees outside. The least I could do for my own two kids was show them how to grieve.

At age sixty-one, in a campground in western Minnesota a long way from a hamlet in modern-day Croatia, I found myself unpacking not only the grief of Leah's illness but my entire family history. I was learning how to forgive: my parents for that which they could not express, and Leah for an illness that neither she nor I could control.

Most important, I was learning how to forgive myself for my imperfections and to grieve for Leah's ceaseless struggle to manage and regain her mental health.

CHAPTER 16

Ob-La-Di

Despite her appointments with her psychologist, DBT classes, meetings with her counselor, support group, and biweekly check-ins with Dr. Carpenter for med tweaks, Leah continued to struggle. One morning she woke up early for her weekly one-on-one DBT appointment.

"Today is Tuesday, not Wednesday," I said.[1]

"Oh. I'm going back to sleep for fifteen minutes."

Three hours later she hadn't risen from bed.

I couldn't fix her and needed to live my own life. I signed up for an intermediate tennis class through community ed. When not bemoaning his shoulder injury, the instructor talked too much and reminded me of Jonathan Winters impersonating a community ed teacher bemoaning his shoulder injury. But it was a funny, healthy escape with people who were not clinically depressed, and when the eight-session course ended I continued to play a couple times a week with several other participants. On Friday evenings, for the thirty-first consecutive summer, I played softball

---

[1] Note the nonjudgmental observation of fact learned from hundreds of dollars' worth of therapy (cf., "You fucked up, Leah").

with the Loons in our recreational league in St. Paul. My fellow team-mates and I marveled how we had spent more than half our lives playing ball with the same group of aging men and their now adult sons.

A few Loons knew about Leah's illness, as did several Loon wives, women who had known Leah early in our marriage when she still at-tended our games and bluffed enthusiasm while watching Loons mis-play fly balls week after week. Talking to your closest friends about your wife's mental illness is hard enough. Telling your softball pals' healthy wives who are out having a good time was dispiriting and felt like a be-trayal to their happiness and Leah's dignity.

"I'm so sorry," Coach Dan's wife said to me.

"Well, Mary, everyone has problems."

"Are you taking care of yourself, Zucke?"

My God. Why could such a simple question get me choked up?

"I guess. I guess that's why I'm playing softball tonight with these Loons."

TO PASS THE TIME and try to get her brain working, Leah and I played Scrabble a couple times a week. She had trouble spelling and sometimes I'd give her some help with a word, and we changed the rules so she could always go first and could use proper nouns. I would win all the time, but it was fun to spend a little bit of quality time together like that.

Still, because I tried to get out of the house a few evenings a week, I kept asking Leah if I was leaving her alone too much. In truth, I hoped she would answer no. Everyone said it was up to Leah to fig-ure things out and not my job. But our anniversary was coming in late July and I couldn't shake the guilt of her sitting alone in the house day after day reading novels achingly slowly, except when she was at a doctor's appointment.

"It's okay," Leah insisted. "I'm glad you're taking care of yourself."

I felt bad for Leah, but I was bitter about her illness, grieving the relationship I had lost.

I estimate that half the people in my support groups for those involved with someone with a mental illness are seeing a therapist themselves. That doesn't mean 50 percent of the people who live with someone living with a mental illness end up in therapy. It could be that people who go to a support group are so messed up they also need a therapist. Or it could be that people who open themselves up to their support-group peers recognize they can benefit from professional counseling. Or it could be the other way around. Or, sadly, it could be that people who might most benefit from a support group or counseling never avail themselves of either.

I, for one, appreciated Crystal helping me "peel back the layers," in her words, of what was eating at me. One day she taught me a trick called bilateral stimulation[2] to steady my nerves when Leah's behavior set off a pang of anxiety. Make a fist, Crystal instructed, and tap at your thighs. Left, right, left, right. A minute. Two minutes. Longer. Or tap your feet. Or do any kind of rhythmic movement, back and forth, left side, right side, back and forth, back and forth. Crystal told me that watching ping-pong or tennis players rally across a net has a related lenitive, hypnotic effect. (Somehow that back-and-forth movement actually worked, and I've often wondered if Leah's bipolar disorder was the best thing that ever happened to my tennis game.)

Crystal knew all about the previous summer's mania, how I imagined Leah levitating a butcher's knife, her head spinning, her eyes

---

[2] See "What Is Bilateral Stimulation?" Anxiety Release, https://anxietyreleaseapp. com/what-is-bilateral-stimulation/.

popping out of her face, screaming gibberish at me that sounded like she was speaking in tongues.

"I wish I had never seen *The Exorcist*," I told Crystal. "I *know* it wasn't Leah; it was her illness. But I can't get past those memories."

"You know, because bilateral stimulation is working, I really think you'd benefit from EMDR."

I first learned about eye movement desensitization and reprocessing in the late 1990s after reading and editing a pair of psychology dissertations[3] on the subject. I read that EMDR has been used to treat U.S. veterans of the Iraq and Afghanistan wars who are suffering from posttraumatic stress disorder. According to the U.S. Department of Veterans Affairs' National Center for PTSD:

> After trauma, people with PTSD often have trouble making sense of what happened to them. EMDR helps you process the trauma, which can allow you to start to heal. In EMDR, you will pay attention to a back-and-forth movement or sound while calling to mind the upsetting memory. You will do this until the way you experience the memory shifts and becomes less distressing.

I resisted the notion that I had experienced trauma. Trauma? Trauma was an army lieutenant watching his squad getting blown to bits by an IED, or a child losing her mother in a Syrian refugee camp. Moreover, although I was a Jewish English major whose people believed in biblical miracles and Isaac Bashevis Singer, I was a positivist,

---

[3] P. A. Finley, "Eye Movement Desensitization and Reprocessing (EMDR) in the Treatment of Sex Offenders" (PhD diss., 2002), ProQuest (AAT 3068413); G. B. Soberman (1999). "Eye Movement Desensitization and Reprocessing (EMDR) in the Treatment of Conduct Disorder with Preadolescents and Adolescents" (PhD diss., Walden University, 1999), https://elibrary.ru/item.asp?id=6683688.

skeptical of any form of new-age quackery. I associated EMDR with hypnotism and figured I'd be hyperaware and distracted, pictured myself taking mental notes for the fictional version of the trance, pictured myself falling asleep and clucking like a chicken.

But I sure was curious how EMDR worked.

"Okay," I said to Crystal. "How about next week?"

HER OFFICE was located on the second floor above a popular ice cream store in a commercial area in a south Minneapolis neighborhood. I was envious of the apparent happiness of the customers on the outdoor patio, smacking away at expensive cones, blissfully indifferent not only to the calories they were consuming but the grief I was about to unload on my therapist.

Despite having read about the technique, I didn't really know how this was going to work. Before the EMDR treatment began, Crystal brought out a control box called a TheraTapper. It was about the size of a cigarette package and had a pair of attached wires. On the end of each wire was a pulsar, called a paddle, which resembled a vinyl coin holder. At the command of the therapist the paddles vibrate back and forth between your two hands.

Crystal instructed me to gently grip the paddles in my fingers and test out the buzzy feel of the good vibrations. She asked me if I was ready and I said yes.

"Okay, close your eyes and take a few breaths. Breathe deeply. Just relax. Breathe. Breathe some more."

"Keep your eyes closed," I heard her say. She told me to let go and really relax and just breathe, to picture a place that gives me comfort.

I thought about the beach in Oregon where Joey had taken me.

That was too cold, so I pictured the beach in Tulum I had visited with Leah about a year prior, then the private beach in New Jersey where my old friend Michael from sixth grade and I liked to hang out.

"Focus on that place and just breathe," Crystal said, and after more breathing, more relaxation, a few moments more of steady breathing, I was there at the ocean. Crystal told me to breathe and listen to the sounds, asked me what I could hear, and I said the waves and the gulls. The waves, I said again, tuning out the vague voices I'd hear from the patio of the ice-cream shop below Crystal's window.

And then I no longer heard those sounds. The longer Crystal talked, the quieter her voice became, and the more becalming . . . I don't know how long that went on. Long enough to get me there, to the gentle waves of the surf . . .

As my breathing grew easy, I began to decompose, as if the arteries in my brain were unclogging and the inner stress evaporating.

Moments later I heard Crystal asking me something about the summer before. Something about one event, to let myself go back to that moment, to go with the memory, to see myself there . . .

I am back on the deck of our house, back in the night air when Leah and I and the dyad timer were out there at it until two in the morning. I am aware I am in Crystal's office, telling her all about it, but I am transported onto my deck, chilled by the pinch of the night air, exhausted and drained, fried by the dyad timer, by Leah's endless yapping, by her maddening twist of every word I utter, by her harping on the *crux of the matter*, screaming, *You see? You see?* over and over. Her swearing, her ranting about "I" statements until, after two hours, I can't take it anymore and I exclaim *enough!*

I bolt from the deck and run through the patio door into the dining room. Back to a place that for months I have not wanted to go.

"Tell me what's happening, Jeff," Crystal says. "What's happening?"

Leah is chasing me now, and I slam shut the bedroom door behind me (and at this point Crystal must have pressed a button on her little machine; I am aware the paddles in my hands are vibrating), and I turn off the bedroom light and hide under the blanket on our bed. I hear Leah chasing after me into the bedroom, screaming at me, turning the overhead light back on, yanking the cover off the bed. I see her monster eyes popping out, looking like she's going to bludgeon me. I'm shrieking, *Go away, Leah! Go away!* But she won't, she just keeps yelling at me, *This is how you deal with your feelings. You just hide under the covers, you see? This is the crux of the problem!* The paddles in my fists are vibrating like mad, back and forth, and I can hear Crystal's voice, more urgently, "What's happening, Jeff? What's happening?" I run out of our bedroom, down the stairs, and I hear Leah chasing after me down the hallway, feel the paddles in my hands pulsing back and forth, back and forth, hear Leah screaming at me, feel myself grip the doorknob to the downstairs bathroom. I push open the bathroom door, slam it shut, strip naked, hear Leah screaming at me, picturing those psychotic eyes, and I pull open the glass shower door and slam it shut (paddles pulsating back and forth, back and forth). I'm deluged in the spray of the shower. I'm gasping for breath, curled into a ball at the bottom of the shower, the hot water washing it all away. *Leah,* I'm hollering at Crystal, *leave me alone!*

Leah, screaming at me, "Why are you afraid of me?"

Drowning in despair, I beg her, "Please, Leah. Please go away. *Please!*"

"I'm not going to kill you!"

I'm plugging my ears with my fingertips, hear only the force of the hot water spray roaring in my skull like ocean waves. *Please, Leah!* Yelling, begging. *Will you please . . . just leave me alone? Just LEAVE ME ALONE?* until I don't know how long but at last I can tell Leah is gone. The hot water is running down my body, I'm gasping . . . the paddles in my fists gradually stop pulsating, and then Crystal brings me back. I am in her office, and once again I hear vague voices from the ice-cream shop below.

Afterward, I stagger around the streets of south Minneapolis for a half hour, woozy and depleted, wondering what just ran me over.

DON'T TRY THAT at home.

Crystal and I talked about it at a follow-up appointment a week later. I still have no idea how any of this stuff works. I don't understand where the eye movement or desensitization fit in. Some therapists use lights, some a wand. Some use earphones and sounds.

Some people need several sessions of EMDR. For me, once was enough. I can tell because while reliving that story just now I sniveled only once.

IT WAS JUNE 2016. One of my Baltimore cousins who had been to the California wedding fiasco a year earlier invited Leah and me to another wedding. I had more than a few doubts about Leah making the trip, not the least of which was that she would have to face the extended family for the first time since all hell broke loose when she was manic a year earlier. I was on my anti-mental-illness-stigma kick, but I had to be realistic. Although Leah didn't remember much about what went on at the weddings, the relatives no doubt did. They have generous hearts, and a few of them have "issues" of their own. But after she had been holed up in our house for eight months, I was dubious about whether a fancy-pants East Coast wedding was the place for Leah to emerge from her cocoon.

Fortunately, so was she.

I bought a solo plane ticket and planned for fun on my own. First, I'd fly to New York City to see my daughter and son-in-law, and then take a southbound New Jersey transit train to howl at the ocean with my friend Michael.

"Let's just say we have a lot to talk about since last summer," I warned him.

From there I'd take a train to Baltimore, attend the wedding, feel the love, and then fly back to Minneapolis feeling guilty but refreshed.

It's fine, Leah repeated. Don't feel bad. Just go.

SARAH HAD HEARD about a minor league baseball team that played in Coney Island and thought it would be fun to take the subway down there and attend a game.

"I don't know anything about it, Dad. I've never even been to Coney Island."

"Me neither. Our people lived in that part of Brooklyn for a while. But no one took me there when we used to visit New York from Pittsburgh."

We rode the F train south from Carroll Gardens, through the neighborhoods that sounded like the set of *The Honeymooners*. Bensonhurst, Homecrest, Gravesend. After about a half hour we landed at the chaotic Stillwell Avenue station.

"Okay, this is weird," I said, as we made our way toward the beach past the original Nathan's hot dog shop and the amusement park. "Your great-grandparents might have walked in this exact spot with your bubbee a hundred years ago."

It was a late afternoon, and the beach was jammed.

"Your bubbee told me that during a heat wave families used to sleep out here."

"Okay, that sounds disgusting."

"It was before air conditioning."

Dominicans. Puerto Ricans. South Asians. They looked different from our people, but they had come to America for the same reason ours did: for the freedom to do nothing on a warm June evening.

At the edge of the ocean we dipped our feet into the water, and then headed to the ballpark.

The home team, the Brooklyn Cyclones, were a Mets' farm club in the Class-A New York–Penn League. We were dueling the Hudson Valley Renegades in a game with epic implications for world peace and interplanetary justice. Okay, neither of us cared who won, but we both liked going to baseball games. The stadium was lovely, a classic minor league park, a field of lush green grass in a crowded American city, grandstands up close to the field, the smell of hot dogs and the salty air of the sea, the sound of laughter, the buildings of Brooklyn bathed in fading sunlight. I hadn't been so relaxed with my daughter in years.

"Too bad your mother isn't here."

"Too bad *your* mother isn't here," Sarah said.

I smiled. "Yeah, your bubbee would have loved this. When her family lived in the Bronx their bakery was only a couple blocks from Yankee Stadium. In Pittsburgh she used to take me to Forbes Field when I was little."

We watched some guy flub a ground ball, and then there was a second error on the throw.

"How have you been dealing with your mom lately?"

We were sitting down the third-base line, about even with the edge of the outfield. A left-handed batter walked up to the plate, and we watched for a foul ball to come our way.

"I know that at some point you and Mom are going to get old," Sarah said, turning to look at me, "and at some point Joey and I will have to deal with it. I just didn't think it would be this soon."

We stared at each other. Since she was a baby, people told me how beautiful our daughter was and how much she looked like Leah. I rarely saw the resemblance, or maybe I rarely looked that closely. But in my grief, as the sky began to darken during a night game in Brooklyn, New York, in the year 2016, what a bewildering and enchanting moment, staring into my daughter's face and seeing her family history etched in her brown eyes.

"We have to hope she'll get better, Sarah. And for your information, I'm not old."

By the sixth inning we were bored. The evening had cooled off, and we had a long ride on the F Train back to her apartment. We were hungry and found a noodles joint near the Bergen Street station. We ate bowls of pho, and then we walked the rest of the way to her place through the chilly night air. A century after my mother toddled around the streets of New York City, I felt closer to my firstborn than I did to any human on the planet.

A COUPLE OF MORNINGS later I rode the New Jersey Coast Line to spend time with my friend Michael near Red Bank, and from there I took a train to my cousin's wedding in Baltimore. My brother David flew in from Phoenix with his family and acknowledged the emotional trapeze on which I was swinging. Then he told me to shut up and enjoy myself. We Jews are bred to do that: the tradition of stomping on a glass during the wedding ceremony is a reminder that in our greatest moments of joy we must still recall the sorrow in the world and vow to repair it, and then we eat and dance.

What a delight to see the extended family during the wedding. This was the Winerman side of my family tree, first, second, and third cousins spread across the country, generations united not by place as the shtetl of our forebears but by Instagram and Facebook and atoms of DNA. Just look around at this Winerman clan: Ulcerative colitis. Learning disability. Social anxiety disorder. Celiac disease. Obesity. Cancer. Cancer. Cancer, cancer, cancer. Heart disease. Emphysema.

Senility. Undiagnosed insanity. This extended family of mine was the front-end collision of genetic pools.

"Do you promise to have and to hold," the rabbi said to the *khatan* and *kalah*, "from this day forward, for better, for worse, for richer, for poorer, in sickness and in health?"

Kenahora! I wanted to shriek. Beware the evil eye! *Der mentsh trakht un Got lakht!* Man plans, and God laughs!

My niece Rachel was there, at least physically. A member of the Winerman clan only through marriage, she was my nephew Marty's wife of about ten years who struggled with her own demolition derby of physical and mental health problems. She had been diagnosed with bipolar disorder at age twenty-three and was an anti-stigma crusader happy to discuss her own illness with me. She had been prescribed a smorgasbord of meds in only the previous few months—Lexapro, Paxil, Wellbutrin, Topamax, Lamictal, Gabapentin, probably a partridge and a pear tree. She had recently completed an outpatient hospital treatment plan and electro-convulsive therapy, or ECT, of which she was a proponent.

Added to the maladies that wedding weekend, Rachel had just undergone eye surgery and could barely see a thing during the ceremony, and from a few rows away, my mental illness radar blipping, I could tell she was having a tough time.

During the reception, Rachel found some peace outside the hotel lobby, and I found her there and sat down next to her. We talked little that evening; she needed the night air, and the best I could offer was an uncle's quiet understanding. I don't know how long we sat there or if anyone even knew where we were. Sometimes the less said the better.

MONTHS LATER, Rachel told me the whole story.

She and my nephew Marty had had a nasty, bipolar-fueled spat before the wedding, one so senseless and grotesque that I felt like I was staring at Leah and me in a funhouse mirror.

"I'd just had that surgery on my eyes," Rachel recounted, "and it had been a rough day. About an hour before the wedding, Marty and I had this big stupid fight over a pair of *shoes*."

"A Shoes Incident!" I exclaimed.

"It's just so ridiculous. I had gotten these beautiful silver high-heeled shoes for the wedding, and I really wanted to wear them. And Marty is saying, 'Why don't you wear the purple sandals instead?' And I'm yelling at him, 'Because they're *ugly* and I *want to wear the silver sandals* because I'll never have *another chance*.' Finally Marty said, '*Fine. Do whatever you want to do*.'

"So, of course, because of my eye surgery I can't see a thing at this wedding, and Marty is guiding me and I'm afraid we're going to walk into a post and I'm screaming at him, '*Watch out for the post!*' And people are saying hello to me, and I could only say hi back to them if I recognized their voices. Because I couldn't see anything. I'm almost tripping over myself and I'm yelling at Marty, '*You're walking too fast.*' I was *so nasty* about it, and I know it was embarrassing for him. All because I'd insisted on wearing these *stupid* silver high-heeled sandals.

"I was just being stupid. I should have just said, 'You're right, Marty. I should have worn the ugly purple sandals.' And of course no one is even *looking* at my shoes in the first place!"

I babysat my nephew Marty more than forty years ago when he was an infant. I worry about him, living with that kind of volatility. Every so often I ask Marty how he's holding up.

"It's a long story," he'll say stoically—but I never hear the long story. I don't think anyone does.

The ghost of my stoic deceased father. As Rachel told me, "Marty is a very private person."

And how are you holding up, Uncle Jeff, living with Aunt Leah's illness?

I'm not stoic. I wrote a book, *pu pu pu*.

Rinse, Repeat

CHAPTER 17

July Is Bustin' Out All Over

We were treading water. Dr. Melnick couldn't fix Leah, nor could Dr. Carpenter.

"Doctor," I said, inhaling deeply, "she's just not getting a whole frickin' lot better."

"Leah, do you agree?"

She had no ability to describe her emotions and mood. "I don't know."

"In that case," Dr. Carpenter told Leah, "let's stop the fluoxetine."

I studied Leah, who stared at Dr. Carpenter blank-eyed. Leah was in her my-brain-is-broken mode, wasn't tracking, couldn't remember what pharmaceutical goulash she had been swallowing—and who could blame her?

"Sorry. Prozac. I forget to use the brand names."

Whew. Rather than increase the dosage of her antidepressant and risk mania, Dr. Carpenter was giving up on it altogether.

"Instead, I want to start you on lurasidone," she said. "It's an antipsychotic."

Now we're talking, Doctor. *Lure-ass-i-done.* A no-nonsense

antipsychotic. Hey, can I have some, too? *Lurasidone.* Sounds like an orgy in an opium den. Bring it on!

"The brand name," Dr. Carpenter explained, "is Latuda."

I'd seen the ads everywhere. Flowers and rainbows. The land of Oz. Side effects may include weight gain, weight loss, increased libido, reduced libido, or growing a second head. As usual, Dr. Carpenter told Leah each new medication can take two to twelve thousand weeks for improvement to present, depending, I gathered, on the whims of God or the mating rituals of walruses.

Desperate for a miracle cure, Leah and I rushed back across town to Walgreens, where she was on a first-name basis with her pharmacist. There we began the next phase of Leah's *journey*—a word I would grow to despise, with its phony overtones of a thrilling sightseeing tour across the Egyptian desert on a camel rather than our reality: a whirlybird ride inside a Category 4 tornado.

SOMETHING CHANGED.

Not even a week after I returned from the wedding on the East Coast, Leah's mood rebounded, like a floodlight illuminating a cave. In my journal I wrote, "I got my wife back!"

Over the course of a couple of days she met friends for coffee. She suddenly had the energy to go for a bike ride with me. One afternoon we went to a matinee and then had dinner at a restaurant.

"I'm going to start working again on my El-El-Cee," Leah said. "I have some new ideas. I'm going to be meeting with people at the university."

For the first time in nine months, my wife was no longer a zombie. The Latuda actually did flip her internal mood switch.

And my stomach turned into knots. The turnaround was so rapid that I was unnerved. Each time Leah voiced her anger about some affront I felt a kick in my teeth. When she scolded me for loading the dishwasher improperly, I experienced a physiological pang, a slight tightening of my chest, my gut percolating.

Add that one to the Latuda packaging with the other eight million warnings: "Side effects include castigating your spouse for improperly loading the dishwasher."

Two days later my colon was vellicating, churning up mystery stools jagged by shards of my latest nightmares and inklings of Leah's high-speed dash up the entrance ramp to mania. I needed my support group fix *and I needed it now.*

"Off to my group," I told Leah. "May stop somewhere on my way home." Argentina, if you're going manic.

I unloaded on my group that night. I couldn't figure out if I was supposed to celebrate Leah's improvement or if I had every reason to believe I was about to get bowled over by a train. For months I had anguished over Leah's depression. Now I was anguishing over her apparent recovery. Recalling her speeches about what a self-centered prick I was, I had enough self-doubt to admonish myself for overreacting.

The consensus was that, for now, I just had to take it one day at a time. Wait and see what happens, my support group people said. And in the meantime, you have to take care of yourself.

I WROTE THIS in my journal: "Leah looked beautiful tonight."

A byproduct of severe depression is not only its effect on a person's melancholy but on his or her physical bearing. During the worst of the depression Leah was loath to bathe, wash her hair, change her clothes, or brush her teeth.

But as her spirit arose from the ashes of her depression, she once again attended to her hygiene. Her eyes came to life. She laughed. Her hair was radiant. It lifted life into my slumbering loins. You'd think she was one of those models in a Latuda ad gathering bouquets of wild daisies in the pasture of a Kentucky horse farm.

In contrast, my imperfections and inadequacies were back on parade. I did a bad job pulling weeds. I didn't rub lemon oil on the wooden frame of the bathroom mirror. I didn't make it to the dry cleaner. I didn't vacuum the floor of her closet.

"I thought I did."

"Look under the shoes."

"I vacuumed the front part. I guess I didn't vacuum under your stuff."

"Look at the dust! Vacuum it right!"

I couldn't imagine Heshie's wife Judy berating him for improperly vacuuming her closet, in part because I couldn't imagine Heshie picking up a vacuum cleaner. How did most marriages work? Was it assumed the wife would vacuum under the shoes in the closet? Was I just another irresponsible chauvinist like most men? Or was I an idiot for listening to Leah yell at me?

She didn't have *time* to do *everything* around the house. She had *nine months* of depression to make up for. The *garden* needed her attention. (It did. I mowed the grass and kept the raspberries watered and grew some beans and peas, but that was about it.) Texts and emails and Facebook posts needed writing. Grandiose plans popped up overnight like toadstools. Meetings and lunches were arranged with her former colleagues to build her delusional consulting firm, Leah & Associates, LLC.

"They need me more than I need them," Leah gloated.

She continued her DBT counseling with new vigor. DBT classes were great! Her DBT counselor was great! She was learning so much!

"Everyone would benefit from DBT," she decided. "You should do it. You would learn about mindfulness."

"Okay."

"So will you do it?"

"No."

"I have to trust her doctors," I texted my brother. And if Leah really went off the rails, we had the crisis plan posted on the refrigerator door. Our so-called emergency contacts had our backs.

Leah & Associates, LLC, had a *brilliant* idea. People with depression need their five senses to be stimulated. She learned that in her DBT class and the hospital. See, she could buy *really cheap* scented candles, tactile stimulants, savory treats, soothing oils and soaps. She could buy inexpensive straw baskets and put together delightful gifts she would call Soothing Sacks and peddle them for $12.99. It was a *million-dollar* idea, she told me.

[Silence.]

"Why aren't you being more *supportive*?"

[Silence.]

"So you're going to sit there and brood, just like your mother."

[Silence.]

SHE WAS LATE getting out of the house to meet a friend for dinner. I kept my mouth shut, thinking, *She's making her own bed; she can lie in it.*

From Marya Hornbacher's memoir *Madness: A Bipolar Life:*

[My husband] withdraws. He won't talk. We try therapy; he sits there on the couch, clenching his jaw, able to discuss only the things I'm doing wrong, how I'm disrupting his life. He doesn't speak about what he gave up for me. He doesn't mention that he doesn't know who I am, how to talk to me, what to do with me, what a marriage is supposed to be like. And I don't know this any better than he does.[1]

Paradoxically, despite the triggers that churned my digestive system, after so many months of her depression I was relieved to see Leah regain some energy and purpose.

Because all this vigor was better than her lying around in bed all day. Wasn't it?

---

[1] Marya Hornbacher, *Madness: A Bipolar Life*. (New York: Mariner Books, 2008): p. 223.

CHAPTER 18

The Corrections

The abrupt switch to mania coincided with the increased
dose of lurasidone [Latuda]. This combined with the wors-
ening of mania, despite treatment with divalproex sodium,
made us suspicious that lurasidone had induced his mania.
. . . The abrupt resolution of his symptoms of mania occurred when his dose of lurasidone was reduced. . . . It is
conceivable that with the popular use of lurasidone for the
treatment of bipolar depression, more patients may experience an unexpected switch to mania. Lurasidone should
also be added to the list of atypical antipsychotics that can
induce mania.[1]

Crystal suggested that to counteract the vestiges of my mania-
inspired fear and loathing, Leah and I needed a "corrective experience."
I liked that notion: I should *correct* my anxiety and its resulting effects
on my gastrointestinal system, which felt infested *Alien*-style with snakes.

---

[1] Mark Kanzawa, M., & Olga Hadden, "Case report of a switch to mania induced
by lurasidone," *Therapeutic Advances in Psychopharmacology* 7, no. 2 (February
2017): 91–93.

I should *correct* the sense that decades of love was a mirage and I was, in essence, the worthless shit whom Manic Leah had berated all summer.

Things did gradually improve.

"Leah and I have been talking," I wrote in my journal, "and mostly listening."

We spent time together weeding the yard. We hiked through the woods in county parks, one day on a trail a few miles long. Miles! We went to a movie, and we held hands. We talked about making a trip together out east to visit our friend Anita when she felt well enough. We talked about our lives together.

Occasionally, we laughed. One morning while looking through the obituaries she asked me if I would have married her had her name been Shmekela Farvus.

"I wonder if she went by Sally."

"I think I'll change my name to Shmekela."

"That was my first wife's name. Please don't."

On July 29, 2016, Leah and I had the special dinner I'd been waiting for since my birthday more than nine months earlier. That late July evening I was a happily married husband again with my loving wife on a warm night by Lake Minnetonka. We'd spent half our lives raising children, establishing our careers, traveling the world, celebrating milestones, mourning the deaths of parents, sending the kids to college, and attending our daughter's wedding.

In support group we remind each other to see the individual first, not the illness. Take it one day at a time, we tell each other. Remember what you like about each other.

Leah and I still shared our goofy sense of humor.

"What do you like about me?" Leah asked me after we ordered dinner.

"Just your hair. What do you like about me?"

"Just your Horowitz nose."

"So what are you majoring in?"

This was one day, one evening, when I looked into my wife's eyes and saw her, Leah, the woman I married so long ago, rather than her mental illness. Just the four of us: she, my Horowitz nose, her thick hair, and an erotically delicious piece of flounder, celebrating our anniversary.

OVER THE NEXT FEW DAYS Leah typed furiously on her laptop and iPhone, emailing and texting me and many friends, relatives, and former coworkers her fervent plans and announcements. I was deluged by daily notifications and reminders, and I kept losing track of what mattered because each one was urgent and exuberant.

Although her inclinations were grand, her plans were grandiose— and a marital Bay of Pigs Incident seemed imminent. There was the Must Buy These Plane Tickets to South Korea Tonight Incident. (We didn't.) The Setting Up the Printer Instruction Sheet Incident. (Who knows? I mentioned it in my journal.)[2]

Describing a manic episode, Marya Hornbacher writes:

> I'm not the least bit tired, and spend the day running around,
> fixing, cleaning, planning to save the world next week. I don't
> have the slightest idea that I'm spinning off into the strato-
> sphere—lack of insight, one of the first signs that hypomania
> is moving into full-blown mania.[3]

---

[2] Although the Printer Incident was an epic ordeal at the time, I forget the details. Which is instructive: One way to improve your mental health is to take the long view. In the grand scheme of things, it might be better to step back and disengage from the havoc. I wasted way too much energy submerged in senseless skirmishes.

[3] *Madness*, 223.

The technical word for that lack of insight is *anosognosia,*[4] one of the worst aspects of mental illness for a friend or family member. In essence, it is a symptom that prohibits a person from recognizing that he or she has a mental illness. It is not denial, it is unawareness: The person does not know he or she is sick. It precludes rational discussion. It incites defensiveness and distrust. It feeds on itself, pushing loved ones further and further away from each other.

I HAD LITTLE IDEA what Leah & Associates was actually up to or what business Leah was planning except that she was planning to be a consultant, although what she planned to consult about, and with whom, was a big mystery.

She told me she arranged to meet in the fifty-four-story Wells Fargo Building in Minneapolis with a junior executive from Wells Fargo whom I called the Python.

"She said she can help me with my El-El-Cee and get a checking account set up and they don't charge anything—"

"Anything?"

"I just *said* that they don't charge *anything*! Because they're just trying to get my business. I need you to drive me downtown because I don't know where to park. You *need to be supportive* of me on this."

I knew not to attempt a prudent conversation with a person who was zipping around in a hypomanic drone ten stories above the rest of us. So in lieu of igniting an explosion because of my continued *lack of support*, I reluctantly drove Leah to the bank and then walked around the skyways moping while she met with the Python.

---

4 Xavier Amador. TEDx Talks, "I'm Not Sick, I Don't Need Help," October 2017, video, 18:02, https://www.youtube.com/watch?v=NXxytf6kfPM.

A half hour later Leah called and told me to join her in the Python's office. The mystery deal was sealed. The Python, who was wearing enough makeup to coat a Boeing 747, was all smiles. She offered to drive out to our house to help Leah get her office garbage dump cleaned out and business files organized. All we needed to do, the Python said, was get Leah's LLC set up with Mr. Thomas over in the small business office.

Oh, and, by the way, the Python said, Leah and I should talk about buying long-term care insurance before I turned sixty-two.

Life insurance! So this whole thing was a scam!

"Our financial guy said we don't need life insurance," I hissed at Leah.

We were transported through the fallopian tube of the Wells Fargo skyscraper to the uterus on the fourth floor to see Mr. Thomas, who, it turned out, was on a different computer system than the Python. He said he couldn't see on his system whatever information the Python had just entered into the company's Nutty Idea Database on her system. And unlike the Python, Mr. Thomas was not amused by my revved-up wife going off on him about *why aren't you on the same system* because this is a waste of my *time* and all I need is to open my LLC's *checking account*, et cetera, et cetera.

Poor Mr. Thomas. He was a mid-level grunt in an evil bank. I pictured him meeting his pals for happy hour, describing Leah as some crazy bitch he had to deal with that day.

You know what, Mr. Thomas? She isn't a bitch.

She has a mental illness, and her children and I love her.

LEAH WAS WOUND UP after the meeting so we ducked into a Bruegger's bagel shop for a snack. Because of the gluten I can't eat bagels, but whatever. She was hungry and we had *so much* to *discuss*.

"I'm so pissed that their fucking *systems* weren't linked," Leah said. "How stupid is that?"

"Given I just spent an hour on a summer day piddling around a downtown skyscraper, I couldn't agree more. And what's this about buying insurance?"

I despised that kind of sarcasm, nothing but my leaky anger, and it sure as heck wasn't an "I" statement. Leah started in on my *condescension* and how I always stick up for the power structure even if it's fucking Wells Fargo, and that might have been the first time that summer I heard a *lorem ipsum* yada yada rant.

"Goodbye, Leah. I'm walking home."

"See? See? That's the *crux* of the problem!"

There I went again, running away from our *communication problems*. It was four miles from the Bruegger's to our house, not a bad walk on a summer day, across the little bridge over the pond in Loring Park and then through the Walker Art Center's sculpture garden, on up Kenwood Parkway, and then west past Cedar Lake. Plenty of time to contemplate packing up my car before Leah got home and driving to Arizona to David and Lois's house.

"You can't do that, Jeff," our emergency contact and friend Emma said when I called her. "If you need to get out of town, fine, go. But stay in Minnesota. You can't go that far away."

"If there's an emergency, Arizona is a three-hour flight away . . . well, three months with stops in Quito, Bangkok, and Tanzania."

"Don't leave Minnesota," Emma repeated.

That afternoon Leah suggested that, since I was unwilling to go to DBT, I should go with her to a marriage counselor at the same clinic.

Oh, for crissake. Marriage counseling the previous summer had been an epically demoralizing and expensive waste of time, like repairing a severed arm with Elmer's Glue. At best it had been a tool to empower Leah while the docs tightened the lasso around her mania. At worst it exasperated me so much I wanted to smash a tire iron through someone's car window.

Looking back, I wonder where I thought all this was heading and why I was acting so cowardly and indecisive. I was already spending a couple hundred bucks a month at my own therapist's office rationalizing Leah's behavior, trying to figure out my options and an appropriate response. Dr. J had bought a two-bedroom townhouse, and once again I was hiding out for the night with him, lacking any kind of a plan. Once again I passed the days on the commode with drippy stools, once again taking Ativan to settle my stomach and my nerves.

I suspected it then and I know it now: I was trying to maintain hope, but I was doing it unrealistically. Deeply in denial, I was like someone staring at a weather radar screen that showed a hurricane barreling down the coast, ignoring the sheriff's edict to head inland. I thought I could wait it out. I thought there were enough safeguards in place to prevent Leah from again going completely off the rails. I trusted her psychologist, her DBT therapist, and her psychiatrist, who kept me hoping the miracle cure was close at hand.

In my journal that night I wrote, "I can't win. If I talk to her, she screams. If I keep quiet, she screams. I cannot control her hostilities and toxicity and personal history and coping mechanisms. I am not an angry person and need to do a better job of setting boundaries. I will not be disparaged by myself or others. I must be respected. I will not engage in hand-to-hand combat."

True enough. But I can't believe I was sticking around while writing these idiotic affirmations in the first place.

On the other hand, where was I supposed to go?

I HAD NO IDEA what Leah was actually doing. I just knew it involved texting for hours at a time, banging away on her cell phone keyboard with one finger like an old-time reporter. She bought a three-hundred-dollar ergonomically designed desk chair she told me to assemble but never used. She told me to get rid of the ugly metal filing cabinet we'd bought a hundred years ago at Target because she would be getting hired and we could afford to buy decent furniture. She bought a few dozen hanging files and manila folders and a set of office supplies during a three-hundred-dollar shopping spree at Ikea, which was okay because the tax guy said we could write it all off.

Because of all that typing and because no one ever told Leah to use her thumbs to tap a message on a cell phone and not her forefinger, a ligament or some goddamn thing in Leah's wrist snapped and so did my fuse. But she was an expert problem solver so she informed me she required my *support* now because she was putting together all her projects and she would need to dictate her ideas to me and I would type them out for an hour or two a day, which was not too much to ask, was it? *Was it?*

"I have my own job to do!" I yelled back at her. "Maybe if you weren't sending so many text messages it wouldn't have happened!"

"*I was there for you in Ayvalik for four days!*" she yelled back.

Touchdown, Leah.

She *had* been there for me in Ayvalik, when we were traveling through Turkey a few years earlier on a work trip of mine and I wrenched my lower back. Leah brought food to our hotel room, lifted me off my hands and knees so I could take a leak, managed to find me a doctor. She never once got sore at me, never once blamed me for screwing up my back, never said an unkind word the four days it took to get back to Istanbul.

So helping her type her stupid business proposal really wasn't too much to ask, was it?

She would dictate, and I would obey.

WE MET for our weekly bullfight presided over by Casper the Friendly Ghost, the cordial but otherwise invisible marriage counselor we began seeing at the DBT clinic. From the get-go Leah blathered on in those sessions uncontained, revisiting how it was *exactly* the same as what happened in Tunisia when the Chauncey Greene contacted me. Then Leah listed the rest of her grievances about how for thirty-six years I had been controlling her.

"Actually, we've known each other thirty-four years."

"A-*ha!* You see? You *see?* That is *exactly* an example of what I am talking about."

I sat on the sofa clutching a throw pillow against my chest, begging the Friendly Ghost with my eyes to put a cork in Leah's trap.

Leah snickered, "Why are you hiding behind a pillow, Jeff? Are you *afraid* of something?"

People with mood disorders are annoyingly self-focused, and someone as smart as Leah can be a stealth bomber attacking her loved ones' weaknesses. I resisted the temptation to throw the little pillow at either Leah's head or Casper's apparition.

"Leah, you have bipolar disorder," I said, changing the subject. "You were hospitalized twice."

In response, Leah told the Friendly Ghost that since she started taking Latuda she was all better, that this was the real Leah, and the only reason she was hospitalized in the first place is because Jeff had railroaded her into it, which all goes back to what happened in Tunisia, the problem being the time zone change *lorem ipsum dolor* and she's fine now and Jeff can't *deal* with her creative energy because now she was going to be a professor at the university and would *not* go back to the hospital unless she gets committed.

Sounds good to me, I thought.

"And if I get only four hours of sleep, that's *my* fucking business,"

Leah said. "And my psychologist, my DBT counselor, and my psychiatrist all say I'm doing FINE!"

Maybe Casper the Friendly Ghost was hearing a haiku, too.

> My psychologist,
> DBT counselor, and
> My shrink say I'm fine.

More likely, Casper was bored out of her mind and was wondering
what to cook for dinner.

I NERVOUSLY KEPT our emergency contacts apprised of Leah's
ascent into mania. They were, with one exception, Leah's friends more
than mine, and I had misgivings about communicating with them behind her back. On the other hand, Leah and I had posted the signed
emergency mental health plan on the door of the refrigerator, worded
in a way that ceded our friends and me power to intervene in an appropriate manner if she became unmoored.

Melody Moezzi called hypomania "the most beautiful land I know":

> I know of no other place where you can keep up so much
> energy without sleeping or eating, finish in a day what would
> take most people a week, abandon so many of the self-esteem
> issues that prevent you from meeting your full potential,
> be the life of the party, guiltlessly increase your participa-
> tion in "pleasurable activities" and engage in so many more
> "goal-directed" behaviors. Why lose that sense of invincibility?
> Why *ever* come down from that?[5]

---

[5]   Moezzi, *Haldol and Hyacinths*, 180.

Why come down from that? Because it leaves family members like me drained and aloof and physically and emotionally exhausted—which Leah took to heart.

"I'm not a disorder," she texted me. "I am a person."

Fair enough. But so was I, and I was barely hanging on.

Looking back, I am astounded by the idiocy of my trying to defuse a time bomb while chewing on a figurative corn dog. I should have called it quits when she tore the emergency plan off the refrigerator and threw it in the garbage. It would have been a perfect exit line, Shakespearean in its tragic finality: *Love looks not with the eyes, but with the mind; and therefore, dear one, I must take leave in my Mazda and leave thee behind.*

Soon thereafter she spent a night in a suburban conference center, living it up in a bubble bath to show me just who's mentally ill around here and who's not.

A text message from Leah:

AUGUST 25, 2016

It seems you are putting a lot of energy into trying to convince me that I am manic. If I suddenly said that I was, what would happen next? Would all your anger and unhappiness go away? Would we then have no marital problems? What would have to happen for you to be happy now? My being committed to a psych ward?

I didn't write back because there's nothing you can say in response, which, depending on your point of view, is either avoidance or a boundary, and when you are in my shoes you will doubt yourself no matter what you choose to do.

MY ST. PAUL FRIENDS Chuck and Maureen invited Leah, me, and a crowd of accomplished beer drinkers I barely knew to a barbeque. As usual, Leah and I drove separately, and once she finally arrived, I stayed out of her way, amused and mortified as I watched a total stranger. She was revved up and bounced around the party like a racquetball, gasconading her grandiose plans to her flummoxed audience until she said goodbye and drove the hell off.

A few minutes later, a notoriously foul-mouthed Irish friend of the hostess, a woman named Deirdre, exclaimed, "What the *fokk* is wrong with *that* one?"

I was pissed by *that* one's stigmatizing tone. Although Leah was driving me crazy, I was suddenly proud of my wife. As Leah has said, she is a person not a disorder. She is enduring an illness she never asked for but one that is hidden in America's collective attic like a forgotten bag of rags, leaving her and millions of others alone in a fundamental and terrifying way. What the *fokk* was *your* excuse, Deirdre?

Yet I, too, was maddened by Leah's manic behavior and continuing calamities those weeks. She paid a neighbor kid, Elroy, to dig a rain garden in the front yard. Two years later that became the Jeff Will Fill in the Hole with Eight Bags of Wood Chips Initiative. She hired Elroy and another kid to be her footmen at a Sunday brunch she held in the Twilight Zone. She spent a couple weeks trying to meet the deadline for an application for an arts grant, complained I wasn't supporting her, and then missed the submission date.

In response, I struggled to overcome my anger. In theory, after hearing such stories from dozens of participants in my support groups and reading numerous books on mental illness, I should have forgiven myself for my thoughts and actions. In reality, it's a wonder any marriage survives that kind of stress.

My support group buddy Jack Lemmon insists his wife's dual

diagnosis of severe depression and alcoholism is a gift. They've been married even longer than Leah and I, and he told me his wife has been sick nearly the whole time.

"Her illness has made me a better person," Jack has said more than once. "I'm kinder. I'm more patient. I've learned so much about mental illness. I've met so many good people."

"Sure, Jack," I've replied. "It's the gift that keeps on giving."

Depending on the week, he credits or blames his deep Catholic faith for making him stick with his wife so many years. I honor that. The beauty of the support groups I've gone to and friendships I've made is that we don't judge each other. We listen closely, ask questions, and support each other's choices. In that regard, Jack's right: Leah's illness has made me a more tolerant, less selfish person too.

At the same time, Jack says he suffers from "NGS," or Nice Guy Syndrome. When he bemoans the sacrifices he has made—especially compared to his wife's reluctance to get help for her problems—I want to tell him to stop being such a nice guy. In fact, I wonder if those of us caring for someone with a chronic illness would benefit from a satellite picture of our lives. We're blind to understanding that our "new normal" isn't at all normal. Housework overload. Child care responsibilities. Financial hardships. The absence of sex.

Separate bedrooms.

I thought I'd misheard when a spouse in my group mentioned "my room" and "his room."

Leah and I became that couple. In her hypomania, Leah spent half the night banging around the kitchen, starting new projects, not finishing others, and, just like the previous summer, cluttering the dining room and living room with reams of paper. When I wasn't crashing on Dr. J's couch, I slept in my son's old bed, emerging for endless trips to the bathroom, my bowels resembling the Dinty Moore stew I feared I would be heating nightly over a campfire if conditions at home worsened.

But I knew none of this was normal. I was waiting out the catastrophe. In case I could no longer take Leah's rage and needed to make a run for it, I kept a duffel bag packed with clothes and a month's supply of my cholesterol pills, sleep meds, and Imodium. And I withdrew five hundred dollars in cash from an emergency slush fund.

I started to formulate a plan.

One warm day in late August, Dr. J and I met our friend Kate for happy hour at the pavilion at Como Lake in St. Paul. This was a summer afternoon we Midwesterners treasure. Couples pedaling paddleboats in the pond. Moms and dads pushing children around the walking path past the ducks and geese like Leah and I used to do when our kids were little.

Kate, Dr. J, and I sat on a bench out on the boat pier, enjoying a beer in the sun, or in my case a Seven-Up to settle my stomach. I was pretty well living with Dr. J at that point. Leah had recently upbraided him, too, when he dared to suggest her drinking wine might be a mistake given the meds she was on.

That's when David called me.

"This is your brother," he said. "I need to talk to you."

He sounded angry and I walked over to the pavilion and listened as he jumped down my throat. "You have *got* to get Leah off our backs about Thanksgiving," he snarled. "She keeps texting me and emailing me and demanding an answer to what we're going to do for Thanksgiving and where we're going to go and she won't stop badgering me and we really don't want her here and you have *got* to tell her we cannot *deal* with her—"

"David. David, stop," I said.

"—constant emailing and texting about Thanksgiving—"

"Stop, David! Stop! She's out of her mind, David," I blubbered. "I don't know what to do. David, I just *don't* know what to do."

He could hear me snarfling into my T-shirt.

"Please, David," I begged him. "Just don't yell at me. Please?"

It was one thing to lose my wife. I couldn't bear to lose my brother.

The next day we spoke again and agreed that if the bottom fell out of my marriage, David and I would spend a couple weeks camping together out west, like the Lone Ranger and Tonto.

My most pressing concern was finding someone to give some love to our pet turtle and Leah's associate, Lollipop.[6] I talked to Elroy's parents, and they told me Elroy would be glad to watch Lollipop for as long as necessary.

I had a plan. I assumed it meant a week or two at most on the road. Something would give in the meantime.

---

[6] One of my friends asked me if I was afraid I'd come home and find Lollipop boiled in a pot of water à la *Fatal Attraction*. Bipolar disorder, as far as I know, isn't that kind of illness. Or Leah isn't that kind of pet owner.

CHAPTER 19

My Kind of Town, Chicago Is

One of the marriage counselors said that to get along better Leah and I should eliminate the question "Why?" Instead, we should just accept and respect each other's choices.

So, when Leah started prattling again in italics, I didn't ask why she was all of a sudden *excited!* about her latest *great!* idea: attending her fortieth high school reunion in Chicago. She dug out her yearbooks and joined a class reunion Facebook group, and I practically shouted, "Fabulous! You should do it!"

And leave me the hell alone for a long weekend. I could get the house organized, cook some meals, and sleep in my own bed.

But there was *even more* to it: Leah would drive to Chicago and then I would fly there for like *ninety! dollars!* a couple days later. On the way Leah would stop in Milwaukee and treat herself to a nice hotel, snap some photos she could somehow use in the class she claimed to be co-teaching at the university, and hand out her business card. She would keep receipts for the mileage and tolls and hotels because she could deduct the costs as business expenses, and I envisaged one or both of us ending up in a federal prison. ¡No *problema!*

"You'll fly in on Saturday and I'll meet you at O'Hare and we'll attend the reunion with the Mickey Marks, who we can pay for because he's *poor* and he's *lonely* and we can afford it. Then you and I can drive back together after we spend a nice day at Millennium Park."

I couldn't help myself. I pictured Leah getting into a fight in a bar with a Klan member in southern Wisconsin, or, worse, my rescuing her from the Cook County psych ward because of some *massive misunderstanding* by some *asshole Chicago cop* and paying off a ten thousand-dollar bill.

Thus, out of self-interest and marital duty, I agreed to be her ersatz bodyguard and valet, and anyway, how lousy a time could I have at my mentally ill wife's fortieth reunion when all I had to do was show up and eat and drive the seven hours back from Chicago with her on Labor Day?

Psychedelically lousy.

I slept at home with Leah Wednesday night, like Ward and June Cleaver. Thursday morning Leah woke up sobbing before dawn. She wouldn't say why, so instead we made love for the first time in weeks because even though I thought about moving to Namibia and becoming a lobster fisherman I still loved her deeply and always will.

Also I am a male, et cetera.

I stopped by the dry cleaners to pick up Leah's party dress and then drove her Honda to get the headlight fixed so she and the car would not be ground into deer sausage on the way to her harebrained fortieth high school reunion and that's what a husband does for his wife before he hides out all day in his buddy's basement.

The plan was for her to leave Minneapolis at noon, stop overnight in Milwaukee, about a six-hour drive, and meet her poet friend the Mickey Marks in the Chicago Loop the next morning. But via text updates I saw noon become one o'clock, then two o'clock, then six in the evening because she'd gotten on the phone for two hours with her estranged brother's old friend living in Boston who was going through a rough time of it with *his* wife, who actually *had* bipolar, Leah said, and the guy *really* needed her support.

When I arrived home from Dr. J's at seven o'clock I found Leah's backpack in the dining room containing, most notably, her medications. The previous summer she had traveled to Tunisia and missed her dosage and sent me on a four-month voyage to the intergalactic asylum.

Of all the things to forget—her medications!

"Dear?" I said, when I called her. "I noticed your backpack is here with your meds."[1]

"Oh, shit," Leah said.

Now what? Do you leave the house at seven o'clock in the evening with your wife's backpack and medication and blow off your one-way ticket to O'Hare and drive to Milwaukee and arrive at one in the morning? Or is that enabling behavior and codependent and even more idiotic than her forgetting her backpack? Or do you just move to Nepal and teach English in a Sherpa night school?

I stayed put and played my piano for a couple hours.

From her Facebook posts I could see Leah was stopping along the interstate to take pictures of *interesting* homeless people near the exit ramps. It had something to do with the Photojournalism Division of Leah & Associates, LLC, a photo collage or PowerPoint presentation of the street people of central Wisconsin, which was somehow related to the graduate course her LLC was co-creating to teach or designing for someone else to teach. I was bewildered and could only trust her and God almighty that she wouldn't sign a contract for consulting services

---

[1] A commendable "I" statement. As opposed to: "Why the fuck did you leave your backpack here?"

with the Church of Scientology or miss the turn in Milwaukee and drive straight into Lake Michigan.

She ended up taking a motel room in Madison at two in the morning and never fell asleep. If I were a generous spirit, I would have commended Leah for her independence, intelligence, courage, and resilience. Instead, during a phone call the next morning, we fought a welterweight prizefight. It might have been about the Incident on State Street Story or the How She Scored the Free Room Story. Here are three of the dozens of text messages:

9:32 A.M.

Leah, when we're on the phone and you start accusing me and yelling at me I'm not going to listen anymore. I'm going to start hanging up when you do that.

9:38 A.M.

Leah, no, I did NOT yell at you. There was zero accusation, and I will not have you say that to me. I calmly said I would be glad to listen to the rest of the story when I see you. YOU started YELLING at ME. I expect an apology. If you are not able to understand that, let me know.

9:39 A.M.

When you are calm, then call me. I will also not listen to you talk uninterrupted for 10 more minutes. This does not bode well for Chicago or a ride back from there. I expect to be respected, and that is on you.

I may have checked my journal to review the stuff Crystal told me to say when Leah started berating me. One woman in my family support group has a set of index cards she looks at with canned "I" statements when she's being screamed at by her son with schizophrenia.

11:19 A.M.
Leah, please stop hanging up on me. I must be treated respectfully and not like that. I am not feeling respected, and I will not be bullied.

You may want to write that one down, although it does no good.

SOMEHOW IT TOOK LEAH two days and two nights lodging to drive the 350 miles from Minneapolis to the northern suburbs of Chicago, which she didn't get to until midafternoon on Saturday because she said Google Maps kept telling her the wrong *fucking* way to go.

I followed through on my end of the deal. Maybe I was a martyr or maybe I was afraid for Leah's life if she caused a riot at her high school reunion. Maybe I figured out she wanted me to attend her high school reunion with her because I wasn't an overstuffed slob like those *assholes* she went to school with and she wanted to show me off to those *bitches* she disliked back when Gerald Ford was president. So I just decided to go along for the ride, literally. I flew to O'Hare, took an Uber to the wrong hotel because, ha-ha, I guess Leah hadn't actually made a reservation there, ha-ha, and waited around a couple hours at a different hotel. Then she had me drive a last-minute forty-mile reconnaissance mission to pick up the Mickey Marks. He'd been hanging around all day doing nothing because the original plan fell through when Leah arrived in town too late for the two of them to visit the old high school together at noon, which would have been *stupid* anyway because who cares, she *hated* those people.

I fetched Mickey and returned to the hotel with him. Leah was just starting to get ready, rocking out to her music with a *downbeat* because in DBT she learned that music can be comforting for stress reduction, and, see, this is called the *downbeat* because just listen, *listen*. You hear the *downbeat*? Isn't that calming?

I didn't find the downbeat very calming, especially with Leah going on and on about how calming it was.

SHE LOOKED BEAUTIFUL, far more attractive than Mickey Marks or me. The three of us arrived for the reunion at the Italian supper club a moment before Leah's class photo was to be taken in the parking lot. I noticed a Chinese buffet across the highway and wondered if anyone would notice if I ate there instead and then thumbed home that night to Minneapolis or, say, Key West.

But that would be irresponsible, and I had committed to being there for Leah's show-and-tell dinner—for me an eighty-dollar gluten-free shingle with red sauce. The Mickey Marks and I followed the crowd into the reunion. I couldn't hear myself think because of the loud disco music, and I shouted to a couple people whom I had never before met that it was *great* to *see* them again. They said they couldn't remember me, which made sense because I went to high school in Pennsylvania, but then they said, "Oh, yes! Jeff!" I mentioned taking algebra class together, and now we were old friends again, reminiscing about old times.

I talked to a fellow in Leah's high school class who told me he was a parts guy.

"A parts guy?" I said. I wasn't sure I heard him right with "Shake Your Booty" banging in the background.

"Yeah, parts. You name it. Auto parts, refrigerator parts, lawn-mower parts. Any kind of parts."

"Whoa, whoa," I said. "Slow down. So not the whole thing. Just the parts."

"That's right. Just parts."

He gave me his card and I thanked him and said now I knew where to go for parts.

There were speeches, including one from Leah that no one could hear because of the ruckus, but from what I could tell she sound-ed mordacious, how mean you bitches were back then, but isn't it swell we're all grown up now? I heard some guy ask who Leah was. It was dark and hard to hear, and I don't think many people knew her in high school. She wanted to show people how terrific she looked, which she did, and that she, Leah, had spent her life with me, the Jeff Zuckerman, which entangled me in a more humbling, heartbreaking, and complex ball of emotions than the cosmic forces that put Leah and me together at that moment in that loud, manicotti-stuffed dot in the galaxy.

After a couple of hours Leah hit a wall and she, Mickey Marks, and I left, having spent what it would have cost for three front-row seats at, say, a Paul McCartney concert in London. We drove back to the hotel and Mickey Marks crashed on the sofa bed in our suite.

The next morning I gave him money for an Uber back to his apart-ment, and Leah and I agreed to drive home a day early. We stopped at the Chicago Botanic Garden, about as peaceful a place in Chicagoland as you'll find. We strolled around the Japanese garden, where

when the gold Ginkgo trees glow in the autumn light, for instance—it's easy to overlook the ways in which the Japanese respect for nature and age are revealed . . . If you look closely, though, the effect is evocative, as seamless as a traditional haiku.[2]

Leah played her calming downbeat on her cell phone, and then as we glanced at the glow of the gold ginkgo trees she vilified me nonstop for twenty-five minutes for every grief she ever had about me, about her fucking parents, the fucking universe, and the fucking Big Bang for creating the whole fucking mess in the first place. We had our biggest argument yet about arguing about arguing, and I doubted more than ever our marriage would survive and thought of another haiku:

> Japanese garden.
> Bad place to berate your spouse.
> Next time: the iHop.

ON THE LONG DRIVE back to Minneapolis through Wisconsin, Leah indulged me and sat silent as a monk and typed on her iPhone nonstop for six hours. She took the wheel the last hour with the downbeat playing, which felt like aural waterboarding, but we'd be home soon enough and I wasn't about to ignite a Gulf of Tonkin incident over the downbeat.

My bitterness about the Chicago trip must sound reprehensible. Yet I eventually learned not to deny and punish myself for so many negative feelings but to voice them, understand them, own them, and take charge of managing them. The stress and pain are so intense when feeling trapped in a relationship with someone whose normal identity is being choked by a chronic illness. One woman in my support group

---

2   "Meredith Hubert Malott Japanese Garden," Chicago Botanic Garden, https://www.chicagobotanic.org/gardens/japanese.

says she can't stand it when people call her a saint for sticking so long with her husband, who battles an extreme mental illness called intermittent explosive disorder.

"I'm no saint," she laughs. "First of all, it makes me feel crazy or stupid for staying with him. Second of all, some days I just hate him."

Writer, educator, and researcher Pauline Boss suggested such turmoil is the result of *ambiguous loss:*

> Ambiguous loss is a psychologically distressing event that is outside the realm of ordinary human experience; it lacks resolution and traumatizes and continues to exist in the present. It is not post anything. . . . It is a rollercoaster ride during which family members alternate between hope and hopelessness.[3]

Boss identified two types of ambiguous loss. One reflects a loved one's "physical absence but psychological presence," as in the aftermath of a soldier's disappearance or a child's unresolved kidnapping or a father's abandonment of his children. Conversely, the other type of ambiguous loss occurs when a family member is "physically present but psychologically absent." The classic examples are loving a substance abuser or someone with dementia "or [some] other chronic mental illness."[4]

I had lost track of what happened to the woman I was married to. She looked like Leah, but who was this woman dragging me through a pod of orcas and rending my spleen in half? Would I ever get back the Leah I knew? Would Leah ever get back the Leah she knew?

---

[3] Pauline Boss, *Ambiguous Loss: Learning to Live with Unresolved Grief.* (Cambridge: Harvard University Press, 1999), 24.

[4] Boss, *Ambiguous Loss*, 8–9.

CHAPTER 20

Zuckerman Unbound

Leah had a mental illness, and I was supposed to keep control of my emotions.

But soon after returning from Chicago, we got into a screaming match in our bedroom. A pillow was thrown. Angry words were shouted.

I called Leah a cunt.

"I am so sorry," I said to her. I was ashamed. I had no idea where that came from.

Leah, who had jokingly used the C-word herself, laughed at the absurdity and responded, "It was funny."

But over the following weeks Leah pulled The C-Word Incident out of her anti-husband satchel like a pipe bomb.

"He called me a cunt," she repeated over and over. With Casper the Friendly Ghost. With her doctors. With our friends. With I don't know who else.

But especially with me. For a while all I could do was suck it up and apologize for calling her the C-word, let her rub my face in it, continue to ask her forgiveness, and, as a peace offering, agree to take dictation.

Until one day at the marriage counselor I finally understood I was getting a C-word gaslighting.

"He called me a cunt," Leah told Casper the Friendly Ghost, for the umpteenth time.[1] "Admit it!"

"He already has admitted it, Leah," Casper said. "And he said he's sorry. It's time for you to move on. Or is it more important for you to be right than happy?"

That was the first time Casper had uttered something more helpful than what a potted fern might say.

Leah paused. "I'd rather be right."

"That's nice, Leah," I said. "You want revenge. Is that what they teach you in your DBT class? Retaliation?"

"Yes," she said.

Yom Kippur, the Jewish Day of Atonement, was a month away. "So much for Jewish values," I said. "I've asked for your forgiveness three times in public, so now it's on you."[2]

I wasn't being completely spiteful. Leah knew that particular Jewish tradition as well as I did. And I was trying to save my soul and reason with someone in the middle of a manic meltdown.

That evening I refused to take dictation, and Leah went ballistic. Too exhausted to flee, I hid in my office and shoved a desk in front of the door to keep her from barging in and hurling a hammer at my head. I heard Leah throw a tantrum, stomping around on the dining room floor, slamming the back door, stomping up and down the wooden deck

---

[1] Leah may well have forgotten she'd brought it up before. Memory lapse is common among people with a mental illness, whether inherently or as an effect of treatment.

[2] "Ask the Expert: Apologizing," My Jewish Learning, https://www.myjewishlearning.com/article/ask-the-expert-apologizing/. In fairness, calling one's wife a cunt is not a Jewish value.

stairs outside my office window, slamming the back door again, and then slamming our bedroom door.

She had officially lost control, and her despair was harrowing. Yet I found myself chuckling. In our support group we say we embrace humor as healthy. And Leah and I had now reached a new level of tragicomedy.

That or I was a complete schmuck. Even after all I'd been through, a part of me was nagging myself for not supporting my wife when she needed my help. In any case, I knew I was safe in my office and I'd be moving out soon enough. The only question was when, and how, Leah would get readmitted to the psych ward.

HER TIRADES and tumble into hypomania reverberated across the continent. Three thousand miles apart on the coasts, our children consoled each other about their own noxious interactions with revved-up Mom. If anything good came of her illness, it was that my children and I had become more honest with each other than ever.

Joey was enough of a mess that he, too, started seeing a therapist, a woman who suggested he and Sarah write a letter to Dr. Carpenter detailing Leah's behaviors. I coached Sarah and Joey to keep their letter unemotional.

"Someday I'll write the whole story in a book," I joked. "For now, you should keep it short. Stick to the facts and be specific."

I wrote a letter, too.[3] I listed a half-dozen bullet points and

---

[3]   Regardless of HIPAA concerns, family members can always contact a patient's providers with information. But unless the patient signs the release forms or the family member has guardian status, the providers cannot share information with family members. For me, it became so critical that I have Leah's written permission to have two-way communication with her doctors that I decided in 2017 it would be my "hill to die on," the sacred conditions we all establish for remaining in our relationships.

examples of the change in Leah's behavior over the previous month. I also wrote this:

Dr. Carpenter, I am trying to be objective. Leah seems scared to death that she's going to go depressed again or end up in the psych ward. She doesn't understand that those who love her want that not to happen.

I can't imagine what she's going through. I love her so much. I got my Leah back for about a week last October and a week in July, but I'm losing her again to this awful illness.

She has trust and faith in you, as do I. No matter what you decide with her at this next appointment, on behalf of her friends and family, I am grateful to you for saving her life.

I printed off Joey and Sarah's cowritten letter with mine and dropped them off at Dr. Carpenter's office. I felt like the three of us—especially our kids—were betraying Leah by contacting her doctor behind her back. I also knew there would be an earthquake if Leah found out what we had done.

The next day, about an hour before her next appointment with Dr. Carpenter, Leah picked a fight with me out on our deck.

"Why do you want to go with me to my appointment?"

"Because I care about you. I want to learn how I can best help you."

"That's condescending—"

"Fine. I just want to hear what Dr. Carpenter has to say."

"Don't interrupt me! Why don't you talk about your feelings, Jeff? You only want to go because you don't *trust* me. That's condescending. I know how I'm doing. I'm doing fine. If you can't fucking deal with how well I'm doing, then fuck you because I can tell I'm doing just fine and you should just mind your own fucking business!" *Ipsum lorem amat, et cetera, et cetera.*

Leah was right. I didn't trust her.

She drove to her appointment without me and I brooded all evening with nowhere to go. At ten o'clock she emailed me:

SEPTEMBER 8, 2016

Now I see why a letter was dropped off[4] *at Dr. Carpenter's office, and I wasn't shown it ahead of time. It includes many half-truths and unethical statements—biased ways of stating many of the listed "situations."*

My doctor thinks I'm healthy right now. No med or any other changes. Smooth sailing as far as my mental health is concerned.

With that I started exploring options—a short-term apartment lease or a road trip to Arizona via my friends' places in Nebraska and Colorado. I couldn't keep living out of my suitcase at Dr. J's house, even though he offered to let me move in with him.

For her part, Leah notified me she was taking a trip to Los Angeles.

I EMAILED OUR CHILDREN and told them the nurse from the psychiatrist's office called me. According to the case notes, Dr. Carpenter doubled the Latuda and increased Leah's sleep med. "Continue to monitor for mania," the nurse read from the notes. I hated that my kids were in the middle of all this, but they were adults. And God knows what Leah had been telling them.

Joey called me back after he got off work. "Dad, here's a direct quote on the phone with Mom: 'My doctor said I'm not bipolar and that

---

[4] "Was dropped off"; "I wasn't shown it": admirable avoidance, on Leah's part, of direct accusations via passive voice.

I'm fine, and she didn't change my meds.' I could tell she didn't want me to ask any more about it."

"Did she sound manic?"

"She was calm. She didn't talk over me or anything like that."

"I give up," I said to Joey on the phone. "I don't know what medicine your mother is taking, what her doctor thinks, and I am starting to no longer care."

That stung Joey. Leah was still his mother.

"If you give up," Joey said, "who will take care of her?"

Every parent in my support group struggles with such predicaments. Parents of younger children, in particular, must decide how much to share with their children about their mother or father's mental illness. If we leave our spouses, we ask, what kind of role models are we for our daughters and sons? What kind of role models are we if we stay? And by whose definition of right and wrong are we to make such profound decisions?

On a good day, it can be invigorating to be in your midsixties like I am and find yourself confronting such haunting questions. On a bad day, you wonder if you'd be happier tending to a herd of alpacas on a Peruvian hillside.

To me it felt like a turning point. I had finally let go. I told Joey that his mother had decided to fly to Los Angeles the following weekend and that her hippie friends out there could deal with her. Later in the month she planned to fly to Portland to see him. Joey was twenty-five years old and got along better with his mother than I did. He would manage it well enough.

"Actually," he said, "I'm more worried about something happening to you than Mom. Sarah and I need at least one healthy parent."

TO MY SURPRISE, Leah invited me to her next appointment at the clinic. She probably wanted to let Dr. Carpenter see for herself what a jerk I was. I was eager to hear the straight dope from the doctor and readily agreed to come along.

By now Leah was possessed by the downbeat dybbuk[5] because it was so *calming*. She took to carrying around her iPhone with the downbeat music playing—in her car, walking around, wherever. I hated the downbeat, but even worse was how much she was still *talking* about the downbeat. Still, it wasn't my hill to die on.

When Dr. Carpenter called us to her office, Leah was rocking out on her iPhone without headphones. Without insight. Without basic manners.

At that point I found myself on the stage of a Samuel Beckett play.

*Scene: The office of **Doctor Karen Carpenter**, a psychiatrist.*

Doctor Carpenter: Leah, please turn off the music.

Leah [*caustically*]: I need the music on. [*She moves her head to the beat.*] It's soothing.

Doctor Carpenter: Leah, I need you to turn off the music.

The Husband: Leah, will you just turn off the music?

Leah: Don't tell me what to do. Listen to the downbeat, Doctor. Do you know what a downbeat is?

Doctor Carpenter: Leah, you are hypomanic. I've spoken with your DBT counselor and she agrees. The medication you are taking is making you hypomanic. I will no longer prescribe Latuda.

---

[5] In Jewish folklore, a dybbuk is a ghost who lingers after death and causes trouble for the living. See Shoshana Kessock, "Dybbuk or Demon: Knowing Your Jewish Ghosts and Ghouls," Tor.com, October 2012, https://www.tor.com/2012/10/28/dybbuk-or-demon-knowing-your-jewish-ghosts-and-ghouls/.

Leah: Fine, I'll TURN OFF THE GODDAMN MUSIC.

*Leah shuts off her phone. **The Husband** smirks.*

Leah: Get out of here. Leave. And I'm taking away your right to talk to my doctor.

The Husband: I won't say another word.

Leah: I said get out of here. You are trying to DESTROY OUR MARRIAGE. Doctor, I am revoking my permission for you to talk to him. He may no longer attend my appointments, and I am NOT MANIC.

*The **Husband** rises, reaches for a tissue, blows his nose, and walks toward the door.*

Leah: That is SO LIKE YOU. Just walk away from our problems!

Music begins playing in the background, the Carpenters' song "Say Goodbye to Love," arranged with a downbeat.

***The Husband** exits.*

After the appointment Leah yammered the whole way out the clinic door, up the parking ramp, into the car, and through the payment gate. I sped through a residential area while Leah screamed at me to pull over and *stop* because she wanted to *talk* so just *stop* so we can *talk* for *five minutes* okay *two minutes*. When I refused to slow down Leah grabbed the steering wheel, screaming at me to stop. I lied and said, fine, we'll talk after we get home. Back at the house I packed the car and prepared to head for Nebraska as soon as Leah left for Los Angeles that weekend.

I HAD NO CLEAR IDEA why Leah was traveling to California. We were beyond "discussing" such matters, and I was done counting how much money she was flushing down the commode. I could only hope Leah's safety was not in jeopardy. But my own well-being was at risk, too. A friend shot a virtual tear gas canister at my psyche: "This ordeal, Jeff," he said, "could be shaving years off your life."

I was fed up with trying to be *supportive*. I called Casper the Friendly Ghost to let her know I was through with marriage counseling and I planned to leave the state. I was astonished when Casper agreed and said she would tell Leah that marriage counseling was futile. Nevertheless, although eager to make a clean break from Leah's mania, I was despondent in my journal: "The only way out seems to be separation or divorce. What a thing! But I need sanity. Is that too much to ask?"

I offered to drive Leah to the airport, thrilled she would be leaving me alone. She said she needed to leave the house at two thirty but dawdled an extra half hour. If she missed her plane, so what? I was a caregiver, not a caretaker.

As we were pulling up to the airport terminal, I told her I was serious about leaving town for a long time.

"Are you going to return my phone calls?" she asked.

"I don't know," I replied.

That was the honest but wrong answer. Leah screamed one final "Fuck you!" for the road, jumped out of the car, grabbed her suitcase, kicked the rear bumper, and stomped away into the airport.

She dented neither the car nor my intention to leave town. I planned to camp somewhere Sunday night in southern Minnesota and then drive west and stay with an old friend in Kearney, Nebraska, and then stay a couple nights with other friends in Colorado. I bought my brother a cheap one-way ticket from Phoenix into Denver International and packed my car with two of everything: tents, sleeping bags, and whatever else would be a nuisance for him to bring aboard a plane. David and I would spend a week or two driving around out west and work our way back to Phoenix, and once there I'd figure things out or just wait out Leah's manic episode.

The next day, Leah called me, crying, at five thirty in the morning Pacific time. I was awake, starting a day of errands before I blew town. She said she hadn't slept at all, and she sounded like it.

"I have bipolar disorder," she wept. "Can you pick up my prescription at Walgreens so I have it when I get back to town?"

"Yes," I said.

It was heartbreaking, but God only knew what her mood would be a day later. I was determined to jump off the mental illness merry-go-round at last.

I spent the next twenty-four hours taking care of household chores, packing and loading my car, and running errands. On Sunday morning I drove over to my buddy Dr. J's house to say goodbye and let myself in to his foyer like I always did.

"What's up?" he said.

How many nights had I crashed on his couch? How much crap had I gone through during the past year with my best friend?

"I'm out of here," I said. "I'm leaving town."

I handed Dr. J one of the fifty-dollar bills I'd withdrawn from the credit union. It felt to us both like the cloddish end to a college romance. The look in his eyes was not only not supportive—I think the guy wanted to spit in my face or deck me for such a stupid token of friendship and gratitude. I don't blame him. I was abandoning him, too, without giving him the courtesy of a farewell meal or even a conversation. But he had no idea how amped I was that day, like Steve McQueen preparing for the great escape from the German stalag.

Sure enough, as I was ready to head out of town, Leah texted me from Los Angeles. "Through no fault of my own I missed my flight. : >) Rebooking on American for the next flight."

Smiley face. Ha-ha.

Through no fault of my own I wish I had taken more time to pack and leave properly, buy Dr. J dinner, show my gratitude in a less half-assed way.

But no matter: I was on the road again.

Lamentations

CHAPTER 21

Exodus

B ack in 1980 I had enough of living in Phoenix and the Sunbelt. I loaded everything I owned into a Volkswagen Rabbit and headed off to graduate school in Minnesota, where I met Leah and raised my children in a state I have lived in and loved ever since.

Three-plus decades later I was making the reverse trip, only now I was a dyspeptic old man living like Charles Bukowski. I spent the first night in a state park near the Iowa line eating sweet corn grilled over a campfire. In the morning I was nerve-wracked and paranoid, like I'd pulled off a bank job. Somewhere near Des Moines I discovered I'd misplaced my wallet and pulled over and dug through the bags of food and garbage, convinced myself I had been pickpocketed earlier at a McDonald's. After searching my car another ten minutes I found the wallet in the glove compartment where I'd shoved it, crack-brained.

I headed west and stopped for a cup of coffee in Grand Island, Nebraska. I reached into my backpack for eye drops and spilled a bottle of Ambien onto the parking lot. I picked the tablets off the asphalt and wiped them on my jeans, except for one wedged under the tire of a pick-up truck. I let it go, picturing a rancher wondering why some little old man was diddling his Ford F-150.

UNGLUED

Leah called me when I was outside Kearney. She was back in Minnesota and ranted about the people she was working with on one of her Leah & Associates escapades. I was *supportive* because I didn't interrupt her and none of it was any skin off my ass out there in the middle of a hundred thousand acres of corn and soybeans, and I hung up after barely saying a word.

It's downhill to Denver from there, desolate as the moon, and I cranked up my Mazda 3 to ninety miles an hour. My niece Rachel called me when I was passing through Brush, Colorado, a little east of an asteroid. She wanted me to know that Aunt Leah had been flaming me in emails to friends and our extended family members. "She railed against our whole Zuckerman family. I was really angry, Uncle Jeff. It's a terribly sad situation. This illness of hers makes your brain lie to you, and it's nearly impossible to recognize what is and isn't true."

"Any words of wisdom? From someone with bipolar?"

"I'm guessing she's going to fall into another deep depression."

I was glad Rachel contacted me and thanked her for her candor and concern. She was angry at Leah, and I envied her compassion. But I needed to focus on where I was (in the middle of nowhere, testing my courage to drive a hundred miles an hour in my Mazda) and what I was doing (I had no idea).

My divorced friends in Colorado let me crash at their houses for two days and nights so I could get some work done on my laptop and earn some money. I had known them long before their divorce. They seemed to be faring well and, like Roberto and Yolanda and Fender and Laura, they gave me hope that I had come out of all this in one piece.

I heard on the hourly news that day that a severe thunderstorm was ripping through the Twin Cities, and I texted Leah to ask her if she was okay and if there was any damage to our house. She was still my wife and it was still my house and I hoped neither one of them had been injured.

She called me back later and launched into a twelve-minute mono-logue (I timed it) about her grievances and plans and creative initiatives.

"Okay. You didn't ask a single thing about me."

"Fuck you."

Joey spoke to her a while later and had to remind Leah how to have a conversation. She went off on him about how many lies I had been saying about her.

I was in no hurry to return to Minnesota.

A COUPLE OF DAYS LATER I picked up David at the Denver airport and tried to forget about the horror show in Minneapolis. We planned to take a day or two to drive toward Canyonlands National Park in Utah, camp there, then work our way to Bryce Canyon and the north rim of the Grand Canyon and arrive in Phoenix in about a week. I wanted to camp every night, but David said no because there was already snow in the mountains and he was a less adventurous moron than I was.

We stopped at a motel in Grand Junction during a rainstorm and the next day drove through snow in a mountain pass before setting up camp along the Colorado River in the high desert near Moab. That evening David blew off some steam about Leah's nasty email blasts and how she had been mistreating me. As much as I agreed with him, I was plenty torn. She had a medical illness, man! Maybe I had benefitted from reading books about mental illness. Maybe it helped to have gone to so many support group meetings. All of us vented, but you had to get over it and find more positive ways to deal with your loved one's illness.

Which, of course, is easier said than done. I understood David's predicament. Messing up my life was one thing, but Leah had dragged my brother and everyone else into our melodrama. I know that he wanted to slap some sense into me for not letting go of Leah and the madness back home. At one point, with the splendor of Arches National Park in the background, he snapped a picture of me staring at my cell phone and then berated me for being a pathetic chucklehead.

"Actually," I told David, "Leah forgot something on the plane when she came back from LA and she went to the airport lost-and-found to pick it up and left the car in a tow-away zone right in front of the terminal and when she came out a bunch of cops met her with their rifles drawn, but it was okay because she explained it was a sociological experiment and she wanted to see how they'd react to a white woman compared to a black woman and it was all just a big misunderstanding and she says she is going to go for a beer with one of the cops.

"Also, my neighbor is concerned because your sister-in-law left the front door wide open all day again, supposedly to scare off potential burglars, and my neighbor wanted me to know it seemed like Leah had lost her mind."

David apologized, felt embarrassed for scolding me, said he still couldn't comprehend just how bad things were.

"Welcome to my world," I replied.

But he was right. I shut off my phone, and if Leah complained I would tell her there was no cell service in the wilderness, which was often true.

We found a deserted, rustic campground and cooked hot dogs and a can of soup over a campfire. The next morning I heard him stomping around outside his tent because he felt like he had spent the night on Pluto and the closest cup of coffee was fifteen miles away. I should have brought a cookstove, but we were roughing it like the Lone Ranger and Tonto.

We spent hours hiking through Bryce Canyon, bowled over by the reddish-orange hoodoos formed a hundred million years ago, long before any human being named Jeff wondered if a burglar was going to jimmy the latch on the screen door of his house and help himself to his wife's jewelry box, MacBook, and never-used replacement iPad.

Let go of it, man, I told myself.

UNLESS YOU HIKE the trails into the Grand Canyon, you can't really get the scope of its enormity. In my twenties, I trekked a couple times the whole way down from the south rim to the Colorado River, once in a single day despite the warning sign: "Under no circumstances should you attempt to hike from the rim to the river and back in one day!" Forty years later my brother and I rented a room in the lodge at the north rim, where the national park was more desolate and tranquil. We spent our days hiking into the canyon and around the park above. One night around ten o'clock, after David had called it a day, I wandered over to Bright Angel Point with my journal. In the light of my cell phone I wrote, "Leah would have loved it here in the old days. I miss the Twin Cities. I miss my kids. It feels like I'm delaying the inevitable. Stalling, for fifteen months now, trying to love someone and getting nothing in return."

On the edge of the rim of the Grand Canyon the empty blackness was spectacular. "Whoa," I said aloud. "Look at the Milky Way!"

Such a sublime moment. I had so much to be thankful for.

I thanked God that night for all of my good fortune. I was sixty-one years old and had outlived my father. All my bones and joints still worked. Leah and I had two healthy children with good jobs who loved each other and loved us. I had the support of friends. Thanks to Obamacare we had health insurance. I was making a living freelancing on my laptop. Our house was warm in the winter and air-conditioned in the summer, and our mortgage was paid off. We had clean water to drink and plenty to eat. Both our cars worked. We were removed from the suffering of war. In another month Hillary

Clinton was a sure bet to be elected the first female president. My big brother and I were staying at a lodge at the edge of the Grand Canyon. In the darkness I could see the wonders of the universe and touch the mystery of the earth's creation.

"Dear God," I said aloud in the darkness, "couldja please heal my sick wife?"

DAVID NEEDED TO RETURN HOME to Lois and other obligations that did not involve scooping his brother's remains out of the bottom of the Grand Canyon. It's an eight-hour car trip around the north rim of the canyon and on through the Martian desert to Phoenix. As we headed south at Bitter Springs, I had that familiar ache when a vacation is ending and you have to return to the real world, which in my case also involved a manic wife from whom I had run away.

In Flagstaff we pulled off into a restaurant and waited out a thunderstorm. The sky was as dark as my mood. I'd driven halfway across the country and had no better plan than when I left Minneapolis. As much as I loved my brother and Lois, I wasn't gaga about holing up in their home in Phoenix until God knows when. In 1978 I had freeloaded off them for seven weeks until I'd found a job, which in family lore had become the crazy loser uncle, ha-ha, who lived with David and Lois for seven years. Ha-ha-ha.

"Stay as long as you want," David assured me.

So I spent an uncertain month doing freelance work from my brother and sister-in-law's dining room table, cooking meals for them, and playing softball with David in an old-man's morning pickup league in Scottsdale. I had an absentee ballot mailed to me from back home, dubious I would return to Minnesota in time to vote in the general election.

One night Leah called David and talked to him nonstop for forty-eight minutes (he, too, timed it). I wondered if he read *War and Peace* while she was talking—and worried when he would finally have had enough of his little brother's soap opera.

IT HAD BEEN ONE YEAR since David flew to Minnesota to rescue me during Leah's first hospitalization for mania, when the three of us celebrated the Jewish New Year in the psych ward by blessing a bottle of hair conditioner. Now here we were, together again, on Rosh Hashanah—and in ways I was even worse off, a vagabond with an uncertain future.

In the liturgy we read: "On Rosh Hashanah it is inscribed, and on Yom Kippur it is sealed who shall live and who shall die, who by water and who by fire, who by strangling and who by stoning. . . ." The list goes on and on, a poetic dirge of misery and repentance that no Jew I know takes literally but only as a friendly warning to get your shit together.

Nevertheless, after abandoning my sick wife, I had what to fear for the future. I borrowed a pair of my brother's dress shoes and found a guest seat near the back of a Scottsdale synagogue, next to a family who seemed a lot more normal than mine. The mom told me she was a pharmacist, and when I mentioned Leah's illness, she offered a woeful look and said she'd pray for Leah.

Which is what Leah needed. Back in Minnesota, my wife had shown up at our synagogue amped like she was attending a Metallica concert. Ours is a notoriously unpretentious and compassionate Reform Jewish congregation, known for its self-proclaimed "radical hospitality." From what friends were texting me, Leah wore a flannel shirt and jeans to High Holiday services, and someone else asked me if Leah had decided she was a lesbian, which I found hilarious but unnerving. Apparently

Leah and a gentile friend from her support group sat in the front row of the temple and Leah never shut her mouth and made a spectacle of herself. She was telling people I intended to keep driving west for the next few weeks, farther and farther west, like there was a suspension bridge to Japan. Her geographical disorientation and rants left me feeling pitiful and dismayed and more than a teeny bit spiteful. But as usual, I was twirling in mixed emotions. I pictured Leah in that sacred space, burning yet more bridges, emitting chaotic fumes as artlessly as Pepé Le Pew. I hoped our fellow congregants who had known her for a quarter century could see the poor woman was coming undone.

IF I THOUGHT I HAD PROBLEMS, a couple weeks later Joey agreed to play host to his mother for a very long weekend in Portland. Compared to Sarah and me, he was pretty much a perfect human being and had a magical way with his mother. With prudent planning and insight, Joey predicted, Leah's visit would go just fine. He told me he read a pamphlet with advice on how to talk to someone with a mental illness.

"What did the pamphlet say?"

"It said don't try to convince someone he or she has a mental illness."

We'll see, I thought. *There's a little more to it than that*. But I prayed the weekend would go well—even if the upshot was that meant my own imperfections were indeed the *crux* of the problem.

The brutal details of what ensued serve no purpose other than to further grind Leah's face in her madness. In starkest terms, my poor son ended up working with a therapist over the next month, and it took him a couple of years until he was ready to reflect about the visit's low points during a forty-minute phone call to me: a hypomanic spectacle at a Kinko's; an awkward introduction of his new girlfriend, Catherine

("You're such a little *peach!* You're such a little *peach!*" his hyperan-imated mother repeated over and over); an aptly bizarre night spent hiding under the covers at the Timberline Lodge on Mt. Hood where Stanley Kubrick directed the horror movie *The Shining*; a confrontation with a hotel clerk over a room reservation; a commotion in a gift shop with a manager who threatened to call a security guard on Leah; a teddy bear thrown at Joey's head; a few insistent puffs on a joint; and an open beer bottle in his car during the last-minute dash to the airport.

Et cetera. You get the picture.

Yet revisiting Joey's traumatic experience two years later fur-ther solidified several points. His love for his mother never wavered. He learned about his inner strength and intelligence. He experienced the sad, frightening, and astonishing reality of the inner workings of a misfiring human brain. That even Joey couldn't contain Leah's mania erased our delusions that we could have helped her. He reaffirmed his respect for how well I hung in there until I couldn't take it any longer, and he said I had done the right thing when I moved out for a couple months and left Leah on her own.

And he learned he was able to accept, forgive, and move on—not-withstanding that he told me, "Hey, that book you're writing? It'll be the best book I'll never read."

Chapter 22

On the Road Again

Three weeks after Leah's visit to Portland, Joey got the call.
"The hospital contacted me for some reason," Joey texted me,
"not you. Mom was admitted to the psychiatric ward again."
She must have given them Joey's number, not mine.
"Which hospital?"
"HCMC. Are you going back to Minneapolis?"
Healthy Leah was Cautious Leah and would not have wanted me
to drive home like a madman, which was fine with me because I was
in no rush to return to Minnesota to deal with her latest mess. I loaded my car and headed east from Phoenix on U.S. Route 60 through
Snowflake and Show Low and stopped in Springerville for a long
lunch. On a rural highway in western New Mexico I revved my Mazda
to ninety-six miles an hour, still too afraid to break the hundred-mile-
an-hour mark because that would have been reckless. Anyway, what
was the hurry? The staff on the psych ward could deal with Leah better
than I could.

That anger and guilt took an emotional toll on me. I was bush-
whacked by the idea of driving sixteen hundred miles in three days

to rescue Leah after she had treated me like dirt the past few months. And I had too much time to ruminate about the previous weeks' events. Leah, from what I eventually gathered, had been "acting out"—whatever that meant—at her support group. The facilitator called the police, who met Leah at our house and decided she was no threat to herself or anyone else, unlike me, racing home at ninety-six miles an hour in an eight-year-old Mazda 3.

I had no idea what I was supposed to do about any of that, other than thank people for caring deeply and nonjudgmentally about my wife. I felt terrible for everyone, most of all for Leah. From the sounds of things, she was like one of those listless caged tigers in old zoos pacing psychotically in circles before zookeepers provided the animals with fake savannas to prowl at night.

But it was still a zoo, and Leah was still my wife, and she was still caged inside her own mind.

I SPENT THE FIRST NIGHT in Las Vegas, New Mexico. The next morning, a couple hours into my trip toward home, someone named Andrew called me from the county attorney's office and told me the details. Apparently Leah had been unable to sleep the past few days and drove herself to the ER for help. I pictured that scene: my wild-eyed wife trying to con her way into industrial-strength sleeping pills and the staff trying to cajole her into admitting herself into the psych ER sans fireworks. Maybe Leah at long last knew the jig was up and in her own sick way waved a white flag and surrendered.

Andrew assured me Leah would remain hospitalized beyond the seventy-two-hour hold, and he wanted to know when I'd be coming there to see her.

Actually, I told Andrew, I was driving back from Arizona and I thought I was in Oklahoma, which was sort of out of the way, but it was one of only two states I had never been to, the other being Alaska, which was somewhere I'd rather be than Minneapolis, but Peru sounded good, too, because I'd never been there, either, and do you happen to know if there's a Motel 6 in Cuzco?

I spent the next night in Salinas, Kansas, got lost driving the back roads in Iowa, and hit a thunderstorm in Albert Lea, Minnesota. The evening sky was dark green and ominous and I should have found a motel room. But I wanted to sleep in my own bed for the first time in ages. After inhaling a box of grease at KFC, I arrived home a couple hours later with a killer stomachache.

When I entered my house I glanced at the mountain of accumulated mail in the dining room before I headed to the bathroom. I should have taken a long, hot bath, but I was too wired and took a quick shower and inventory of my life. My gums were a bloody mess. My stomach was a wreck. My wife was in a psychiatric ward. I had no plan. I was exhausted.

I prepared a speech for when I would see Leah in the morning. How before I left town she was not being reasonable. How I understood she felt abandoned. How we could get her well only if she let us help her. How I was sorry she had no insight. That the reason she was in the psych ward was *why* I left town, not the *cause* of her being there. How I had stuck by her not in spite of my family of origin but because of that family, and I was done drinking her poison.

How I was so, so sorry she couldn't see how her illness was destroying our family.

I drove to the county hospital Sunday morning, and this time I spotted Leah's car at a parking meter right outside the hospital entrance, again unticketed. Had I been plugging parking meters all these years for nothing?

I knew the drill. I weaved through the maze of hospital hallways, buzzed my way into the outer alcove of the psychiatric ward, deposited my cell phone in a locker, and waited for the *click* as the door to the inner ward was unlocked. I signed the visitor register, and then a nurse led me to the ICU.

And there was my wife. The whole encounter was awkward, two people who had been married for decades, the husband having slithered away six weeks ago, often incommunicado, the wife in the middle of a manic episode, drugged up, and wired like I feared but not enraged. She had told the staff she was an oppressed minority, an African American Jew, because, ultimately, all Jews go back to Egypt three thousand years ago. For the first time in her life she had clipped a yarmulke to her hair to show she was a proud minority. Or something like that.[1] The poor woman was intensely frustrated about the *misunderstanding* that had resulted in her being held in the lock-up unit because she had come to the hospital only because she needed to *sleep*. Leah would have a commitment hearing on Thursday, which she said was *bullshit* because she was getting out at five o'clock that afternoon because she was there *voluntarily*. I don't think Leah understood she had volunteered to stay there until the doctors gave her permission to leave.

I escaped quickly without an ado, saying I would be back the next day. After collecting my belongings from the locker in the safe space I sat on the bench outside the door to the ward, breathing calmly, tap-tapping my thighs like Crystal had taught me.

Monday was Halloween 2016. My buddy Dr. J came over for dinner and beer and allowed me to make amends for shoving that fifty-dollar bill in his face. We gathered kindling, lit a fire out front in my portable

---

[1] There was also a bizarre *tefillin* (phylacteries) incident, but that would be as complicated for me to explain as a Hindu discussing the forty-nine kinds of Marutganas and fifty-six kinds of Visvadevas. And let us say amen.

metal fire bowl, and prepared to hand out candy. Only three groups of kids stopped by. Dr. J and I joked we had so few trick-or-treaters because word was out the Addams family lived in my house.

On Tuesday I returned to the hospital and delivered clean clothes to Leah. She was out of the psych ICU and in the less-restrictive locked ward, which meant either she was improving or the hospital had admitted new patients who were even worse off than she was. She said she was pissed at me for bringing the wrong clothes, but I had thicker skin than a year ago and knew it was just the illness scolding me.

Back at the house I made payments on more than seven thousand dollars in credit card charges Leah had rung up,[2] recycled a few hundred pieces of junk mail, prepared the deck for winter, cleaned up the garage, and readied the snowblower for the inevitable first blast of snow. I ran errands, including a stop at the post office to mail our kids gift packages that Leah had prepared before she was hospitalized. No matter how ill, my wife's heart was rich in love.

And I knew she deeply loved me.

And I loved me, too. I drove to the credit union and withdrew another five hundred bucks from my slush fund. That afternoon I handed the envelope of bills to a stranger named Helmut who was willing to rent me a room in the house he owned, which is where I planned to live until Leah got better or I moved to Scotland or Peru.

---

[2] Spending a fortune is not listed in the *DSM-V* as a criterion of mania per se. But increased activity, grandiosity, and excess pleasurable and risky activity are criteria often manifested in uninhibited credit card charges. According to people in my support group, $7,000 was peanuts compared to what some spouses ring up while manic. Numerous women and men I know rescind their spouses' access to ATM and credit cards and put them on an allowance.

CHAPTER 23

Breakin' Up Is Hard to Do

Leah, improving with the help of Risperdal, an antipsychotic drug used to treat bipolar disorder, was to be released from the hospital on Monday, November 7. In preparation, I spent Sunday night in my new digs, a room in the upper level of a 1920s-era three-bedroom, two-story house in a residential neighborhood in northeast Minneapolis. I had bonus use of the upstairs sunroom as an office, which was dandy because I was working around the clock to earn money to pay all the expenses from the past couple of months. My landlord, Helmut, told me to make myself at home, which was as unlikely as if I'd taken up residence in a mud hut in Malawi.

Helmut was a young guy and single, owned a pet rat I nicknamed Steve Bannon, and had anti-abortion lawn signs in his yard. The presidential election was coming up in a few days, and the last thing I wanted to do was get into any kind of discussion with Helmut about the candidates' positions on abortion or much of anything else.

I sensed I had made the worst decision of my life. I was sixty-two years old with a backache from sleeping on Helmut's taco-shaped mattress in a spare room with a mystery stench, like English Leather mixed with shellac. I was cold all night and uninterested in Helmut and his stance on abortion and I just wanted to be left alone. Steve Bannon creeped me out and I was pretty sure I was allergic to him and I swallowed a couple Benadryl tablets before I went to bed each night.

I hadn't told anyone where I was living. I was determined not to put any of my friends on the spot if Leah contacted them and asked about my whereabouts.

"Why don't you just live here instead?" my buddy Dr. J implored me again and again.

I would have preferred to give Dr. J the five hundred clams instead of this guy Helmut, not that Dr. J would have accepted that much money. Since his divorce, Dr. J had moved into a warm suburban townhome with a fireplace, a refrigerator full of fresh fruit, a comfortable spare bed, a bottle of whiskey, and, above all, friendship.

I told Dr. J that I was a city boy and I liked Helmut's neighborhood, which was just a few miles from my own. I was hardly planning to abandon Leah or my responsibilities as a homeowner. Importantly, no one, including him, had any idea where I was living. Moreover, I explained to Dr. J, Leah needed to understand I wouldn't spend one more night couch surfing while she continued to berate me and deny she was sick.

Above all, I needed to show myself this was real. I would never again allow myself to get run over by my wife's illness.

ON HER NINTH DAY in the psych ward Leah was discharged and I drove to the hospital to fetch her. She was jacked up, but who wouldn't be when it's your first breath of fresh air in more than a week? After I dropped her off at home, I drove back downtown to donate platelets at the American Red Cross. After a week of walking in and out of a hospital, the least I could do was help a cancer patient getting chemo.

Late in the afternoon Leah waited for me at an Indian restaurant near Loring Park. She was eating a bowl of soup when I arrived. I sat down and ordered chicken tikka masala. Leah sounded snotty and had an edge in her voice. "Are you planning to leave me?"

I said, "I just think things have to be different from what they were."

"Well," she snapped, mimicking me, "*I* think things have to be different from the way they were."

I cancelled my order and walked out.

I was done apologizing for my actions and mistakes, a moment of self-satisfaction that lasted only until I walked into my shitty room in the doleful Haus of Helmut. I was still trying to place that doggone smell. Cabbage boiled in Pine-Sol?

Tuesday was Election Day. I worked all afternoon, and that evening at my NAMI support group I was lauded for doing a good job of taking care of myself. Afterward I met my friends Kate and Maureen in a Mexican restaurant to watch the election results. Because my stomach felt like I had the bubonic plague, I stuck to a couple of tortilla chips and a glass of ginger ale. Kate is Buddhist or something like that, and as the exit polls came in she seemed to transmogrify her whereabouts into an ashram in Dharamshala. Maureen is a flammable second-generation Irish American, and by the time the Michigan vote was announced, I waited for her earlobes to combust.

"I fucking *cannot* fucking *believe* this is fucking *happening*," Maureen groaned.

That night, and often since, I have considered how I have maintained my equilibrium. I was living through the cycles of my wife's mental illness and was simply too worn out to get swept away by politics. I know I should be more involved as an advocate for public policy that battles discrimination and supports the needs of the mentally ill and their families. But that night I finally understood the lassitude of half the eligible citizenry who never bother to vote. In our NAMI group someone reminded us to live one day at a time. The more we focus on the long-term ups and downs of the health and welfare of our loved ones, the more we succumb to melancholy, fear, and rage.

Maybe that's just an excuse for my inaction. Maybe it's because at my age it becomes easier to take the long view of the human condition. Maybe it's from staring at the Milky Way at the edge of the Grand Canyon, contemplating whether God had time to sprinkle magic dust on my wife's noggin.

Or maybe I'm just a tired old man.

IT WAS still my house. She was still my wife.

One afternoon when Leah was out I drove over there to try cleaning it up. The yard needed raking. The furnace filter needed to be changed. The place could have used a scrubbing by an entire hotel staff.

A jammed window in the living room wouldn't lock shut for the winter. When Leah got home, I climbed a ladder and used a lever to squeeze the window shut while she twisted hard on the latch.

"You want a steak for dinner?" I asked her.

"Sure. Thanks."

According to my journal, around six-thirty Leah looked at me and said, "I'm afraid I'm getting depressed."

Here we go again, I thought.

A FEW DAYS LATER Leah texted me: "I didn't choose to have a mood disorder."

It was the first time she expressed insight to me. I was still harbored in my room at Helmut's house, determined not to fall back into the grip of her illness. "Well," I wrote in my journal, "I didn't choose to ignore the emergency plan. And I will choose to leave her once and for all if this continues."

It took only two days for Leah to sink into a black depression.

But I stayed put. I told Helmut that I might need to live in his room for at least another month.

"You're a perfect housemate," Helmut said. "You're never here."

In the coming days Leah was in bed nearly full time again, flattened like a gingerbread cookie after months of relentless mania, and now the downer Risperdal. And I was bitter.

From my journal:

NOVEMBER 26, 2016

Jeff will pay Leah's bills. Jeff will figure out money. Jeff will shovel snow and get her flat tire fixed. Jeff will cook dinner. Jeff will get taxes done and clean the house again and not grumble and give and give and give because Jeff does not have a mental illness.

A WEEK LATER Leah brought up the Chauncey Greene Incident again, and my head exploded. "How many times have we gone over it, Leah? Huh? How many times with how many therapists? If you can't get past it, go find yourself a different husband."

God, that felt good.

"I apologize," Leah said.

I was too worn out to celebrate her insight, too knocked around emotionally to think she finally recognized the damage of her illness to herself and those who loved her.

I could no longer pretend that if I did the right thing I could somehow fix Leah. The only choice was living with Leah during her nosedive into depression (if you can call that living) or flush another five hundred bucks down the toilet at Helmut's house, destroy my back, and soon enough start smelling like cabbage soup myself.

So what was the right thing to do?

I left Helmut's house key in an envelope, blew Steve Bannon a kiss, and moved back home and never saw any of them again. The mystery smell lingered in my duffel bag, which I left in the garage over the winter to air out. What a fragrant reminder to be grateful for the blessing of our home and that, if need be, I had the strength to determine my own future, whatever it might hold.

They say that breaking up is hard to do, but I guess it's easier for some men than others.

CHAPTER 24

The Paradox

The second winter's crash was more disturbing than a year earlier. Leah and I were less hopeful that a magic combination of meds would "fix" her. I lost trust in her support network, since her psychologist, psychiatrist, and the mental health system were unable to prevent Leah's months-long manic episode and free fall into depression. The county assigned another case manager, Betty, to stop by the house once a month and theoretically keep an eye on things. Monica had done no good. Why would Betty be any different?

DBT had failed. Our emergency plan had failed. Had prayers helped?

For Leah's sleep hygiene I bought new curtains that blackened our bedroom like a photographer's darkroom. Her physical health deteriorated. She lost twenty pounds over the course of a few months, and her blood pressure readings sunk to 78/52. Dr. Woody prescribed her sodium tabs and kept her on megadoses of Vitamin D, but that was no cure for what ailed Leah. The problem was her maddening, self-reinforcing bipolar depression.

IN GRADUATE SCHOOL I was most attracted to Leah's intelligence—that and her reddish brown curly hair, thick as a rainforest, luxurious, wild, sensual hair that hung two thirds of the way down her back, hair to hold in my fist and lust for and devour, pounds and pounds of the world's best hair.

"I hate my fucking hair," Leah would complain.

It was a pain to take care of all that curly hair, she repeated a thousand times, especially in the winter, when she would need an hour to wash and blow dry it, *which you just don't understand* because a couple inches under the top layer *it might still be wet* and turn into icicles and *I'll get pneumonia* and *die* just so you could enjoy *my fucking hair.*[1]

In her second major depression Leah gave up on her hair. Her entire hygiene went to hell because, she said, she was too weak to shower, that it was too much work to wash her hair, that she was just going to cut it all off. I offered to drive her and her hair over to the salon at the strip mall and have a stylist wash it and I'd buy her an Arby's roast beef sandwich and then she'd feel like dancing the mambo.

"I'm too tired," she said. She'd rather lie there in the dark, unwashed, eyes closed, ears plugged, and if you're wondering what bipolar depression looks like, there you go.

One winter morning Leah asked me to drive her to Great Clips to cut off all her hair once and for all and let it go gray and be done with it.

It was her hair, and we had had a good ride, her hair and me.

---

[1] Over the course of our entire marriage, Leah has seen me without a beard for only three weeks because, she says, I have no chin. In principle, it seems like if she planned to cut off all her hair I should be allowed to shave off my beard. But what principle that is, I don't know, especially because I have been too lazy to shave since freshman year in college and have no desire to do so now.

At the salon I tried distracting myself in the waiting area by reading a two-year-old *Sports Illustrated*, but I could not stop watching the massacre. The stylist stopped when Leah's hair was shoulder length. I could see that Leah kept telling her to make it shorter, shorter. A few minutes later, Leah looked like her older peers who had come to grips with aging and felt "refreshed" with short hair. But she wanted more off. More, until Leah's hair looked like a crew cut I'd gotten as a little kid.

When the hair-ectomy was finally done, I asked Leah how she liked it because that's what the husband is supposed to do.

"I don't know," she said. That was all Depressed Leah ever said. "I don't know."

It was just hair, wasn't it? It would grow back. It wasn't her breast or ovaries or uterus, and comparing a stupid haircut to a life-changing illness was pathetic of me.

And yet. That haircut was the physical manifestation of Leah's loss of identity. She was now a graying, flat-topped shell of her former self, mired in bipolar depression, unable to bathe herself. She had no job, no hobbies, no definition of who she was.

Or maybe I was projecting all that and it was all about me and my hunger for her hair.

But I don't think so. I loved and married Leah, not her hair. She was the one suffering in the dark, unable to feel. Unable to think. Unable to laugh, or cry, or do anything but lie in bed and whittle away the days and nights of her life.

In ancient Greek mythology there's the paradox of the ship of Theseus. Over many years Theseus won many naval battles. Old planks on his ship would decay and be replaced by new ones, and then, later on, additional planks, and then more, until all of the original planks had been replenished. Was it still the same ship?

With Leah's personality so deadened and now her distinguishing hair so vastly altered, was she still Leah?

Yes, I assured myself.

Alas. Devoid of a career, friends, purpose, hope, and her hair, Leah herself was much less certain.

ONE WEEK before Leah had landed in the hospital during her second manic episode, Dr. Carpenter left her position at the clinic (Manic Leah: "She was caught by ICE and deported"). It took two months for Leah and me to find a new psychiatrist covered by our insurance, a Dr. F, reportedly the smartest chemist in town.

Unlike when she was manic, Leah implored me to accompany her for her initial appointment. "My brain is broken," she kept saying. She said she doubted she could find the clinic on her own (even after we'd been there a half-dozen times), and she was grateful for my driving her and taking notes so we would remember what this Dr. F told her.

"Of course I'll drive you," I said. She had completely forgotten the fights from the summer.

When Dr. F popped into the waiting room, I liked his youthful energy.

"Leah?" he asked. "Come o-o-o-o-n back!"

We hit the jackpot. We got the announcer from *The Price Is Right*.

Although this young doctor may have been affable in the waiting room, in contrast to Dr. Carpenter, Dr. F had the interpersonal skills of a cement block. (About a year later a guy named Henry in my support group ranted about his husband's psychiatrist, whom they called Dr. Frankenstein, and I figured out from his description he was the same guy.)

During that first appointment Dr. F rattled off a list of a few dozen medications, asking Leah which ones she had taken, checking the box on his electronic record. For God's sake, the woman could barely remember how to tie her shoes, let alone recall the generic names of all her past meds. We had dealt with psychiatrists from three different health systems during the past two years and naively thought someone else was keeping track of all this stuff. How could we remember what meds she had taken?

Each time we went to the clinic Dr. F's manner further infuriated me. "Leah? Come o-o-o-o-n back!" he'd holler into the waiting room, and once inside his office he would stare at his computer monitor, read through the list of symptoms dispassionately like he was reciting the ingredients of a pot of chili, and robotically click Leah's answer on the online spreadsheet.

Leah was resigned to following his recommendations. What choice did she have? He was supposedly the smartest guy in town. We met with him every three or four weeks, and each session the doctor would stare at his computer monitor, reading off the same bulleted list of symptoms, checking off boxes on his patient inventory with the bored demeanor of a cashier at Dunkin' Donuts.

"Are you feeling sad?"

"No. I'm depressed."

"How often do you feel sad? Once a day? Once a week? Once a month?"

"I'm not sad. I'm depressed."

"Do you feel like hurting yourself or killing yourself?"

"Occasionally."

"How often? Once a day? Once a week? Once a month?"

"Once a month."

"Cream or sugar in your coffee?"

He didn't say that, but he seemed so disengaged he may just as well have been fixing himself a sandwich.

Ten minutes of rote interrogation later, Dr. F banged a rubber stamp on Leah's paperwork and hustled us out the door. Leah left confused and I left rankled and more hopeless than when we had arrived. We donned our coats and heard Dr. F holler the next patient's name. "Come o-o-o-o-n back!"

It went on like that with Dr. Frankenstein for seventeen months. The meds he prescribed appeared to forestall another manic episode, but I was incensed by his seeming indifference to Leah's leaden comportment and despair. He occasionally admonished her for not exercising, for not getting out of the house. Glaring at me instead of Leah he would snicker, "Hey, I can't help you if you don't follow through on your end." (Which was true, but come on. Did he have to be such a jagoff about it?)

And then, switching his own mental gear shift, he'd shout gregariously, "I'll see you again in three weeks!" and bang his rubber stamp on that appointment's paperwork.

NEITHER LEAH NOR I thought it was safe for her to drive, so every couple of weeks I took her to see her psychologist, Dr. Melnick.[2] I was bitter about flushing more dough down the toilet for what I thought were such inconsequential appointments. Afterward I would ask Leah how it went and she would mumble, "I don't know."

Leah and her medical team were unable to help her resolve a

---

[2] One night a guy in my support group explained the interplay between psychiatric and psychological therapies for those with a mental illness: "It's like two oars paddling a boat," he said. "One oar is the meds, and the other is counseling. You need to row with both paddles to get anywhere. If you use only one oar, you'll end up going in circles." That might be bullshit, but it made more sense to me than anything else I heard or read.

central paradox of living with depression: to get out of bed, Leah had to get better, but to get better, she had to get out of bed.

Stated more broadly, how can we do that which we cannot do but that which we must do?

I've heard that enigma stated dozens of times. I had heard my whole life that instead of wallowing around in bed all day feeling sorry for yourself, you should get up and do something. Do anything. Move your bones around. Go for a walk around the block. Go to a movie. Take out the garbage. Something. Anything.

It makes so much sense. It sounds so easy. Yet for people who are clinically depressed, it's as useless as telling a paraplegic to hop out of her wheelchair and dance the tango.

And over time, for many of us living with someone who is clinically depressed, our reserve of patience eventually runs dry.

But as long as Leah kept trying, I hung in there. We heard about a twice-a-week hospital outpatient program similar to the therapy and classes she attended after her first hospital visit but specially designed for patients aged fifty-five years and older. I schlepped Leah there for four weeks until the therapist said it was doing no good. I then lost a yearlong fight over coverage with the insurance company, and we ended up blowing six thousand dollars for nothing.

She had a CT scan to test for Lyme disease. The results were negative.

She did a DNA swab to see which meds had the best chance of helping her or worst chance of not working or I don't know what the purpose was except that the retail price was five hundred bucks and as far as I could tell nothing changed and once again the neuroscience of all this seemed as random as a weather forecast in the *Farmer's Almanac*.

She tried DBT a second time to no avail, but at least her insurance covered it.

She sought a second opinion at the Mayo Clinic in Rochester, another nine-hundred-dollar out-of-pocket gamble. Dr. F followed the Mayo doctor's med adjustment. Nothing changed.

"What about transcranial magnetic stimulation?" I asked.

TMS is more or less what it sounds like: magnetic fields kick-starting your brain out of depression. It's noninvasive but involves daily hospital appointments for a month, and Leah and I had been told it can lead to a manic episode. Maybe there was a 2 percent chance of that, maybe 50 percent. Maybe it depended on the position of the fourteen moons of Neptune relative to the price of a dozen eggs in Sardinia.

"TMS is not a recommended treatment for patients with bipolar disorder," Dr. F answered passively.

"What about electroconvulsive therapy?" I asked him. Our niece Rachel had suggested it.

"ECT has been shown to be an efficacious treatment in some instances of bipolar depression," Dr. F answered. Translated into human: Sure, try it and see what happens.

SO IT HAD COME DOWN to electroshock therapy. Dr. Melnick called ECT "barbaric," and it sounded that way: you undergo general anesthesia and have your head wired to a machine that sends electrical juice into your brain, which, in turn, induces a seizure, changing your brain chemistry (no one knows exactly how). Over a series of ten or more appointments the procedure can improve your mood. I pictured a mad scientist's lab in a 1950s movie, a lightning bolt of electricity passing through Leah's skull, a singed scalp, and the overall effect of a lobotomy.

Not so, we were told.[3]

Leah's experience with ECT—and mine—was frightening and comical and ultimately futile. We met with the hospital psychiatrist, a Suzanne Somers clone, for an evaluation one week ahead of time and answers to our concerns. I had concerns, all right, including what's up with all the gaudy makeup around your eyes? But Dr. Somers was confident in the efficacy of ECT, or at least there was little risk of long-term damage.

In desperation, twenty pounds underweight, with a blood pressure of 73/50, and glued to her bed all day, Leah consented to the treatment.

The ECT clinic had its own little waiting room with a half-dozen patients, their designated drivers, and a trio of overworked staff members, all of whom were sympathetic and frantic. They managed the human assembly line and apologized for the disorder and the unwieldy blood pressure machine they dragged through the crowded lobby. While one patient was getting an IV, another was wheeled inside to get knocked out by the anesthesiologist, another was getting zapped by a doctor, another was coming to in the recovery room, and so on, an amusement park ride into the voltaic funhouse. Leah's appointments were scheduled for ten o'clock in the morning, which I know because just as my sweetie-pie was getting a jolt of electricity to her noggin, Drew Carey was airing in the waiting room. Contestants dressed as giraffes and parsnips were guessing the price of a patio grill, and I sat there wondering who decided who is crazy in this world.

---

[3]   For starters, see "ECT, TMS and Other Brain Stimulation Therapies." To learn more, see NAMI, https://www.nami.org/Learn-More/Treatment/ECT-TMS-and-Other-Brain-Stimulation-Therapies and "What Is Electroconvulsive Therapy (ECT)?" Patients & Families, American Psychiatric Association, https://www.psychiatry.org/patients-families/ect. You'll find other websites with evidence and anecdotes steering you away from these treatments.

Nearly vegetative on the way home from the first treatment, Leah recovered quickly and by that afternoon was talking about attending a Minnesota Twins game. "Maybe we can ride bikes to Target Field," she said.

I prematurely emailed friends and relatives my happiness about ECT. Alas, we never biked to a ballgame or even attended one. Leah spent the next day in bed and barely ate a thing.

Three weeks later, after seven more ECT treatments, unilateral and bilateral, Leah's mood had not improved, and the staff threw in the ol' electrodes. We had been warned about memory loss, and that was Leah's experience, particularly in the short term—even months later, to some extent. But over the long haul most of her memory returned, and we laughed recently about the *Price Is Right* blaring when she woke up from electro-shock treatment. Whether or not ECT is barbaric, or whether any specific patient should try it, someone else can decide. It just didn't help Leah.

CHAPTER 25

Any Way the Wind Blows

Back in that old neighborhood of mine in Pittsburgh, where I'd stopped during my sentimental journey just as Leah was becoming undone, lived a most peculiar man.

Mr. Prentice lived two doors up the street from our house. He was a bit older and taller than all of our dads, silver-haired and handsome. No one knew his first name or anything else about him. No one ever talked to him. Supposedly he worked at a parking lot downtown, but a few older kids claimed he had a pet alligator. All of us, even our dads, were afraid of him.

There were no little Prentices, but you would occasionally see Mrs. Prentice. She was six or seven feet tall, with a mass of blond hair flying all over the place, and she scared the bejeebers out of us. Sometimes we'd see Mrs. Prentice floating down the street like an apparition, or in her front yard in her pink bathrobe, leering, scrutinizing the street as if she were waiting for a bus or a werewolf. I watched Mrs. Prentice stand by the front curb and water the street with a garden hose, like she was growing pansies in the concrete or whatever she thought she was doing.

One spring Mr. Prentice planted about a thousand balsam fir trees all around his backyard, a couple dozen rows of sweet corn and squash, and who knows what else. He dug up a few hundred jagger bushes in the woods and transplanted them all around. Maybe he wanted to impede the deer we never saw, but more likely he just wanted to keep the kids out of his yard when one of us hit a Wiffle ball over there.

Three times we counted the men in white lab coats corralling poor Mrs. Prentice. She would disappear for weeks at a time, and the only sign of life there was Mr. Prentice, whom we would spy on, tilling his little backyard farm. By the end of summer he had rows of corn much taller than we were, surrounded by brambles loaded with thorns and blackberries we dared not touch. Every year that border of trees and jaggers grew thicker and thicker until you'd need a machete to hack your way through it. By the time we went to college there might have been twenty or thirty Wiffle balls in his yard.

Our parents aged and moved away, as did we. I don't recall Mr. Prentice's house ever being put up for sale. I know that not one of us said goodbye to him or his wife.

In June 2017, two years into Leah's illness, the raspberries flowered first in my garden, and then the tomatoes and the zucchinis.

And I was exhausted. I was overwhelmed by my responsibilities, embittered from caregiving and *being supportive*, and deadened by Leah's lethargy and the contagion of her depression. Some days she barely talked, and the silence was unnerving and soul-crushing. I was mad at Leah, mad at her psychologist, mad at Dr. Frankenstein, mad at bipolar disorder, and mad at the world.

In July, when I picked the first raspberries of the summer, I recited the ancient Hebrew prayer in gratitude for the fruit of the earth.

As far as I know, no one heard Mr. Prentice's prayers.

I hoped that God was listening to mine.

THAT SUMMER I played softball with the Loons, joined a tennis club, and rode my bike around town, building up to my annual autumn ride in which I try to bike my age in kilometers. I was in good shape, but that September day I was running on fumes at 59 kilometers. With only three kilometers to go, it became a psychological rather than physical struggle.

"I think I can, I think I can," I said aloud to myself, and when I made it to 62 kilometers, I got off my bike and did a celebratory jig out on the trail.

When I got home and told Leah, she said admiringly, "It's so good that you can do that."

"Those last two miles were sheer willpower," I replied—and in an instant, two years of anger and frustration with her and her mood disorder boiled over. "Tell me when you're going to do what your doctors are telling you to do! Are you just going to stay in bed under the comforter all day? I for one can't let life pass me by!"

"You're acting like I want to be this way!" Leah snarled back, defeated, like an old dog who'd been swatted by a newspaper.

What a phenomenal jerk I was. She had a medical illness. Without fail she took her medication. For nearly a year she had not complained about me. She thanked me for every little thing I was doing for her. She was suffering in a sea of sadness, her entire being bulldozed by a psychological battering ram over which she had no control.

Over which she has no control, I repeated to myself. *Have you learned nothing the past two years?*

The next day I bought her a bouquet of alstroemerias, the variety of flowers she chose for her wedding bouquet, and I set them out in a vase on our dining room table.

"I wish I could enjoy them," Leah murmured, sunken in anhedonia.

"Oh, Leah. I am so, so sorry."

I truly was. If those flowers didn't make her feel any better, at least they liberated me of my anger and took a chunk out of my guilt.

She never went a day without telling me how much she loved me.

IN OCTOBER 2017 I noticed Leah's mood finally beginning to improve a little. Maybe it was Dr. F's med tweaks, or maybe her sessions with her psychologist. We started going to the movies, to restaurants, for walks by Cedar Lake. She no longer lay in bed during the day; instead, she spent her afternoons in the living room, reading the news on her cell phone. She saw her doctors. We played Scrabble a few times a week. She took her pills. She went to bed on time each night. Unlike some depressed people, she did the laundry. She emptied the dishwasher. She encouraged me to do what I needed to do to live my life.

Those were victories, according to the people I trusted.

"Hey, at least she's doing the dishes," my support group friend Henry said. "I tell Steven, 'Listen, Steven, I'm not asking you to landscape the yard. I'm asking you to *mow one blade of grass.*'"

"Yeah, well, Leah needs to spend time with other people," I muttered.

I tried a home health aid agency for caregivers and found a young woman to do light housework and take walks with Leah. I needed the help, but paradoxically it felt like I'd reached rock bottom. I was hiring someone to be my wife's companion.

WE FOUND another marriage counselor, and right up front I put Leah's mental illness on the table. Miriam was the first therapist who got it. She was our age and a straight talker and said the chitter-chatter about communication problems was all well and good, but the problem in our marriage was Leah's bipolar disorder.

See? I wanted to say to Leah. *See?*

We both respected Miriam's intelligence and candor. When she occasionally nailed me for being dishonest and uncommunicative, I sat there and took it on the chin.

"All right," I said during one session. "You want me to be honest about my feelings? I feel like I can no longer trust Leah."

"And why is that?"

"Because she lied about how she was feeling when she was manic and lied to me about what her doctors were telling her."

I could see the hurt on Leah's face, but I had resolved to quit playing games and to finally be honest.

"How does that make you feel when you hear that from Jeff, Leah?"

"I don't know. Sad, I guess."

I closed my eyes and shook my head. I was shutting down again, blockading Leah's misery and brain fog behind my own emotional wall.

"Jeff, what are you feeling?"

"This *feels* pointless," I said.

"Well, that's on you, Jeff," Miriam said. "It might be painful to Leah, but you both need to be honest with each other. That's the only way you'll rebuild trust."

At my support group I announced we finally found the world's greatest marriage counselor. "What's her name?" someone asked me.

"No way," I said. "It's hard enough to get an appointment as it is."

In January 2018, for a birthday present and in gratitude for all my brother had done for me the past sixty-plus years, I invited David to accompany me on a vacation in mid-May. Having driven across the Oklahoma panhandle on my way back to Minnesota, I had only one state left to visit: Alaska.

"What about Leah?" David said.

"I bought flight insurance. You know what? If we can't go, we can't go."

I kept working and saving money, and in February Leah was well enough to take a trip with me to Florida, where we relaxed for a few days on a Gulf Coast beach.

In March 2018 Leah started volunteering once a week at a Minneapolis elementary school. One day she even met her friend Jill for coffee.

I made plans for my trip to Alaska with David, confident Leah could handle my absence for a week. I told David that at long last she was doing better.

ONE EVENING my support group buddy Jack Lemmon said he'd thrown in the towel.

"Every time we meet we say that we will never give up hope. Well," he said icily, "I have. I've lost all hope my wife will ever get better."

Oh, Jack, I thought sadly. "You know, man, it's not just about giving up hope for our loved ones. We can't give up hope in ourselves!"

I loved what I said that night. I really believed it. I'd ridden up and down the mental illness roller-coaster for almost three years, and at least I had learned something.

Yet despite my encouragement for others, in April 2018 I finally burned out, too, and ranted at our next marriage counseling session.

"I'm *feeling* fed up with Leah's bipolar disorder and her anhedonia," I barked to Miriam. "I'm *feeling* angry because I can't help Leah or help myself. I'm *feeling* sad because Leah is so depressed. I'm fed up with Leah's semimonthly appointments with Dr. F asking her if she's sad and Leah saying no, she's depressed, and him asking if Leah feels like hurting herself or killing herself and Leah answering yes, and him saying how often and her answering 'once a month' and him asking whether she wants any goddamn onion rings or French fries with her order."

I guess I expressed my *feelings,* which is something else I learned to do since Leah got sick.

"Caretaker burnout is a real thing," Miriam said. "It sounds like you need a vacation."

"I'm supposed to go to Alaska in mid-May."

"Well, that's a few weeks away. Where could you go for a few days in the meantime?"

"I'd like to go to New York to visit my daughter and see my friend on the Jersey shore."

"Leah, how do you feel about Jeff going to visit his friend and Sarah for a few days?"

Leah nodded her head.

"Jeff, are you satisfied with Leah's answer?"

"It would help if Leah actually said yes."

"Yes. I said you should go."

So I did. On the first Tuesday in May I flew east for a quick trip that would get me back to town by Friday evening to lead my support group. I spent that first evening and Wednesday with Michael. We hung around the beach and laughed like nitwits. On Thursday afternoon I rode a train into Manhattan and met Sarah for happy hour after work. She was a millennial techie in a job I didn't understand, and my all-grown-up daughter glimmered as she walked toward me in her black A-line work dress. Smiling when I saw her, I marveled at the woman Leah and I had created and raised and who had found her own way into the world.

About a half-hour later Sarah and I met Seth for dinner in a noisy midtown restaurant for an extraordinary moment of healing.

"Hey, so, guess what, Daddy?"

I gave Sarah a look.

"Daddy, I'm pregnant—"

"*I'm going to be a grandfather!*" I howled, and the two of them laughed and hid behind their menus.

Sarah said she had already told Leah, who texted Sarah right then and told her to call. My head was spinning, astonished by the joy of impending grandfatherhood. I was happy—joyful for myself and Leah, elated for Sarah and Seth, even grudgingly delighted to buy them each a New York dinner.

That night, back at their apartment, I tried calling Leah, but there was no answer. She must have gone to bed already.

Rats. I couldn't even share this joyous moment with her.

THE NEXT MORNING I took the train from Penn Station to Newark International. It had been three years since I dropped off Leah there curbside, just as the first inklings of her mental illness were jabbing my gut, before her metamorphic trip to Tunisia, before *the Chauncey Greene Incident* and the *crux of the issue* and *words mattering* and *I statements* and cops and two summers of madness and two winters of melancholy.

I hadn't yet talked to Leah about Sarah's news and called home.

No answer.

Oh, brother, I thought. On a bad day Leah would plug her ears and lie in bed all day in the dark. In my absence was Future Grandma Leah again shutting out the world?

In only two weeks I was supposed to meet David in Anchorage for a once-in-a-lifetime adventure. How would Leah manage without me?

When the plane landed in Minneapolis that afternoon, I once again tried calling Leah's phone. There was no answer, and then I called her again. I called her again, and then on the light rail to downtown I called her cell phone and then the house phone. I called again. Finally, when I called once again, Leah picked up the phone. "I was resting," she said, almost inaudibly, and the kerosene in my colon swirled.

I hurried off the train and hailed a cab and ten minutes later I hustled into the house.

"Leah?" I called, running up the stairs to our bedroom.

Silence.

"Leah?"

The door was shut and I burst in. The curtains were drawn, and Leah was in bed, blanketed and immovable in the blackness in which she had lain defeated all winter. I jostled her and she didn't move. I shook her. Nothing. I shook her again, and shook her again.

I shook her again.

Finally her foot wiggled, and I swallowed, feeling the fear dripping down my throat. "Leah," I said, leaning over to her ear. "Leah! *Leah!* Did you try killing yourself?"

"Yes," she whispered.

"Leah," I repeated, in disbelief. "*Did you try killing yourself?*"

Man plans, and God laughs. That God of ours has a strange sense of humor.

CHAPTER 26

Both Sides, Now

I guess a more honest and thorough memoirist would attach a Go-Pro to his head and show the whole truth and nothing but the truth by live-streaming his spouse's suicide attempt and the aftermath.

I guess out of consideration to my family, I'm not the most honest and thorough memoirist you'll ever read.

A lot of it is a blur to me; the rest is a painfully profound memory that I suspect will take years to fully process. Leah was alive. The empty pill bottles were on the nightside table. I didn't want to wait for an ambulance; instead, I somehow got her out of bed and half-carried her through the house. The hospital is only about fifteen minutes away—that afternoon, probably eight minutes. In the emergency room the doctors did some tests and determined she had done no damage to her vital organs. From there she was wheeled into the psychiatric ER for an evaluation.

"There's no place like home," I sighed aloud, once again in the ER lobby.

Screw it, I thought. *She's in good hands. She's not going to die.* I had come home from New York on Friday only so I could facilitate my support group that evening.

"I have a NAMI meeting to attend tonight," I said.

"Go," the nurses told me. "She'll be okay here."

WHAT I REMEMBER:

Rage. What a stupid, irresponsible, chicken-shit thing for Leah to have pulled.

Vindictiveness. Why had her egomaniacal butthead psychiatrist so robotically ignored her answers about her suicidal thoughts, and what had her psychologist done to prevent it?

Conceit. Super-Husband Action Figure Jeffrey had saved Leah's life.

Chuckling. A caustic, exhausted, relieved, and astonished snicker. One more shitstorm on my shoulders.

Despair. How completely hopeless Leah had been. Why hadn't she said anything to me or anyone else?

Guilt. How dare I laugh sanctimoniously, self-pityingly, angrily, like it was all about me. I was the moron who left her alone for three days.

Crying. How profoundly sad that Leah and I could not celebrate Sarah and Seth's news about our future grandchild. (And, to my credit as a loving human being, I still cry as I write about it.)

Dread. What do I tell Sarah and Joey?

And hunger. How could I be thinking of food at a time like that? I guess because I hadn't eaten since before I left for the airport in Newark. On the way to my support group I stopped at a gas station and bought a bag of potato chips and a 32-ounce Sprite. Maybe I would give myself a coronary and end up in the same hospital as Leah.

Normally the facilitator at a NAMI meeting checks in first with an update about the experiences of the past few weeks. Out of consideration, that night I spoke last. I knew that hearing a participant say he had just dropped his wife at the ER after she tried ending her life is a tough act to follow.

The group members let me blow off steam. They smiled. They passed me a box of tissues.

They suggested I needed to be honest with Sarah and Joey and tell them what their mom had done. They stayed after the two-hour meeting. They told me not to blame myself, and they said they'd be thinking about me.

The next day I called our kids. "Your mother had a setback," I said. "She's in the hospital."

"Wait, *what?*" Joey exclaimed. "How could that have happened?"

"She has bipolar depression. You know, Joey. It's like she has a mental illness or something."

I didn't tell them the rest . . . at least not yet.

I waited until Sunday to call my rabbi. She had visited Leah in the hospital the previous year, had suffered through depression herself before switching careers and entering rabbinical school more than a decade earlier. When I asked my rabbi for something—anything—to hold on to, she encouraged me to read the Book of Lamentations.

> From above He has hurled fire into my bones, and it broke them; He has spread a net for my feet, He has turned me back, He has made me desolate [and] faint all day long. . . . Behold, O Lord, for I am in distress, my innards burn, my heart is turned within me, for I have grievously rebelled; in the street the sword bereaves, in the house it is like death. (Lamentations 1:13, 20)

Okay, enough of all that.

I decided to write my own book of lamentations instead.

IT WAS LEAH'S FOURTH ADMISSION to a locked psychiatric ward in less than three years. We knew the drill. The days
were filled with blood pressure checks, meals, group activities, talks
with the doctors, medication changes,[1] and the hubbub of a mental
health unit in a large county hospital. The TV ran constantly—most
often sci-fi and reality shows about drug offenders. I visited Leah at
lunchtime every day, sometimes in the evening as well. We held hands
and watched the commotion around us, bemused by the odd behaviors of her fellow patients, saddened by the lonely spectacle of so few
patients receiving visitors.

The nurses, mental health workers, and hospital psychiatrists were
top-notch: overworked, caring, and smart. They had faith in Leah and
hope for me. The social worker, a woman named Lily, was heroic in her
advocacy for Leah's well-being, her reassurance that Leah would recov-
er, and her support for Leah's distraught husband.

I told Lily about my travel plans to Alaska later in the month.

"That sounds fantastic! You should go."

"What if she's released while I'm gone?" I said, uncertain how Leah
would care for herself.

"It won't be anytime soon. And if she's discharged when you're out
of town, there's an unlocked step-down facility where she can stay until
you get back."

"Leah, how do you feel about that?"

---

[1] That week, for the first time, Leah was prescribed lithium, one of the oldest
pharmaceutical treatments for mental illness. The well-known psychiatrist Kay
Redfield Jamison, author of the best memoir I have read about living with bipolar
disorder, described lithium as her own life-saving drug. The initial dosage seemed
to recharge Leah's batteries, but by the time she titrated to a therapeutic dosage,
she was walking and talking in slow motion, her mind decelerating to a crawl, and
she was taken off the medication.

"I don't know. I guess you and David should go to Alaska and enjoy yourselves."

I couldn't read her face. "Leah, dear. I can never tell what you're
really thinking."

"*Go to Alaska*, Jeff," Lily ordered me. "You have *got* to take care of
yourself."

So I went.

MY BROTHER DAVID was with me in my first state, Pennsylvania, the day I was born, and now, sixty-three years later, he was with
me in my fiftieth state. We roomed together in low-end inns and ate
supermarket food on the cheap. We hiked through mud and snow on
wilderness trails. We laughed at ourselves, two old men slip-sliding our
way across snowy mountain streams, and we watched in silence as bald
eagles soared along the shore of the Cook Inlet. We saw moose and car-
ibou and, from our rickety tour bus in Denali National Park, watched a
mother grizzly bear and her yearling amble along a hillside.

David and I at a lookout on the Russian River in Alaska.
I'm the one on the right who looks like he's carrying a
baby kangaroo in the pouch of his rain poncho.

David kept thanking me for footing the bill, and I kept thanking him for being there for me my whole life, especially the previous three years.

"By the way," he said to me, "how's that book you're writing going?"

"Yes, the book. So I've been talking to this friend of mine, Jim. He's a doctor, about your age. He and his wife had this terrific marriage. She was great. Smart and funny. She got breast cancer, fought it for four years before she finally died last spring. Jim was devastated. It was so hard for him to watch his wife die. The only woman he'd ever been with. Forty-two years!

"You know what Jim said to me? He said what I'm going through is worse than what he'd been through. I said no one should compare tragedy and heartbreak, and Jim said, 'At least my story had an ending.' This book I've been writing is supposed to have a happy ending, David. But it's not happy, and I guess it never ends."

THREE WEEKS AFTER LEAH'S ADMISSION to the hospital for her suicide attempt, Sarah flew home to Minneapolis from New York City and assisted with her mother's discharge. Joey came home from Portland on a Friday night red-eye, and I arrived from Anchorage on Sunday morning at dawn. I walked in the front door, anxious about Leah's mood. I was wired to hug my kids, but they were still asleep, still unaware that Leah had attempted to take her own life.

After breakfast, Leah and I called a family meeting in the living room for the first time in a decade.

"Please put away your phones," she said calmly. "I have something to tell you."

She and I held hands on the couch; our kids sat across from us in a pair of overstuffed chairs, wondering what was up.

Leah cut to the chase. "I was hospitalized because I tried to kill myself."

Sarah, thirty years old. Pregnant. Watery. Stone faced. Stone silent.

Joey, twenty-seven, sensitive like his old man. Gasping, wailing "*No! No!*" and burying his face in his hands. He arose from his chair, lost. I watched him stagger and collapse on Sarah's chair, plunging his head into his big sister's chest. Heard him hyperventilate, watched him hide his face in his hands, his body burrowed in Sarah's embrace. Watched him bury the pain of the endless nightmare of his mother's abysmal descent. Sarah cradled Joey tenderly, gently massaged his shoulders, rubbed his head and his arms, and wiped her own eyes. I watched the tender humanity of two siblings, and I tumbled into the deepest recesses of their hearts, into their grief and their resilience and their love.

Inside my pregnant daughter, a spark of life.

Inside Leah, I knew not what. I strained to see a single tear or a strand of a smile beneath the languid eyes of my love of thirty-three years.

Behold, the Winter Is Past

CHAPTER 27

Hurry, to the Hills of Spices

Actually, for a book without a happy ending, here's a pretty good one.

The following month, Leah began seeing a new psychiatrist—coincidentally, the same Dr. Patek who treated Leah during her first hospitalization. Dr. Patek was working now for a private mental health provider, and her warmth and compassion contrasted sharply with Leah's jaded memory of their last encounter in the psych ward, not to mention the cyborg Dr. Frankenstein she'd been seeing the past eighteen months. Under Dr. Patek's care, Leah's mood stabilized into a less extreme but still stubborn depression over the remainder of the year. Dr. Melnick, Leah's psychologist, retired. After meeting her replacement, I was optimistic this new therapist could help manage Leah's illness in a more productive way.

Confident that Leah could handle my absence, in April 2019 I finally took that trip to Peru I'd been yapping about the past four years. My friends Emma and Shelley organized the tour through a travel agency with ten other acquaintances from the Twin Cities. With the blessing of Leah's doctors and caseworker, and with a promise of daily check-ins via FaceTime, I spent two weeks touring the Sacred Valley of the Incas and Lake Titicaca, tending to some sort of half-assed spiritual reckoning and busting my lungs hiking at 13,000 feet above sea level.

Our guide, a middle-aged Peruvian named Salvador, was a charming and eloquent historian and anthropologist who for two weeks proudly and playfully revealed the commingling of his family's Incan and Catholic spiritual beliefs.

"Check out my family pictures," he said to me, pulling out his iPhone at a hotel bar in Puno. He was drinking pisco sours and I was drinking coca tea to battle altitude sickness after Shelley destroyed me in a ping-pong match two miles above sea level. "Right there, where I'm pointing. Those are my mother's parents."

He laughed while I stared at the photo of his grandparents' skulls adorning a shelf in his mother's home, a custom that honors the deceased family members and is said to protect the household from evil spirits.

He was that kind of guide, and it was that kind of tour.

Which was how I ended up one morning in an open-air shelter under a thatched roof in a pasture high in the Andes Mountains. Seated in a semicircle, our group was taking part in an Incan *challa* ceremony, a rite of spiritual cleansing and gratitude to Pachamama, or Mother

Earth, and a prayer to the *apu* mountain gods to heal ourselves and our loved ones.

The Incan *paqo*, or shaman, who led the ceremony was named Nicacio. He was forty-six years old, but with his ruddy, pockmarked face he looked much older. Atop his head he wore a colorful woolen *chullo*, its strands dangling below the ear flaps and resting on his striped poncho. He spoke no English, but with his mild manner he presented an aura of serenity and perhaps bemusement in the presence of our group of gaping gringos.

The paqo, Salvador explained, was building an altar of offerings—grains, herbs, coca leaves, and the like. The coca leaf, we learned, is a sacred plant in Incan culture, offered to Pachamama in gratitude for a bountiful harvest, connecting the gods' world, the middle world in which we live, and the dark world, as well as birth, marriage, and death.

Sure, why not? If from a continent away this gentle-mannered paqo could cure my wife's dark world—and, for good measure, save the planet from global warming—the least I could do was lock away my North American skepticism for an hour.

I was mesmerized. There was something about Nicacio. His campy earnestness. The sanctity of the traditions. The morning quiet and the misty Andean rain. Grinning as he began the ceremony, Nicacio pulled from his medicine bag a couple dozen offerings wrapped in individual sheets of newspaper, an odd assortment of more than a dozen herbs and spices. Sage, Salvador explained, for cleansing the negative energies. Retama flowers for protection. Different varieties of quinoa and corn, fava beans, more flowers, dried fetal alpaca powder (beats me, but I saw it for sale in the outdoor market). A handful of M&Ms and colorful plastic beads. Then, after assembling the mound of offerings, Nicacio poured on the pile a few ounces of *chicha de jora,* a local corn moonshine, and finally a cup of Coca-Cola, which glued together the whole mess into a conical totem.

"Pachamama likes sweets," Salvador translated.

Man plans, and Pachamama laughs.

Nicacio reached into his woven *chuspa* and began distributing three coca leaves to each of us,[1] beginning with Salvador, and then me,

---

[1] Thankfully, for inhaling. Earlier in the trip, to relieve altitude sickness, I chewed a wad of coca leaves, which felt like biting into a robin's nest.

and then to the others in our group. Then, one by one he stood before each of us and recited a personal prayer in Quechuan.

I'm sure this happened: The shaman paused an extra moment, staring into my eyes intensely, almost through me. I glared back into Nicacio's eyes, and it was like I could sense him looking into my soul, like he could feel not only my heart but Leah's heart erupting in my own. As I had seen Salvador do, I drew the coca leaves to my face, inhaled through them . . . and something spooky happened. For a moment I felt like I couldn't breathe, like I was suffocating. I felt a wave of sorrow sweeping me, through my chest, my neck, my mind, through those little leaves. An overwhelming anguish for Leah, the pain she had suffered for four years now. The uncertainty. The grief. The loss. I felt tears leaking down my cheeks. I said nothing aloud, but I called out to anyone who could hear me. Pachamama the goddess of Mother Earth, Miriam the prophetess of the Jewish people, Jude the patron saint of lost causes, the man in the moon and the entire universe, a silent wail as I yearned for anyone or anything that could at long last heal that broken wife of mine.

It lasted barely a minute.

And then, once again, it was eleven in the morning in the year 2019, and I was sitting in a pasture, high in the mountains of Peru.

A few minutes later Nicacio built an altar of eucalyptus branches, set the offerings atop the altar, and lit it on fire. Up in smoke went the spices and grains and coca leaves and moonshine and Coca-Cola and the sweetness of the morning's prayers.

A few days later, I flew home to Minneapolis. And for the next few months I waited impatiently for Pachamama to heal my wife.

BY LATE SUMMER Leah was still mired in depression. Dr. Patek agreed to add a very low dose of the antidepressant Zoloft to Leah's antipsychotic quetiapine as something of a last resort.[2] Leah knew as well as I did the risk of antidepressants, but she was desperate.

"If you start showing signs of hypomania from it," I said to Leah in front of both of them, "and you ignore the warning signs and what your doctors and I say, I won't stick around this time."

"You'll divorce me?"

"I will leave town and figure things out."

The remarkable thing was that I didn't say it threateningly or as an ultimatum. Leah and I had already discussed that boundary with Miriam, our marriage counselor. We had come a long way, and it was simply a fact. Leah was an adult and could make an adult decision.

After about ten days the Zoloft kicked in. For a few days Leah seemed a little revved, but with her psychologist's help we talked through it. Over the next weeks Leah and I and her doctors could mark her improving mood. She smiled and had oomph in her voice. She could describe her mood more robustly. She started cooking dinners again. She did a little housework. We played Scrabble, and she didn't need my help. She laughed. She started going to yoga classes for the first time in three years, and a week later she began exercising on a treadmill. She went to movies with friends.

It was a blessedly gradual improvement. One day while reading the obituaries in the morning paper she jokingly asked me if I would have married her had her name been Mindel "Fanny" Klutchman.

---

[2]   Had an antidepressant not worked, Dr. Patek was ready to enroll Leah in ketamine treatments. Ketamine, a former party drug, was approved by the FDA as a promising treatment for major depressive disorder. See "FDA Approves New Nasal Spray Medication for Treatment-Resistant Depression; Available Only at a Certified Doctor's Office or Clinic," *News & Events*, U.S. Food and Drug Administration, March 5, 2019, https://www.fda.gov/news-events/press-announcements/fda-approves-new-nasal-spray-medication-treatment-resistant-depression-available-only-certified.

She was getting her sense of humor back. And for the first time in four years, I was getting my wife back.

AS OF LATE FEBRUARY 2020, Leah has been sticking to a beneficial schedule. When she wakes up each morning, she plugs her earbuds into an app on her phone and meditates in the quiet of our living room. She participates in a couple of monthly book groups, and she volunteers twice a week at a nonprofit agency that serves families in need. She invites me to her monthly appointments with yet another new psychiatrist, the most engaged one yet. She co-facilitates her weekly NAMI support group. She ends her day at the same time each evening, takes her medications, tells me she appreciates me and the good things in our lives, and without fail she aims for a full night's sleep.

It took three years, but Leah's hair grew out of its depression, too. It hangs below her shoulders again, as luxurious as ever, with faint reddish tints mixed into the long brown tresses. She joined an international Facebook group for women with curly hair, which she no longer hates or wants to cut off.

In short, Leah is the thriving embodiment of why those of us living with a person living with mental illness continue to hope for a better future in a realistic way.

And the rest of our family?

In December 2018, Sarah and my brother's daughter each gave birth to baby girls.

In September 2019, Sarah, Seth, and their baby moved from New York City to Minneapolis. They live a seven-minute car ride away from our house. Pretty much anytime they ask, Grandma Leah and Grandpa Jeff are happy to babysit.

On New Year's Eve 2019, Joey married Catherine, "the little peach" whom Leah met in Portland three years earlier when she was manic. Three years since Leah and Joey's night together on Mt. Hood in a Stephen King horror story. Four-and-a-half years after Sarah and Seth's wedding, after the dyad timer, the Shower Stall Incident, the TSA fiasco, the worst of Leah's undiagnosed mania.

In the months leading up to the wedding in Portland, Joey and Leah hadn't seen each other face to face. He fretted about his mother's mood, for such is the family fallout from an illness like bipolar disorder.

"She's doing well, Joey," I reassured him. "I booked a daytime flight to Portland. We talked about taking breaks from the family gatherings if Mom's getting stressed out. She'll go to bed on time. I'm not worried at all. You remember about 'corrective experiences'?"

"Yeah. Maybe this will be the corrective experience I need."

About one hundred people attended the wedding. Dr. J and Anita couldn't make it, but Heshie and Judy made the trip, along with Emma and Shelley. My brother signed the ketubah. Sarah and her cousin Tova led the march down the wedding aisle, carrying their baby daughters, a pair of second-cousin flower girls in matching velvet dresses. Joey's childhood buddies, the boys with the apartment reeking of bat turds and washing machine sludge, stood in crisp dark suits, all grown up, groomsmen at Joey's side.

Catherine and Joey were married under the same chuppah that Leah had sewn for our own wedding. Aunt Lois and Seth were among the four who held the chuppah upright. And when in a centuries-old tradition Joey stomped the wedding glass with his right foot, with profound joy I felt like at last the bane of Leah's instability had been shattered.

One thing bothered me. During the ceremony, as I looked out at the guests, I noticed that my brother, seated in the second row behind Sarah, Tova, and their babies, spent the entire ceremony staring at the floor. I couldn't imagine what David found so annoying. Although it wasn't the most traditional Jewish wedding in the past three thousand years, the words were reflective and solemn. The bride looked beautiful in her long white wedding gown, the groom looked dapper and as happy as I had ever seen him, and love lit the ballroom that evening like the gentle glow of the moon.

A while later, in the men's room, away from the hubbub of the reception, I asked David why he wasn't watching the ceremony.

"I was counting the floorboards."

I gave him a quizzical look. The floor was made of narrow wooden slats, like a bowling alley.

"I was totally overcome. I couldn't stop thinking, 'This is a miracle. A true miracle.' I watched Tova and Sarah smiling, but I couldn't watch the ceremony. I could only think of how well Leah was doing compared to how chaotic her mind had been during Sarah's wedding, before we understood what was wrong with her. And all the pain, frustration, and despair that all of us went through for so long. Especially you, my brother. 'This is a miracle,' I kept thinking, and I felt like I would lose it right there if I didn't distract myself. So I counted the floorboards."

"How many were there?"

"Sixty-five."

He made that up. It's how many years he had known me.

Joey and Catherine splurged on a swing band. For the most part the musicians played jazz standards, but by prior request they played the traditional wedding dance song "Hava Nagila." There's a photo of the bride and groom, frog-eyed and terror struck, hoisted high in the air on chairs by their strongest friends, as their parents and friends circled around them in a joyous dance of the hora.

BUT WAIT. What happened to the leading man?

These days I spend a few hours a week playing with my grand-daughter. My stomach is fine, *pu pu pu*. My tennis game continues to improve—although I rarely win a match against Seth. Leah and I practice "Yoga with Adriene" on YouTube four or five times a week. I'm planning to complete a sixty-six kilometer bike ride this autumn. I donate platelets at the American Red Cross. I co-facilitate a monthly support group meeting for partners and spouses of people living with a mental illness. And I thank my lucky stars each day for my family and friends, without whom I surely would have fallen apart.

People in our support group come and go. Some have been attending longer than I have. Some have disappeared. Some have gotten divorced. Some have hung on, and some, like me, offer words of hope for ourselves and our loved ones.

The mental illnesses change little. Agoraphobia. PTSD. Attachment disorder. Borderline personality disorder. Depression. Intermittent explosive disorder. Schizoaffective disorder. Severe anxiety. Suicidal ideation.

Bipolar, bipolar, bipolar.

In our group each month we share our experiences and what we have learned. Like what it actually means when people remind you to take care of yourself. Like learning to forgive yourself without guilt for setting boundaries. Learning about resilience and how to counterpunch the stigma of mental illness. Learning to appreciate the power of friendship, humor, and hope. Learning that although my life with Leah will continue to change, I'm better equipped to deal with it. Learning that a caring doctor is the best medicine. That meds quit working but new treatments get developed. Learning the best thing any of us can do is go to bed at night and ask ourselves if we were as loving as we could be that day.

I learned it's okay to have a love–hate relationship with my wife's bipolar disorder. Her illness nearly destroyed our family, but love turned out to be the glue that held us together.

And if, as my support group friend Jack Lemmon says, these are all gifts, then I learned that my cup runneth over. God might laugh at my plans, but for now I might just be . . . the luckiest man . . . on the face of the earth.

Afterword

Justice, justice, shall you pursue.
Deuteronomy 16:20

A s I described in the final chapter, Leah reengaged with the world after her newly prescribed medication mix clicked in September 2019. Over the next half year she adhered to a strict schedule of exercise, meditation, and sleep. She benefited from strong rapport with her new psychologist and psychiatrist. She spent her days volunteering, attending movies and plays, cooking, and visiting with friends. Together we babysat Sarah and Seth's toddler, upon whom we lavished our love after the three of them moved to Minneapolis. Meanwhile, seventeen hundred miles away in Oregon, Joey and Catherine enjoyed their first winter as newlyweds. What an unexpected, hopeful way to end the book I had been banging out for two years.

That is, until everything changed. First, the beginning of the COVID–19 pandemic; then, on May 25, 2020, an African American named George Floyd gasped "I can't breathe" more than twenty times during a lethal arrest by four Minneapolis police officers. Over the following four days, fifteen hundred Twin Cities businesses were vandalized, looted, or destroyed,[1] and protests against police brutality, especially against black Americans, erupted in two thousand U.S. cities and dozens of countries around the world.[2]

The city of Minneapolis was more than a backdrop for this book. I described our first apartment in a diverse neighborhood not three blocks from where Mr. Floyd was killed, as well as our home in a mostly white neighborhood a few miles away, where we have lived the last-quarter century. I chronicled how throughout the chaos of Leah's illness I found solace and refuge among the area's parks and lakes. I mentioned birthday and anniversary walks with my wife along the Mississippi River. I described Leah's interactions with local police. I depicted how Leah, a former hospital social worker and public health practitioner, spent four years as a patient whirling around an imperfect but functional mental health system. And, in hindsight, I told a love story about two white Minneapolitans largely shielded from the inequities and racism that tarnish many American institutions in the 21st century.

Nearly twenty years ago the George W. Bush administration published "Mental Health: Culture, Race, and Ethnicity,"[3] which documented the gross disparities in access to health care between Whites and non-Whites. "Ethnic and racial minorities in the United States," the report concluded, "face a social and economic environment of inequality that includes greater exposure to racism and discrimination, violence, and poverty, all of which take a toll on mental health."

---

[1]   https://www.startribune.com/minneapolis-st-paul-buildings-are-damaged-looted-after-george-floyd-protests-riots/569930671/

[2]   https://www.nytimes.com/interactive/2020/06/13/us/george-floyd-protests-cities-photos.html

[3]   https://www.ncbi.nlm.nih.gov/books/NBK44243/, chapter 2.

As of June 2020, black Americans were dying from COVID–19 at twice the rate of white Americans.[4] The U.S. Department of Health and Human Services indicated Blacks are three to four times more likely than Whites to experience serious psychological distress in their lifetime.[5] In addition, according to the U.S. Department of Justice, nearly two thirds of women in jails or prisons have a history of mental illness.[6] Lesbian, gay, bisexual, and trans youths are five times more likely than straight youths to attempt suicide.[7]

"My brain is broken," Leah often murmured as she battled bipolar disorder. I responded with encouragement, prayer, and, at each meeting of my support group, a mantra-like avowal to never give up hope. Miraculously, Leah has been spending the COVID–19 crisis in our garden, planting, weeding, and watering the perennials. The hope she inspires and the prayers of gratitude I recite for her continued well-being are not to be dismissed. But what about those whose hopes have been shredded by racism, discrimination, and the inadequacies of our health care and criminal justice systems? The nation's demand for racial justice after George Floyd's death and the uncertainty and fear caused by the pandemic are reminders that we must heal not only the minds of those ill like Leah but the hearts of an entire nation.

---

[4] https://www.apmresearchlab.org/covid/deaths-by-race

[5] https://www.minorityhealth.hhs.gov/omh/browse.aspx?lvl=4&lvlid=24

[6] https://www.bjs.gov/content/pub/pdf/imhprpji1112.pdf

[7] https://www.cdc.gov/mmwr/volumes/65/ss/pdfs/ss6509.pdf

Support Groups

F riends, family members, and medical and mental health providers have helped keep me sane—literally. But no one "gets it" like the participants in my support groups.

Local chapters of the National Alliance on Mental Illness (www. nami.org) offer support groups for family members and friends as well as persons with an illness. State affiliate websites list details about when and where groups meet. I've also attended both in-person and online groups sponsored by the Depression and Bipolar Support Alliance (www.dbsalliance.org). I'm told Al-Anon meetings can be beneficial, too, particularly for friends and family members of persons with a dual diagnosis.

The NAMI family support groups that I've attended follow a specific model. They are volunteer-led by people who are caring for someone with a mental illness. The meetings last from seventy-five minutes to two hours, and in my experience the time goes quickly. They're fairly informal but they follow a consistent format:

1. We read the group guidelines and principles of support. (See www.namicolumbusga.org/programs/family-support-group/.) The groups are run essentially the same throughout the country.

2. Each participant then spends three to five minutes discussing what has been going on at home the past couple of weeks (although no one is required to talk).

3. If someone is in the middle of a crisis, he or she can ask for more time to talk about the crisis and ask for support and resources that might help. The facilitator usually leads a discussion about common themes that have arisen.

4. As a wrap-up we try to figure out how we'll take care of ourselves in the weeks ahead or which principles of support have been useful.

Some of the best things: NAMI groups are designed for listening, empathizing, asking questions, and offering personal experiences and perspectives. Only rarely does anyone offer advice, and no one judges your choices. Although they're a safe place to vent, group members try to bring it back to something positive. That may be self-care or another perspective—or it may be the reminder that our loved ones never asked to have an illness.

And best of all: we remind each other that humor is healthy and we will never give up hope—even if it means hope only for our own well-being.

APPENDIX B

Books and Other Fancy Stuff

I wrote *Unglued: A Bipolar Love Story* in part because of the dearth of memoirs focused on those caring for and loving a person with a mental illness. The following books were invaluable resources.

- Amador, Xavier. *I AM NOT Sick. I Don't Need Help: How to Help Someone with Mental Illness Accept Treatment.* New York: Vida Press, 2012.

   Free download at https://www.nami.org/getattachment/ Learn-More/Mental-Health-Conditions/Related-Conditions/ Anosognosia/I_am_not_sick_excerpt.pdf. A psychologist by training, Amador spent several frustrating years trying to convince his brother he had schizophrenia. He finally understood he was going about it all wrong and developed the LEAP approach: Listen, Empathize, Agree, Partner. (A link to his TEDx Talk appears later in this appendix.)

- Boss, Pauline. *Ambiguous Loss: Learning to Live with Unresolved Grief.* Cambridge, Mass.: Harvard University Press, 2000.

  After dealing with the deaths of five family members over a fourteen-month period around 2010, I thought I recognized and understood grief. Only upon reading Boss's book did I comprehend I was experiencing a different kind of grief, the ambiguous loss stemming from my wife's mental illness. See www.ambiguousloss.com for more information.

- Fast, Julie, and John Preston. *Loving Someone with Bipolar Disorder: Understanding & Helping Your Partner*, 2d ed. Oakland, Calif.: New Harbinger, 2012.

  The best how-to book I've come across. Julie Fast writes from her experience and knowledge as someone who has battled bipolar. The book is loaded with real-life couples' scenarios, many of which hit home; "reality checks" that dampen our unrealistic expectations; and practical guidance on dealing with and at least trying to head off interpersonal fireworks in our homes.

- Frankl, Victor E. *Man's Search for Meaning.* Boston: Beacon Press, 2006.

  The classic Holocaust survival book and introduction to logotherapy.

- Hornbacher, Marya. *Madness: A Bipolar Life.* New York: Mariner, 2008.

  A candid, funny, and familiar story for anyone with bipolar and their loved ones. Hornbacher is a Minneapolis writer married to a guy named Jeff. As I read the book I kept wanting to hear Jeff's perspective, which is another reason I wrote my book.

- Jamison, Kay Redfield. *An Unquiet Mind: A Memoir of Moods and Madness.* New York: Vintage Books, 1996.

  A psychiatrist, Jamison is the most eloquent and knowledgeable writer I've read on the experience of living with bipolar illness. Every memoirist should read her, even if you're not interested in mood disorders.

- Larsted, Bob. *Witness to the Dark: My Daughter's Troubled Times.* Self-published, CreateSpace, 2013.

  A father's piercingly honest, sometimes funny memoir about how he coped with his daughter's schizophrenia. Health care providers, administrators, and policy makers should read it to see how broken the mental health system is.

- Lukach, Mark. *My Lovely Wife in the Psych Ward: A Memoir.* New York: HarperCollins, 2017.

  I liked it a lot. So did hundreds of thousands of other readers. I would have liked to have read more about Lukach than about his wife, which is why I focused this book on my experience.

- McInerny, Nora. *It's Okay to Laugh (Crying Is Cool Too).* New York: HarperCollins, 2016.

  Another Minneapolis writer. (I'm seeing a pattern.) She's funnier than I am and apparently more resilient.

- Moezzi, Melody. *Haldol and Hyacinths: A Bipolar Life*. New York: Penguin, 2013.

  A memoir of an Iranian-American woman's coping with bipolar disorder and a chronic pancreatic disease. The husband is portrayed as saintly, which is fine—but as in other memoirs, that depiction contrasts with the narrator in *Unglued* and most spouses in our shoes who complain, worry, fear, and struggle with guilt and rage.

- Saks, Elyn R. *The Center Cannot Hold*. New York: Hachette, 2015.

  A profound memoir of turmoil and hope for those with schizophrenia or those who love someone who has the illness.

- Sheffield, Anne. *How You Can Survive When They're Depressed: Living and Coping with Depression Fallout*. New York: Three Rivers Press, 1998.

  An exploration of the five stages of "depression fallout": confusion, self-doubt, demoralization, anger, and the desire to escape. Sheffield tells you how to survive it.

Other Fancy Stuff

- Amador, Xavier. "I'm Not Sick, I Don't Need Help." TEDx Talks. YouTube video, 18:02. Posted October 2017. https://www.youtube.com/watch?v=NXxytf6kfPM.

- *bp Magazine*, www.bphope.com.

  I get free weekly newsletters and bloggy emails a couple times a week and sometimes forward them to my wife.

Beware of the hyped-up ads from drug companies, but the content is good.

- Depression and Bipolar Support Alliance (DBSA), https://www. dbsalliance.org/support/.

- Gilmartin, David. *Mental Illness Happy Hour* podcast. http://www. mentalpod.com/.

    I like the logo on the website.

- Greenstein, Luna. "The Best Movies About Mental Health." NAMI blog, December 20, 2017. http://www.nami.org/Blogs/NAMI-Blog/December-2017/The-Best-Movies-About- Mental-Health.

- MakeItOk.org. http://makeitok.org.

    Lots of information, stories, podcasts, and resources about how we can fight discrimination and stigma of mental illness.

- McInerny, Nora. *Terrible, Thanks for Asking* podcast. https://www. ttfa.org.

    Award-winning podcast that cuts through the chitter-chatter.

- National Alliance on Mental Illness (NAMI). http://www.nami.org.

    With links to state chapters.

- National Institute of Mental Health (NIMH). http://www.nimh. nih.gov/.

    A smorgasbord of factual information and research. The science is solid and current, and the website is easy to navigate and written in plain English.

- National Suicide Prevention Lifeline. 1-800-273-8255.

  When in doubt, call. I got a human being right away when I did.

- Sandwell, Ian. "The 20 Best Movies About Mental Illness That Get It Right," GamesRadar+, October 10, 2018, https://www.gamesradar.com/best-movies-about-mental-illness/.

Acknowledgments

I am grateful to Joe Gredler, Brenda Hudson, and Laura Westlund for their extraordinary friendship and encouragement from the beginning to the end of this project.

Thanks to Daniel Edelson-Stein, Scott Edelstein, Jay Isenberg, Bruce Lackie, Jay Lieberman, David Mathieu, Jamie Patterson, Laura Savin, Kevin Schwandt, Laurel Walsh, my brother David, and my wife for their generous feedback; Emily Hitchcock from Boyle & Dalton; and especially Heather Shaw and Hillary Wentworth, for their gentle flogging and professionalism as editors.

Thanks to Leah's medical team for saving her life.

Finally, thanks to our friends, our children and their spouses, and my extended family, and to Laura Niewald, Debra Rappaport, the National Alliance on Mental Illness, and the men and women in my support groups for gluing me back together.

Jeffrey Zuckerman is a freelance editor and writer. For many years he directed the writing center at Walden University and taught writing and editing classes at the University of Minnesota. In earlier careers he was a newspaper reporter, social worker, barroom piano player, stadium vendor, and short-order cook. A native of Pittsburgh, Jeff co-facilitates a support group for the National Alliance on Mental Illness and spends his spare time playing tennis, kayaking, ice-skating, fishing, and teaching his granddaughter about his childhood hero, Roberto Clemente.

He and his wife live in Minneapolis.

Connect with Jeffrey at www.jeffzuckerman.com.

CPSIA information can be obtained
at www.ICGtesting.com
Printed in the USA
FSHW020315070221
78300FS

9 781633 373761